Chicken Soup
for the Soul.

101 Ways to Think Positive

Chicken Soup for the Soul: 101 Ways to Think Positive
Amy Newmark

Published by Chicken Soup for the Soul, LLC www.chickensoup.com
Copyright ©2025 by Chicken Soup for the Soul, LLC. All Rights Reserved.

The publisher gratefully acknowledges the many individuals who granted Chicken Soup for the Soul permission to reprint the cited material.

Front cover illustration courtesy of iStockphoto.com (©Orla)
Back cover and interior illustration courtesy of iStockphoto.com (©iridi)
Photo of Amy Newmark courtesy of Susan Morrow at SwickPix

Cover and Interior by Daniel Zaccari

Publisher's Cataloging-in-Publication Data

Names: Newmark, Amy, editor.
Title: Chicken soup for the soul : 101 ways to think positive / Amy Newmark.
Description: Cos Cob, CT: Chicken Soup for the Soul, LLC, 2025.
Identifiers: LCCN: 2024947492 | ISBN: 978-1-61159-107-1 (paperback) |
    978-1-61159-343-3 (ebook)
Subjects: LCSH Conduct of life--Literary collections. | Conduct of life--Anecdotes. |
Happiness--Literary collections. | Happiness--Anecdotes. | Optimism--Literary
collections. | Optimism--Anecdotes.| Self help. | BISAC SELF-HELP / Motivational and
Inspirational | SELF-HELP / Personal Growth / Happiness | SELF-HELP / Personal
Growth / Success
Classification: LCC PN6071.C697 C48 2025 | DDC 158.1/02--dc23

Library of Congress Control Number: 2024947492

PRINTED IN THE UNITED STATES OF AMERICA
on acid∞free paper

30 29 28 27 26 25   01 02 03 04 05 06 07 08 09

Chicken Soup
for the Soul.

101 Ways to Think Positive

Amy Newmark

CSS

Chicken Soup for the Soul, LLC
Cos Cob, CT

Changing your life one story at a time®
www.chickensoup.com

Table of Contents

①

~Expect Good Things~

②

~Silver Linings~

❸

~Reframe It~

❹

~Surprise Yourself~

❺

~Let It Go~

❻

~Count Your Blessings~

❼

~Find a Role Model~

❽

~Change Your Perspective~

❾
~Face Your Fears~

❿
~Keep Going~

⑪

~Reach Out and Connect~

⑫

~Keep the Faith~

Chapter 1

Expect Good Things

I Know How This Works

*Visualize this thing that you want, see it, feel it, believe
in it. Make your mental blueprint and begin to build.*
~Robert Collier

We were seated in an outdoor holding area on a bench with the rest of the studio audience, waiting to be ushered inside. The year was 2002, the place was Los Angeles, and the show was *The Other Half*, a male version of the women-centric morning show, *The View*. This incarnation featured hosts Dick Clark, Danny Bonaduce, Dr. Jan Adams and Mario Lopez. The production assistants and show interns were handing out clipboards containing a questionnaire for us to fill out. The questions hinted at the day's topic of discussion: dating disasters. I was sandwiched between my eighteen-year-old niece Jessica and my best friend Lisa, coaching them on how to answer the questions.

"They're trying to find someone who will make good TV," I explained. "Think of the funniest dating disaster you've ever had, one that may have also happened to other women. Something relatable and lighthearted, yet slightly humiliating."

Both Lisa and Jessica laughed, and I said, "See, now you're getting it."

My "dating disaster" had to do with a fellow who pulled up outside my house and beeped his horn rather than come to the door to escort me to his car.

"He completely ruined the moment," I wrote on the questionnaire. My mother was supposed to open the door, usher him inside, and tell him I'd be right down. He had denied me my grand entrance.

I saw the smile on the intern's face as she collected the clipboard, and scanned what I had written.

"Can you tell me a little bit more about this?"

Now that I'm a writer, I understand the concept of the "elevator pitch," but I had no idea what I was doing back then. All I knew was that I was minutes away from seeing Mario Lopez in the flesh (yes, he's better-looking in person, just in case you thought that wasn't possible), with the prospect of talking to him on camera. I turned on the personality like I was there for an audition. In a way, I suppose I was.

Other women were getting interviewed just like me, sharing their dating-disaster stories, hoping Mario, Danny, Dick or Jan would talk about it with them on camera. But I felt something more than hope. I felt like it was actually going to happen. I started to visualize it in my head: Mario approaching me with a microphone, the two of us laughing along with the rest of the studio audience as I discussed my rude date.

As we filed onto the soundstage, I actually began to get flutters in my stomach, sweating even though the studio was freezing. I realized I was experiencing stage fright. As the three of us took our seats, I caught the eye of the production assistant who'd spoken to us, and she smiled at me. I turned to Lisa and said, "They're going to interview us on the show."

"How do you know that?"

"Just a feeling," I said. I'd had it from the moment they handed us the clipboards. Even though the production assistant who'd spoken to me had also taken the time to chat with a few others, I was confident my story was going to make it on the air.

Sure enough, right after the entire audience was seated and the crowd warmer stirred us into the proper level of excitement and anticipation, the assistant approached us and squatted between Lisa and me.

"When Dick talks to you, I want you to tell your story just like you told me."

She turned to Lisa and advised her to do the same. I couldn't believe it. Both Lisa and I had been chosen to speak on national television.

Suddenly, the show was beginning. The four hosts took the stage amid much applause and enthusiastic whooping. They bantered through their opening routine and introduced the topic. Then, Mario Lopez was standing beside me, holding a microphone in front of me as I relayed to Dick Clark and everybody in the entire studio — not to mention the television-viewing audience — my dating-disaster story. It played out almost exactly as I had envisioned it.

It was an incredible moment, exhilarating and somewhat surreal, even if not entirely unexpected thanks to my positive thinking.

— Rachel Remick —

A Dreaded Doctor Visit Ends in Magic

Nobody can be uncheered with a balloon.
~Winne the Pooh

I was seven years old and had just moved with my grandparents to Anaheim, California. I would have to go to a new school, make new friends and, worst of all, get updated vaccinations.

As I sat on the crinkly paper on the doctor's exam table one week before school was to start, with my legs dangling over the end, I dreaded the moment when he would say, "Time for your tetanus shot." The only thing I knew that would make the pain of a shot worthwhile was the balloon I had been promised.

I took that shot like a champ, without so much as a quiet "Ouch." While I waited for the doctor to come back with my balloon, I thought about all the cool things I was going to do with that balloon: I was going to tie it to my doll's arm and pretend she was floating away, only to rescue her at the last minute. I was going to tie it to my dog's tail and pretend she was from outer space and had landed as a scout to report back on whether Earth was a suitable planet on which alien dogs could live. And I definitely planned on rubbing the balloon on my hair to make it stand on end so I could look like a member of KISS, my favorite band at the time.

The doctor returned with a concerned look on his face and delivered the tragic news. "I'm sorry, but we're out of balloons."

All my big plans for that balloon popped faster than that balloon ever would have. I was devastated.

The entire way home, my grandma kept telling me that I should think positively, and everything would be okay. We had a pack of balloons at home that I could blow up. Well, I positively knew that those balloons would never be as good as the balloon from the doctor's office. First of all, we didn't have a helium tank to make the balloons float. And, more importantly, I hadn't had to sacrifice anything for those balloons.

We pulled into our driveway, and I trudged into the house, my day ruined by shots and no balloons. I went straight through the house to the back patio door, ready to go outside and tell my dog all my troubles, when I looked out and saw the most amazing thing my seven-year-old eyes had ever seen. Our entire backyard was filled with floaty balloons! I screamed in delight and ran through them, twirling in circles and stirring them this way and that.

We lived less than a mile from Disneyland. As it turned out, when the wind was just right, the balloons released from the daily parades would land neatly in our backyard.

I will never forget that day of whirling through those balloons and thinking they were all for me because I had to get my shots. And I will never forget my grandmother telling me throughout my life that if you just think positive thoughts, everything has a way of working out in the end.

— Leyla d'Aulaire —

The Robe

Great things happen to those who don't stop believing,
trying, learning, and being grateful.
~Roy T. Bennett

I t all started when I needed a new winter robe. My thin bathrobe looked pretty ratty after many years of use. But money was tight, and there were plenty of other things on the priority list ahead of replacing my robe. On a teacher's salary, I had enough to pay bills but not much extra.

It was Christmastime, and I received wonderful gifts from parents such as Starbucks gift cards (I don't drink coffee, but they didn't know that), Christmas cookies, candy and assorted classroom supplies. And then I got a fifteen-dollar gift card that had real promise. My colleague Verlene was a teacher's aide at my school and a dear friend. I gave her a Christmas coffee mug courtesy of Starbucks, and she gave me a Macy's gift card for fifteen dollars.

I didn't ordinarily shop at such a swanky store, but I looked forward to browsing. I waited for an after-Christmas sale to make the most of my fifteen dollars. Then, I went on a robe hunt. I kept a good attitude and knew I would get something. Then, I decided to find my *perfect* robe because I knew I could. Suddenly, I just *knew*.

I headed for the clearance racks at the back of the women's department. That's how I always started shopping. The sign said that all merchandise in this section was 75 percent off. *That's a good sign,* I thought (pun intended). I looked for nightgowns and robes, and there it was: On a rack near the back wall hung the most fluffy, soft, cozy-looking, long winter robe that I had ever seen. It was white and looked like something a "real housewife of somewhere" would wear while lounging around. Then, I realized I hadn't checked the size. I held my breath as I looked at the tag. It was the perfect size—*my* size. Then, I searched for the price tag. The white tag had started with some number that started with one hundred dollars but had a yellow tag over it. The sale price was $55.99. I did some quick calculations and began to believe that I could be the new owner of the world's most perfect robe.

I stood in the back of the store and quickly put on the robe over my street clothes. I ran to a nearby mirror and spoke out loud as I admired the well-fitting, beautiful garment. "I knew I would find you!" I said to the robe.

As I walked to the checkout, I began to pray that everything I calculated was accurate because I knew I had to have that robe. When it was my turn, the clerk rang it up, and the price began sliding downward from $159.00 to $55.99. Next, she calculated the 75-percent clearance savings and told me the total was $15.04. Then, I pulled out my $15.00 gift card and handed it to her. She ran that through and presented me with my grand total of four cents. I replied with a smile, "Do you want a credit card, or is cash okay?" I joyously pulled out a nickel, handed it to her and said, "Keep the change."

I went home, put on my glorious robe, and wore it for the remainder of the evening. Ten years later, I still have it. It's finally getting to the point of being gently used, and I may have to buy a new one soon. But how could this robe ever be replaced? I know that the miracle of a four-cent robe will never come again. On the other hand, maybe I could get a three-cent robe. You never know… It could happen!

— Laura McKenzie —

Uber Lucky

Within all of us is a divine capacity to manifest and
attract all that we need and desire.
~Wayne Dyer

We were driving into Manhattan with our out-of-town guests, Sara and Chris, who started out as our son's in-laws but quickly became our friends. As we zipped down the highway, we hit a giant pothole. Seconds later, one of the tires blew, and we had to pull off to the side.

There were ten other cars along the side of the highway, all with flats from that pothole. Unfortunately, my husband's car, a Tesla, doesn't have a spare, not even a donut. That's a great example of misplaced positive thinking, right? This was actually the third time we had been stranded by a flat tire because that car has no spare.

Our useless hunk of steel would need to be removed from the highway on a flatbed truck, but it would have to wait its turn behind all the other cars with flats. There was no way we would get to the play on time.

Just days before, I had scored front-row seats to one of the hottest plays on Broadway, *Patriots*, about the rise of Putin and the Russian oligarchs. It was only in New York for a few weeks, so we wouldn't get another chance to see it.

How did I get those seats? The same way I always buy theater tickets: last minute, and through the theater's official ticket seller so there is no mark-up from Broadway.com or another ticket broker.

I'd been doing this for years. I might know months ahead of time that we're going into the city for a theater weekend, but I'll wait until Wednesday or Thursday of that very week to buy our tickets. And I always get great seats because theaters usually hold back a handful of their best seats for VIPs, just in case.

Years ago, we got four tickets to *The Book of Mormon*, even though it had been sold out for months, by buying tickets for Friday on Thursday. We scored two great orchestra seats and two front-row mezzanine seats, which happens to be my favorite place to sit because no one is blocking your view. Those tickets must have just been released that evening, part of the stash the theaters were holding onto for those theoretical VIPs.

We get to see all the most popular shows by waiting and then pouncing.

My best example of how lucky we get with tickets was the weekend in 2023 when I got last-minute tickets to two Tony Award-winning shows. An hour before the first show on Friday night, I got an e-mail saying that it was canceled due to illness. Now, we were really talking "last minute!" I went online and got us two fifth-row center house seats for *Six*, another Tony Award winner. And who should sit down next to us but Zibby Owens and her family. Zibby is a big deal in publishing, and I was thrilled by this serendipitous meeting. We had been on each other's podcasts and talked on the phone but had never met in person.

Then, on Saturday, as we finished up at a museum, I decided to quickly check for *Harry Potter* tickets. We had wanted to go to the matinee, but when I had checked the day before it was sold out. Suddenly, two great seats showed up, so I grabbed them, and we hustled over to the theater.

Then, that night, we went to another Tony Award winner, *Take Me Out*, which is loosely based on the Yankees. All I knew was that it was about baseball, so I thought my husband would like it. When I had looked at available seats a couple of days before, there were two front-row orchestra and two front-row mezzanine seats available. I wasn't sure, but then I decided to go for the front-row mezzanine so we wouldn't be looking straight up for the whole performance. That turned out to be a wise decision because I had no idea that all the actors are totally nude during shower scenes in the locker room. Never have I been so relieved that I didn't take front-row seats!

A couple of months ago, my daughter and I were going into the city for one night to see a couple of plays. On Wednesday night, I asked her what she wanted to see on Saturday for a matinee and an evening performance. She said *Harry Potter* and *Hamilton*, two plays I was happy to watch again.

When I went online to check on the theaters' official ticket sellers' websites, there were only a handful of seats available, but there they were, my babies—the exact same seats my husband and I had gotten last minute for *Harry Potter* and the exact same seats we had for *Hamilton*, too—front row of the second section in the orchestra, so there was no one in front of us, and we were first out the door for the race to the ladies' room during intermission. If you don't frequent Broadway shows, here's a tip: RUN to the ladies' room during intermission. If you don't, you will be standing in line for twenty minutes.

And now, back to my luckiest break ever with theater tickets. There we were with our flat tire, sitting on the side of the highway twenty miles from the theater district. I turned to Sara and said, "I wish we could somehow get an Uber to materialize here on the side of the highway and take us to the city." Not ten seconds later, a black Toyota Camry pulled over and parked on the shoulder in front of us. It seems like ninety percent of the Ubers in New York City are black Toyota Camrys so I got excited.

I got out of our car, ran up to the driver and said, "Are you an Uber driver? If I give you $100 in cash, will you take us to the theater district right now?" (A lesson to all those people in the generation behind mine, including our four grown children: *You should still carry cash.*)

Our savior agreed, and after he concluded that his inflation device would not reinflate the Tesla's destroyed tire, Sara and I jumped in his car and were off. We even got to the theater in time to use the ladies' room *before* the play started and also in time to learn from the box office that we could give the two unused tickets to friends for another day.

Our husbands stayed with the car, and while they were sorry to miss the play, they ended up having a fun afternoon. It took many hours and two flatbed rides to get them to the Tesla dealer, and both times they got to drive the car right up onto the flatbed and sit inside it high up on the back of the truck.

Meanwhile, Sara and I watched the play, which was fabulous, and then, despite the rain, immediately scored another Uber — weirdly, it was a Tesla — and were driven back to the suburbs in style, in time to meet our husbands, with their two new front tires, for dinner.

— Amy Newmark —

An Unexpected Angel

*Angels are not mystical creatures from another realm; they
are the manifestations of love and kindness in our lives.*
~Deepak Chopra, The Ultimate Happiness Prescription

In the blistering heat of 90 degrees Fahrenheit, I watched the elderly woman struggle with a walker, laden down with bags of groceries. I was driving north, and she was walking south. I'd seen her before, each time feeling guilty I didn't offer her a lift.

But how can I safely stop in the middle of a busy road to help anyone without obstructing the late-afternoon traffic? That was my reasoning. It resolved my guilt... temporarily.

This day, however, the guilt got to me. I got into the far-left lane and made a U-turn. Slowing down, I opened the window and called out, "Need a ride?"

I knew I was upsetting the drivers around me, but I no longer cared. The woman looked drained, with sweat pouring down her weary face.

"Let me help you with your groceries," I added.

Getting out of the car, I placed her walker and bags into my trunk. I helped the woman into the passenger seat, and we were off.

"Bless you, child," she said. She no longer looked elderly, just worn out.

She directed me to go farther south. It seemed too far for her to walk every day. She explained that she usually took a bus but had missed the last one. She worked as a bagger at the nearby grocery store.

After a few blocks, we passed under a bridge where several homeless people had taken up residence. She asked me to pull over. I hesitated. *Please tell me this is not where she lives,* I thought.

Thankfully, it wasn't. She rolled down her window and called out to a couple, "Y'all come by later. It's spaghetti night tonight." She waved and smiled, her smile erasing ten years off her face.

We continued south, chatting as if we'd known each other for years. Her name was Ida. She had grandchildren. I have grandchildren. She loved cats. I love cats. She gave me tips on her spaghetti sauce. I found her delightful.

Suddenly, I realized we were on the "wrong side of town." It was starting to get dark, and I began to feel uneasy. We continued down unfamiliar streets until she finally pointed to an old apartment building where she lived. Several rowdy young men in their early twenties had congregated around the entrance. They were smoking something and appeared threatening. Some were on motorcycles, and one, wearing a hoodie over his bushy, long hair, was staring at me intently — too intently — and smiling.

Hoodlum! I thought. I was getting more and more uncomfortable, but Ida seemed fine. I stopped the car where she had indicated and opened the trunk. Ida directed a couple of the guys to help with her cart and groceries. She thanked me, and I drove away as fast as I could.

Luckily, my car had GPS because I would have had a problem getting home — especially since it was getting dark by then. Nevertheless, I drove slowly, preferring to stay on the residential streets rather than unfamiliar highways. Once I knew where I was going, I turned on the radio and played some familiar music. Suddenly the peaceful atmosphere was interrupted by the roar of a motorcycle behind me. I must admit it made me nervous. Slowing down, I was hoping he would pass me.

I recognized the biker from the apartment house — the one with the hoodie and bushy hair who kept smiling at me familiarly. He didn't pass me but continued to drive at the same speed as me. I realized he was waving for me to stop.

It would soon be getting dark. No way was I going to stop for an ominous stranger on a deserted street. I tried to speed away as fast as I could, but it didn't deter him. He raced after me again. Getting increasingly anxious, I tried to use the phone feature in the car, but it said something like, "No telephone detected." In a panic, driving haphazardly, I reached down for my purse to retrieve my cell phone. I had to call 911.

With my eyes on the road, one hand on the wheel and the other hand searching on the seat next to me for my purse, I felt an empty seat. My purse wasn't there!

"Darn! She stole my purse!" I may have used stronger language. *So much for acts of kindness,* I thought.

Meanwhile, the guy on the bike stayed close to me and even tried to get in front of me, signaling for me to stop. Then, I noticed out of the corner of my eye that a purse was on the floor of my car. Yes, there was a purse, but it wasn't *my* purse. Keeping one eye on the motorcycle dude, I reached down and retrieved it. With one hand, I dug around in the strange purse searching for a phone. But there was none. The perp was right outside my window, waving. Waving my purse! I couldn't believe my eyes.

Tears of relief streamed down my face.

Meanwhile, a police car had stopped in front of us. The policeman got out and, with his hands at his waist near his gun, started to approach the driver of the bike. But when he noticed that the situation was being resolved peacefully, he paused, watching cautiously from a distance.

I pulled over to the curb, and the young man stopped his motorcycle by the passenger side. Through the window I had opened, he handed me my purse.

"Grandma sent me to give you this. She picked it up by mistake. She is so sorry." He was still smiling. This time, his smile didn't appear threatening, simply gracious. I was speechless as I handed him his grandma's purse, and then he took off.

Groping in my purse, I quickly found my wallet. Retrieving a few dollars, I waved at the young man to stop. I wanted to reward him ever so slightly, but he had disappeared into the night.

I did manage to yell, "Thank you!"

I never had a chance to say I was sorry for my thoughts. Just because he was young and looked on the "wild side," I assumed he was a criminal.

Here was a young man — an angel, really — who went out of his way to help a stranger, expecting nothing in return.

I had been feeling so smug about doing a small act of kindness, but I learned something else that day: Sometimes, we think we know a person's character because they don't conform to what we believe is the proper, suitable way to be. They may not drive a stylish car, live on the "right" side of town, or dress in what we consider to be fashionable, but who's to say they are not equal to or better than we are?

— Eva Carter —

Focus On the Good

Blessed is the influence of one true,
loving human soul on another.
~George Eliot

"I'll never again be well," I'd wept, wondering how many more days before my husband would grow weary of hearing my fear-filled sobbing. My patient husband had done everything he could think of to make my struggles easier and to come up with a solution that would make the unbearable pain disappear. But the pain had not disappeared, nor had it diminished.

"A concussion," the first ER doctor had said. There was no telling how long I would feel as unwell as I had been feeling. And the blinding headaches and vomiting? One and then another doctor would shake his or her head. "We can only suggest things that might make you more comfortable: a warm bath, a nap, relaxation therapy. We can even prescribe medications for the migraines, but there is no guarantee."

"No guarantee, no guarantee" began to torment me day and night like an unwelcome echo. I was in horrendous pain, but no one could tell me when it would cease — or even if it ever would.

Days after suffering my numbing fall and the shock of something seeming to explode inside my head, I was sent by my primary care physician to a speech therapist. The weekly visits with the young therapist seemed to help some, but the pain continued to keep me in bed for hours at a time. I slept in the afternoons with the aid of a prescribed sleeping medication. I lay awake nights listening to the clock in the next room and noting how even the smallest sounds thrummed in my brain and throughout my entire body. While I would never have believed such a delicate sound could feel like someone in the next room wielding a hammer, the ticking often made me literally sick to my stomach. I'd even begun to keep a bucket beside my bed because I never knew when I might lose what little I may have eaten for supper.

Not once had I experienced such bewildering pain in my entire seventy-plus years. I was grateful for the young speech therapist and the encouragement she gave. I was also grateful for the physical therapist who helped with my balance and taught me how to walk without tripping or stumbling.

"But I'll never again be well! I'll never again be well!" I would tell myself as I tossed at night and tried desperately to sleep.

"Babe," my husband would say as he held my hand and prayed, "you've got to stop telling yourself it's all over or that you'll never again be without pain."

But how could I lie to myself? The truth was the truth; I was in bed more than I was out. I'd missed special occasions with my children. I'd even missed out on an unexpected visit from my New York City granddaughter who'd flown all the way to Montana to surprise me. Her mother, my youngest daughter, had arranged the visit and even paid for the trip. It was to have been a delightful time of dining and shopping. But I'd been forced to return to my bed where I could only weep and think, *I will never be well — never be well — never be well.*

Not until my third or fourth visit to the ER did I begin to feel that healing might become a possibility. An ER doctor I'd not yet seen came to sit in a chair beside my bed as he closely studied my chart. This doctor was older — like me. His hair was silver — like mine. And he wore the kindest expression — unlike the bitterness and pain that had begun to change not only my behavior but my physical appearance.

I didn't have to look into my mirror to know I'd begun to wear a strained and uncaring expression. I no longer cared if I hadn't washed my hair. Were my nails chipped? Did anything I wore look like a put-together outfit? I wished I could die. I'd been keeping to myself for days. I couldn't even go out for a hamburger with my husband or delight in my daughter and granddaughter when they'd made all that effort and spent all that money to see me. Friends had come with hot dishes for our suppers, but when I tried to eat, I'd lose everything in my stomach.

"You've lost too much weight," one friend said, as if I didn't already know that I'd grown so thin that I had a difficult time keeping my denims up to my waist. All because I'd tripped. All because the tripping had slammed my forehead into a wooden door frame, and now I would be spending the rest of my life in bed and in pain, disconnected from everything and everyone I loved.

I turned my head to look directly at the doctor who was still sitting in that chair. He was still saying nothing, looking over my charts and the reports that had been filed by the other doctors. Except now, he was looking directly at me. I could barely keep my eyes open. The prescribed medications hadn't exactly deleted the throbbing pain, but they were at least helping me sleep.

"You'll be released in a bit," the doctor was saying as if this was good news. But then what? Go home where I would spend hours and days in bed, in the dark, cut off?

"But, before you go, I want you to know…" He hadn't smiled, but there was something in his expression that suddenly made it easy for me to relax. "I want you to know," he was saying again, "that you are healthy, and you will get well."

I was healthy? I would get well? No one had even once suggested that my concussion would be resolved with a happy ending. And well? I hadn't felt well for too many weeks. Yet this doctor with some age on him like me and silver hair like mine was nodding as he placed his hand on my shoulder. And then, before I could respond with even one word, he was turning toward the exit. He would no doubt be attending to another patient, but he looked back over his shoulder and smiled. "Remember, you are healthy," he said, again nodding. "And you will get well."

And I did. Not that night, not the next day. Not even within the next week or month. But daily, when the pain would threaten to pull me under or I would begin to feel there was no use in trying, I would recall the kindness on the face of one ER doctor and hear him say, "Nancy, you are healthy, and you will get well."

And then one morning, the waiting ended, and I experienced what had been promised. It was not as soon as I had anticipated nor in the way I had imagined, but I was made well.

— Nancy Hoag —

Not Kidnapped

*The purpose of human life is to serve, and to show
compassion and the will to help others.*
~Albert Schweitzer

My brother's wedding brought us to Mexico City. It is a beautiful place with amazing food, but it also has an alarming crime rate, including kidnappings of tourists. Before arriving, my sister-in-law-to-be, who lived there, relayed all the safety tips.

"Never get in a red-and-gold cab. Those aren't licensed, and anyone can paint their car, abduct you, steal your money, and make you empty the ATM," she said. Her smile didn't match the severity of the warning.

"Check. Avoid red-and-gold cabs," I replied.

On the day of the wedding, my husband and I were to be separated. My sister-in-law had arranged for my mother and me to have our hair and makeup done in my hotel room. Once our transformation was complete, we'd head to the hotel shuttle to take us safely to the wedding pictures at the venue, which was only across the street. We could have walked if it weren't for the heels we were spending the next twelve hours swelling in.

We stood outside our hotel awaiting transport. In Mexico City, weddings are formal affairs. We were wearing gowns, so the locals knew there was a wedding.

A coach pulled up in front of us, and the hotel staff whisked us into empty seats. All the other rows were full of people in gowns and tuxedos. The occupants were having animated conversations in Spanish.

I don't speak Spanish.

We asked the driver if we were on the right transport, and the answer was a nod. Hundreds of Spanish-speaking people were going to my brother's wedding. I had only met five of them at that point, and all of them were currently at the hotel smiling for the camera, so it was reasonable to assume the driver was correct.

The van headed in the direction we were going when I realized that everyone else had plans to attend the same wedding—and it wasn't my brother's.

The van turned around and drove past our destination. We objected. The driver nodded and said, "After."

We drove about ten minutes when my mother panicked. She tried to ask the driver to let us out. Her hysterics stilled the conversation. It was a buzzkill for sure. But the driver said, "Not safe."

I prefer safe, so I acquiesced.

By the time we got to the van's destination twenty minutes later, my mother was in full boil. She was certain she was going to miss her son's wedding. I was certain we wouldn't but thought it was going to be tight to get in the pictures before the church. I was also certain that no amount of tequila would be enough for me if my mother wasn't in those photos. One of the other wedding guests consulted with the driver in Spanish and turned to us. He said he would drive us back.

Then the driver and all the passengers left us alone on the bus. We waited. And waited. My mother perspired off her smoky eye. No sign of the driver. Finally, I got out and talked to the porter at the venue. He told me we had caught a private vehicle, and they could not transport us back because the family had hired them to drive their guests.

Shit.

I asked the porter to call us an official cab. A white one.

What arrived was a slightly battered red-and-gold cab.

As my mother was objecting, I shoved her into the backseat, ducking her ginormous hair out of the way like a perp in a cop car. We needed to get to the wedding, and I have a completely unhealthy faith in people. So far, it had paid off.

We had been updating my husband and stepfather the whole time, but it was time to tell them we were on our way in a red-and-gold cab.

My mother has a lovely, even voice — except on this occasion. She was speaking to her husband in a decibel reserved for a hockey game when your son was in goal.

"We are in a red-and-gold cab with a driver who doesn't speak a word of English. I don't know where we're going, and I don't know if we're safe. He is a crazy driver, and I don't even know if he knows our destination."

Way to tip our hat, Mom. When she got off the phone, I took hold of the conversation and turned her face to mine. "Mom, we have a great driver. He is going to get us there in time for the pictures and the wedding."

"He's driving like a crazy person!" she insisted.

"He's driving like every other driver in Mexico City, and he doesn't want to be in an accident, either. I have faith that he knows where he's going, and we'll be fine. We are traveling in the right direction. All we can do is be patient."

I believed every word, and I must have sold it because my mother calmed down. We spent the next twenty minutes sweating off our three-hour makeovers. Turns out, the real threat of a red-and-gold cab was no air conditioning.

There wasn't much conversation until I said, "Here we are, Mom. We are on the road we need to be on. Not long now."

That is when the driver said in perfect English, "Is it your son's wedding you are going to?"

My mother's face turned many shades of red, but I turned many "shades of relieved" that my faith in humans had helped us.

The driver congratulated my mother and gave me a knowing wink. We made the pictures just in time. My mother and I looked like melted crayons, but we were there.

No one kidnapped us.

Maybe our driver was an honest guy, making a living driving a car. Maybe he suspected, and was right, that we were carrying nothing but a phone and lipstick in our clutches and gave us a break from his planned kidnapping.

What I learned is to never bad-mouth someone who has your safety in their hands, even if it is in another language. Having faith in people will never let you down.

I'm not saying that the power of positive thinking saved us from a kidnapping, but it saved us from a potential disaster. The wedding photos, however, were not saved from disaster. Our colorful story was all over our faces.

— Kristine Laco —

My "World Series" Moment

Dare to visualize a world in which your most
treasured dreams have become true.
~Ralph Marston

I stood in the batter's box, looking out at the pitcher's mound. Standing on the mound was none other than the legendary New York Yankees relief pitcher, Rich "Goose" Gossage. There were two outs, the bases were loaded, and my Philadelphia Phillies were trailing by three runs in the decisive Game 7 of the World Series. As I dug into the batter's box, the gravity of the moment was not lost on me. The Philadelphia crowd roared in anticipation, a sea of fans clad in red, and their last hopes were pinned on me and me alone.

Gossage glared with his signature menacing stare complete with his Fu Manchu mustache. He received his signals from his catcher, paused, and went into his windup before unleashing a 100-mile-per-hour fastball. Time slowed to a crawl. The ball cut through the chilly October air. I took a mighty swing that was followed by a distinctive CRACK. It's the sound that only a baseball hitting a bat just right can make. The sound echoed throughout Veterans Stadium; it was so loud that it temporarily drowned out the 50,000 Phillies fans who were in attendance. The baseball soared into the night sky, clearing the left-field wall. The fans erupted, and I could hear the radio call from legendary Phillies announcer Harry Kalas.

"Here's the windup... the pitch from Gossage, a swing... THERE'S A DEEP DRIVE TO LEFT.... THAT BALL IS OUTTA HERE! THE

PHILADELPHIA PHILLIES ARE THE WORLD CHAMPIONS OF BASEBALL!"

Arriving at home plate, I was met by the legendary Phillies third baseman, who was waiting to embrace me.

"YOU DID IT, KID! YOU DID IT!" Schmidt screamed as he embraced me in a bear hug.

Okay, okay, as any baseball fan knows, none of that actually happened, However, that very scene did indeed play itself out in my mind probably 10,000 times, and it was the catalyst for a kid transforming himself from a very poor hitter into a very good hitter.

So, a little backstory is probably needed here. As a nine-year-old kid playing his first season of Little League, I struggled mightily. My brother, who was two years my senior, excelled effortlessly. It always seemed so easy for him and my other teammates and friends, Brian and Scott. Their swings would cut through the air, and the ball just seemed to rocket off of their bats. It all seemed so natural for them.

For me? Not so much.

That first season, I grappled with a terrible uppercut swing. My teammates humorously talked about my "golf swing." Yells of "FORE!," a mocking reference to a golf swing, would abound.

That season, I finished with a dismal .071 batting average. I collected one solitary base hit in fourteen at-bats. At the end of the season, Coach Kelly, a patient and kind man, delivered his straightforward assessment to me.

"Brian, you have to fix that swing. You have to practice swinging level every day from now until next season!"

Determined to improve, I also sought advice from my physical-education teacher, Mr. Perkins. Like Coach Kelly, Mr. Perkins was also very patient and kind. As a kid, I always thought Mr. Perkins resembled an Olympic athlete. He was young, physically fit, and a natural at just about every sport imaginable. I approached Mr. Perkins and sought his advice. Mr. Perkins not only took the time to demonstrate proper swing mechanics but also emphasized the power of visualization and believing in myself.

He said, "You have to believe in your swing from the first moment you step into the batter's box right up to the point of contact. If you can combine proper technique with what you EXPECT to happen, you will become a better hitter."

That's all I needed to hear. If both Coach Kelly and Mr. Perkins believed in me, I needed to follow their advice and begin believing in myself. From September until the following April, rain or shine, I diligently practiced my swing. I had an old, thirty-ounce Bake McBride wooden bat that was held together with nails and electrical tape. Each day, I would take at least one hundred swings with that old bat. With each swing, I envisioned the baseball rocketing off of that bat.

Eventually, I began to envision hitting a game-winning home run in the World Series off of Yankees legendary Hall of Fame relief pitcher Rich "Goose" Gossage. I believe I chose Gossage because he was the walking embodiment of an intimidating pitcher. In my mind, if I could hit a homer off of the Goose, I could hit a homerun off of anyone.

The next season, I showcased significant improvement. I batted a respectable .285 and even began hitting doubles and triples. Every time I stepped to the plate, I expected success. By the age of twelve, I made the all-star team, and that season I hit my first legitimate home run. Admittedly, it wasn't off of Goose Gossage.

Fast forward to age fifteen. My team, the Knights of Columbus, were playing in our local Hot Stove league championship game. It was late in the game, and my team was leading by a run or two. I stepped to the plate. We had runners on first and second base. Ironically, the pitcher was a player who would later become a high-school teammate. Objectively, he was a much more talented player than I ever was. As I stood in the batter's box, the echoes of both Coach Kelly and Mr. Perkins replayed in my mind.

Coach Kelly said, "Swing level and hard, use your hips, drive the ball!"

Meanwhile, Mr. Perkins' voice was saying, "Just know that the ball is going to make contact right in the sweet spot of the bat!"

I took a deep breath.

The pitcher wound up and threw his pitch, a fastball. I swung, and there it was — that distinctive CRACK! I knew the result of the swing long before the ball cleared the left-field fence.

That home run was not the proverbial game-winning hit, but it did shift the momentum of the game, which we won. For six years, I had practiced positive thinking, and finally my dream of hitting a crucial home run in a pivotal game had come true. That moment was the absolute pinnacle of my baseball career.

In high school, the very pitcher from that championship game excelled as our team's starting second baseman. I, like many teenagers, became distracted by life, lost focus, and ended up spending most of the time on the bench. Like many kids before me, my dreams of a baseball career ended well before making it to the major leagues.

Regardless, I will always have my proverbial "World Series moment." While the home run didn't come off of Goose Gossage to win the World Series, and there was no iconic radio call from Harry Kalas, and Phillies legend Mike Schmidt wasn't there at home plate to celebrate that great moment, the memory of that one triumphant swing remains etched in my mind and exists as a testament to the power of hard work and positive thinking.

— Brian Michael —

Becoming a Gracious Receiver

It is not giving up, it is accepting.
And the light will enter. Always does.
~Kamal Ravikant

Losing my entire right leg, including my hip and pelvis, to bone cancer at thirty-two years of age was going to be hard. I knew that. But, two weeks before my biopsy results came in, I had a dream that my life on one leg would be filled with purpose. And, if I chose to live my life as an amputee, it would most certainly be a life that mattered. We had one son at the time, and I even foresaw the birth of a second son.

I didn't tell anyone about the dream. I just wrote these words in my journal: "After the dream I had last night, I know I am going to lose my leg, and it's going to be okay."

The dream was so vivid and reassuring that I walked into the doctor's office with a sense of acceptance and calm that neither the doctor nor my husband could quite accept. The doctor must have explained to me three or four times that he was going to have to amputate my hip and pelvis before the aggressive cancer moved to my lungs. He explained that chemo and radiation were not options. The only thing that would save me was this drastic and radical surgery to remove my entire leg, hip and pelvis on my right side.

It was December 22, 1987, and he wanted me in before Christmas to do the surgery. I calmly asked him if he could guarantee me another Christmas. He shook his head sadly and said he couldn't do that.

I smiled, knowing the dream had reassured me of many years of life to come as an amputee, and said, "Well, I'll tell you what. I am hosting a baby shower for my best friend. Our three-year-old is expecting Mommy to be there on Christmas morning to open presents with him. I want to celebrate Christmas and New Year's with my family and friends. We have a wedding to go to in the new year, and I want one more night of dancing on two legs with my husband. I've checked my calendar, and I'm free on January 6th. Will that work for you?"

His mouth opened, but no words came out. Finally, he nodded and said, "I'll make that work." And so, on January 6, 1988, I became a right hemipelvectomy amputee — one of the rarest types of amputations.

After the surgery, I recuperated at the G.F. Strong Rehabilitation Centre in Vancouver. I suffered excruciating phantom pain where it felt like someone was poking me with an electric cattle prod in the limb that was no longer there. I struggled to regain my strength and learn how to walk on crutches. The strength of the dream, however, kept me motivated and pushing through the pain every day.

One day, I stepped on the scale in the treatment room, and the number shocked me. Even without my leg, 105 pounds was far too thin. I felt that I was disappearing, and I was determined to walk to the nearest store to buy myself some chocolate bars and doughnuts to try and get some calories into me. I left the building and started walking.

I don't know where I thought I was going, but I figured there had to be a corner store somewhere nearby. I made my way to a drugstore and walked in on my crutches through the open door as a couple walked out. No doughnuts, but I bought my chocolate bars and wandered around inside for a while before deciding to head back.

When I tried to push open the door to leave, nothing happened. The door was too heavy. I remember looking up as a feeling of despair washed over me. *Seriously? This is what my life on one leg is going to be like? Now, I can't even open a door for myself?* Tears came to my eyes as frustration and sadness built up inside me. During that moment of absolute helplessness, a man appeared behind me. I don't know where he came from. I hadn't seen him in the store earlier. He was tall like my dad, about six feet, five inches. And he had the kindest eyes I'd ever seen. In a voice that was both soft and strong at the same time, he asked if he could help me with the door.

In that moment, I had a choice. I could have refused his help and insist I could do it myself, which was a lie. Or I could do what I did, which was to look up at him with gratitude and say, "Yes, please."

He smiled down at me, and with one hand, as if the door were as light as a feather, he pushed it open for me. With relief beyond words, I said a simple "Thank you," and his reply has helped shape my life as an amputee. He said, "You are so very welcome. It was entirely my pleasure." He smiled down at me, and I watched him walk away with an added bounce in his step.

Was he an angel? I don't know. But those few words have stayed with me all the years since and made me realize that it is impossible to be a gracious giver if someone is not an equally gracious receiver. Both roles are equally important to balance things. Up until losing my leg, I had always been the giver — the one offering to help with doors and lend a hand when needed. Now, it was my turn to learn to accept help with grace.

Everything in my dream has come true. I gave birth to my second son less than three years after my surgery. I've written books, spoken to thousands of people, and appeared on TV and radio shows. And, yes, one of my favourite keynote speeches is about the importance of learning how to be a gracious giver and an equally gracious receiver. Now, decades after losing my leg and rapidly approaching seventy, on most days I am still strong enough to open a door by myself. But if someone offers to help me, I smile and say, "Thank you! That would be lovely!" And I know that, in giving me a hand, they have lifted themselves as well.

— Glenda Standeven —

Silver Linings

Out of the Mouths of Babes

*Life is 10 percent what you make it
and 90 percent how you take it.*
~Irving Berlin

"Daddy, please take me to AstroWorld. Can you? Will you?" begged my four-year-old daughter, Shawn.

I didn't want to go to the amusement park, but what was I going to say, especially when I looked into my daughter's big, brown eyes? It was made even more difficult by the fact that I was disabled (having been shot in the head as an innocent bystander to a robbery). Plus, we were in the middle of a steamy Houston summer. But I continued to stare into Shawn's big eyes, begging me, her father, to take her to AstroWorld. In the end, I gave in.

We stood in line for the first ride, inching our way up for forty-five minutes until we finally got to the front. Shawn climbed onto the ride first, her excitement building, followed by me climbing in awkwardly to sit down next to her.

The ride attendant approached us, buckled us in, and said, "Sir, I could tell by the way you walked that you're disabled. We at AstroWorld have two policies for disabled guests: They get to go to the front of the line, and they get to ride twice."

With these words, the attendant finished buckling us in and walked away to help another group of riders.

I did not think much of the woman's comments. However, my daughter looked up at me, smiled from ear to ear, and yelled with glee,

"DADDY, THANK GOD YOU WERE SHOT!"

At first, I sat there in shock. However, I quickly realized that my young daughter was teaching me something very valuable that day: With everything that is bad, there has to be some good. Shawn was teaching me to always look for the silver lining.

— Michael Jordan Segal, MSW —

11

Appreciating the Little Things Close to Home

Enjoy the little things in life because one day you'll
look back and realize they were the big things.
~Kurt Vonnegut

I wish I were a more spontaneous person. I am not referring to those daredevils who throw all caution to the wind and bungee jump down a precipitous peak. I am not even thinking about those courageous souls who ring in the new year with an icy dip in the North Atlantic Ocean as a member of the Polar Bear Club, or even those free spirits who drop everything at the spur of the moment to join a friend on a cross-country road trip. I just wish that, for once, I could be one of those carefree people who slip into their seats just as the theater curtain rises, or hustle down the aisle of a plane seconds before takeoff, or skip onto the bus to score the last seat as it exits the terminal.

But that's not me. I'm the one who arrives at the theater before the doors even open. I'm the first person sitting in the boarding area in an airport. I have committed the bus schedules to memory, and I always board at the head of the line. Yes, being organized does have its advantages and often ensures a smoother ride. But when life throws you a wild pitch, something that is completely out of your control, the only way to cope is to regroup, reset, adjust your perspective, and think positive.

For years, I had been fantasizing about my retirement. I'm certain many in the Baby Boomer generation share that common dream — the wonderful freedom that accompanies passing the sixty-five-year yard line. As a certified card-carrying Medicare beneficiary, my major healthcare needs would be covered, my 401K accounts would be ready to harvest, and my bucket list would take center stage.

A born organizer, I had planned my first year of freedom down to the most meticulous, minute detail. I was scheduled to leave my full-time position in early 2020. In April, my husband and I would embark on the trip of a lifetime, cruising down the Rhine River, where we would explore European villages and landmarks. Three months later, we would travel to the West Coast to reconnect with classmates we hadn't seen in thirty years. Then we planned to tour the West Coast, beginning with cups of coffee in a Seattle cafe and ending with fish tacos in San Diego. Autumn would find us back in our New Jersey home, preparing to spread our so-called "snowbird" wings to explore a Florida retreat for several weeks that winter.

Wasn't it John Lennon who stated, "Life is what happens while you are busy making other plans"? Well, I certainly did not figure on the pandemic or the impact this virus would have on my long-awaited retirement.

Let me first state that my heart, prayers and thoughts go out to everyone who lost loved ones, jobs, homes, businesses, and careers during this crisis. In comparison, the disappointments and frustrations I experienced seem so minor. However, I felt as if I were living the words of Langston Hughes when he penned the words, "What happens to a dream deferred?" To me, I felt like my long-awaited dream had completely dried up just like that raisin in the sun, with no relief or Plan B in sight. So much for my meticulous organization!

And, one by one, every plan I had painstakingly put in place during the past few years collapsed. The river trip was canceled, the reunion was scrapped, and the Florida vacation was abandoned. Then, the restaurants and diners closed their doors, the movie theaters and playhouses grew dark, and the retail shops and malls were shuttered. The only businesses that remained open were pharmacies, food stores, and hospitals. To gain entry, everyone needed a mask, gloves, and hand sanitizer. When I didn't think things could get any worse, the national supply chain sputtered, and staples such as chicken, paper products, and household cleaners were suddenly in short supply.

I distinctly recall one gray, stormy morning in early April when I spent the day chasing down rolls of toilet paper. I finally unearthed three precious rolls in a deserted pharmacy after kneeling on the wet floor looking through discarded cardboard boxes and newspapers. When I walked back to my car, I remember sobbing, drenching my cloth mask, thinking that I should be exploring a winery in Southern France, not spending the past two hours foraging for rolls of toilet paper in northern New Jersey!

That awful day was certainly one of my lowest points. But I can attest that, once the human spirit hits rock bottom, there is only one directional option. It has to go up... at least somewhat. That day was a turning point for me. I decided I was not going to remain a victim, and my mindset had to change. How could I adjust my thinking?

While I realized that I could not explore Europe, I could walk to our local park, and I did every day. Truth be told, it's a lovely area, with a lake, stone bridge, and winding walking paths. I had just never noticed it. Those solitary sojourns offered me the opportunity to stop, slow down, and truly think how I wanted to spend my time.

While I knew that I could not join my former classmates on the West Coast, I could befriend those around me — the same individuals who would soon be known as "local heroes," the workers in our neighborhood pharmacy, food stores, and municipalities. They became wonderful acquaintances and later friends. They had always been there, but I'd taken them for granted. But now, Benita at the neighborhood pharmacy, Tristan at the local grocery store, and Denise at the township's Public Works Department have become part of my extended "family."

And while I recognized that I could not travel to Florida, I could read about and even channel the spirits of those who battled challenges worse than those I was facing. I became an unofficial expert on the Spanish Influenza of 1918, and reading about the trials and tribulations of those brave souls over a century ago strengthened and changed me for the better. Our book club selected several of these historical fiction selections for discussion over Zoom and, despite the challenges brought on by the coronavirus, all our members signed off from those meetings feeling blessed for the advances made by modern technology.

Looking back, it's been quite a journey — certainly not the one I nor anyone else could have predicted, but I survived and even thrived in a different way. And, I have to report, those walks in the park, those conversations with the neighborhood workers, and those afternoons spent reading in the comfort of my own home brought me something that the long-anticipated European vacation could not. Much to my amazement, I discovered a quiet joy, a sense of well-being, and an overwhelming feeling of gratitude and appreciation for those things closest to home.

— Barbara Davey —

12

Falling Short of a Gold Star

Develop success from failures. Discouragement and
failure are two of the surest steppingstones to success.
~Dale Carnegie

My day was ruined before I even got out of bed. I wiped sleep from my eyes and reached over to the night table where my fingers fumbled toward my smartphone. First things first: scan e-mails.

As I scrolled through messages, I stopped at one from my publisher. My new novel was slated to release in two weeks. Could this be the review I'd been waiting on for months?

I opened the e-mail and spied a link to a pre-publication review. Yes, this was it: the review, the one that had the power to sing the praises of a story I'd enthusiastically written and, hopefully, launch it far and wide. This review was from a notable professional outlet that chose, from thousands of books submitted each month, to pull mine from the stack and give it a nod. In my mind, I had positively imagined the jubilation of this moment... a joyful moment capped with a proverbial gold star! I had never been so proud of, excited by, or had more confidence in anything I'd ever written before.

As I pressed my finger on the blue-underlined link in the e-mail and waited for the review to engage, I inhaled a deep breath as though I were preparing to leap off a very high diving board that would keep me from coming up for air for a long time.

Ta-da!

There it was: the title of my book and the cover. With a swell of pride, I read the review, gasping as I encountered words like "sloppy," "mismatched," "saccharine," and "overly sentimental."

My heart sank. Everything I had imagined — the hope and promise I had planned for — went *splat!* My mental high dive left me to belly flop into the water as if I'd been punched in the gut.

I stayed in bed, stunned by defeat, until my publisher e-mailed a few minutes later. "Disappointed in the review, too... Please don't let this do a number on you...."

But it did.

Sensitivity is what made my writing rich. But that same sensitivity could often be a curse in dealing with life off the page. In my head, and in the larger scheme of things, I knew this review shouldn't be such a big deal. After all, I'd lived through the deaths of loved ones. I'd navigated through labyrinths of love and romance gone miserably wrong. I'd even faced cancer and other physical challenges. But pursuing a dream, giving it your all and making sacrifices, and not having it play out the way you'd hoped and envisioned — the way you'd positively imagined — was just as devastating and heart-wrenching.

I read and reread that review until each scathing word was seared into my memory. How could that critic find nothing worthy in a story I felt was transcendent?

In the week that followed, I started to beat myself up. Soon, I was up to my eyeballs, sinking in a quicksand of self-doubt.

When the novel was officially launched a few days later, I wanted to crawl in a hole. But then, my publisher e-mailed, "Happy Release Day! Trust you're full-steam ahead in promoting the book?"

Happy? How could I possibly be happy promoting a book that was panned?

And there, wallowing in fear and self-pity, the voice of the devil — his insidious, belittling whisper — gave me a jolt. "Why don't you just pack it in, Kath? Admit it, you failed!"

I countered his niggling jeer with, "I'm not a quitter. And I'm not a failure. I'm not gonna let the opinion of one lone reviewer derail everything I've believed in!"

That was it—the moment I decided to take down the streamers at my pity party. How could I not keep my commitment to a book that, despite that one review, I loved and believed in, as did my trusted beta readers, everyone in my writers' group, my editor, and everyone at my publishing company? In my heart, I truly believed this novel would prove meaningful to many people.

Determined, I rolled up my sleeves and spent hours each week querying hundreds of book bloggers and other reviewers. I wrote personal messages, respectfully asking them to read the novel and offer their honest thoughts and opinions online. Like a cheerleader unwilling to give up on a losing team, I rah-rahed and set up giveaways and features to entice readers. I sent out e-mail blasts and snail-mail flyers and postcards to bookstores and libraries, book clubs and specific readers I thought might be interested in the story or pass on the information to others who might be. There were press releases to mail, columns to write for blogs and magazines, and even interviews set up with radio programs, newspapers, my alma matter and podcasts. Through these connections, I was also asked to speak at conferences, schools and assisted-living communities where I told the story of how and why I wrote the novel, what it meant to me, and what I hoped readers would take away from the book.

The more I promoted, the more my readership and royalties grew. My enthusiasm rebounded until the sting of that first review was diluted amid a sea of other reviews—glowing reviews—that poured in. There were hundreds of them, along with personal letters, e-mails, social-media messages from readers—even strangers from other parts of the world—who'd read the story and were not only moved and entertained but were eager to share their own experiences that mirrored themes portrayed in the novel.

Each and every victory became more gratifying than the next. That one simple shift in mindset and attitude diminished my discouragement and empowered me to believe in myself so I could propel my story out into the world. By doing so, the novel ultimately reached those who were destined to find it, those who appreciated my vision. By doing everything in my power to push back against defeat, I wound up vigorously promoting that book and personally connecting with probably even more readers than if I'd received a gold-star review in the first place.

—Kathleen Gerard—

13

The Best Day Ever

*I have learned over the years that the nicest thing I can
do is to just say to myself, "Good Morning Darling,
I love you; we're going to have a really great day today."*
~Louise Hay

It was supposed to be the best day ever. My husband Doug and
I were on vacation with our travel trailer. The Wisconsin summer countryside was breathtaking. But now I was sitting in the
cab of a tow truck with a Doberman Pinscher glaring at me and
growling.

Our truck had an oil-pressure problem, but we were confident
that we could make it home to California in a week to have it fixed.
We were wrong. As we left the scenic Wisconsin Dells, our truck shut
down and we pulled over to the shoulder, unable to restart the engine.

After an hour or so, our tow truck arrived. I had visions of us
having to leave our trailer on the side of the highway, in the middle
of a beautiful yet unknown nowhere. Our trailer and everything we
packed would be vulnerable. I quickly placed a few granola bars and
water bottles in my tote bag.

The friendly tow-truck driver escorted me up into the backseat
of his truck.

"Don't worry about Brutus, ma'am. He's friendly," he told me.

Let me tell you at this point that I am a cat person. I sat down and
smiled weakly at the snarling dog. *Darn those granola bars!* I thought.

I'm a kindergarten teacher, and we start every school day by chanting my homemade rap. "First, we're gonna work. Then, we're gonna play. And we're gonna have a happy, happy day! Say hey!" We repeat that several times until the kiddos are appropriately awake and smiling. Then, we all yell, "Let's have the BEST DAY EVER!!"

And we always do.

With Brutus staring at me, I began chanting this to myself. I spoke directly to Brutus and quietly said, "Let's have the best day ever."

When Doug and the driver returned, they told me the good news that they would be able to tow our trailer along with the truck. The driver headed to a repair shop in the nearby town of Baraboo, about ten miles away.

The owner of the shop looked at our truck and listened to our story. He sat us in his office and began making calls. He called Glen somebody and asked if Glen could borrow John's old truck and wait a few days to get his repairs done. He said yes. The owner did this several times to make sure the people ahead of us were taken care of. He even made arrangements to loan one of his own cars to someone.

He told us that they would get started on our truck as soon as we could park our trailer somewhere. Then, he jumped up, left, and returned with a young man named Chris. He introduced Chris as one of his mechanics and told us he had a large backyard and would be willing to let us park and even sleep in our trailer there. He said he would share electricity, too.

We accepted his offer and parked our trailer in the backyard of a small house a few blocks away. We weren't able to plug into the electricity, but we did hook up to his water. Chris then offered to loan us his car, but we thought that was too much, so we declined.

"Well, it's getting close to dinnertime, so please let me drive you to Main Street. You can walk around, eat dinner, and walk back to the trailer whenever you want." We accepted, but I wondered how far the return walk might be. It turned out that Baraboo was only seven miles from end to end, and the main drag was about a half-mile from his house.

We settled on a family-run pizza place for dinner where we ordered a medium pizza. The owner came out and visited with us while our pizza was baking. Then, he brought out an extra-large pizza. We told him there was a mistake, but he disagreed.

"You folks look hungry! Eat what you can and take the rest with you!" I began to think that maybe this day didn't turn out to be the worst day ever.

After eating, we took a walk around the town square and park. Everywhere we went, we saw elephant pictures, carvings and decorations. There were pictures of circus wagons, and every wall in town had carved elephants walking in a line, each one using their trunks to hold the tail of the elephant in front. Miles and miles of elephants walked in lines.

The next day, we walked over to the repair shop, and the owner told us that they should have the repairs done that day. He asked if we needed anything, so I inquired about a laundromat. He said it was one block down, so we walked over to do laundry. The owner of the laundromat was there, and we offered to give him a few dollars if we could charge our cell phones. He wouldn't accept money and said to please come back to charge anytime.

At the café, we asked the waitress about the town's elephant decor. She said that Baraboo was home to the Ringling Brothers. In 1884, they launched their first tour as a circus. Over the years, they expanded from a wagon show to a highly successful railroad show with 225 employees, touring all over the U.S. Baraboo remained their headquarters until 1918 when they combined with Barnum and Bailey Circus.

After lunch, we spent the afternoon at the charming library down the street and discussed how friendly everyone had been to us. The kindness of strangers was impressive. It was something I had never thought about. We're not used to being on the receiving end of kind deeds, and this was the purest type of kindness. The heart of kindness is to do something for another with no thought of reciprocation. These people would never see us again. They weren't doing these gestures for money. These small acts of goodwill were powerfully uplifting.

That evening, the owner of the car-repair shop called and told us that our truck was ready. As we said "thank you" and "goodbye," the mechanic who worked on our truck asked if he could pray with us.

It was a simple prayer of health and traveling protection.

We felt a small sense of sadness driving away from our new friends. As we made our way onto the highway, I said, "This was the BEST DAY EVER!!"

— Laura McKenzie —

14

Kindling Friendship

When you assume negative intent, you're angry.
If you take away that anger and assume positive
intent, you will be amazed.
~Indra Nooyi

Not long ago, I had a Kindle that was acting up. It wasn't that old, and no matter what I did, it kept telling me that I didn't have any more storage to add new books. Seeing that I only had about thirty books stored on this marvel of technology, I was irked and frustrated.

I needed help. According to the company's website, I had three ways to contact customer service: telephone, e-mail or online "chat." I chose to chat. Immediately, a page appeared informing me that I would be chatting with someone named Chandu. It wasn't clear if my helper was male or female. I steeled myself for a frustrating exchange like ones I'd had before on other websites. I only hoped that this person spoke English!

"Ohh-kay," I murmured to myself as the letters appeared on the screen: "Hello! My name is Chandu. How can I help you today?"

I explained my problem in detail, and he understood right away. After I answered a few questions, he explained that he would need to have virtual access to my device and run it through a few tests. Would I be willing to wait about fifteen minutes while he did this? Of course, I would.

I'd been sitting at my desk, tapping a beat with my pencil when

I jokingly wrote, "So, how's the weather where you are, Chandu?"

To my surprise, the answer came back: "Very hot! I'm in India. Where are you?"

"I'm in North Carolina, USA."

"It's winter there, isn't it? Do you have snow? I love snow, though I've never experienced it."

"We have it sometimes but not very often. North Carolina is in the South."

"Someday, my wife and I will go where there is snow. Right now, she is taking care of our little girl."

"Oh, how old is your daughter?"

"Six months old."

"Oh, that's a wonderful age! They're just starting to notice the world."

"Do you have children?"

"I have five grandchildren."

"How wonderful! You must be so happy!"

"I am. What is your little girl's name?"

He typed out a name that I can't remember now. "It has to do with music," he said.

"That's lovely. Are you a musician?"

"No, but my wife is. Ah, I think I have found the problem with your Kindle. I'm afraid it can't be fixed, but if you will mail in your device, I can arrange for you to be sent a refurbished one. Would that be all right?"

"That would be wonderful, Chandu! Thank you so much! I'd like to send you one of my books." I explained that I was a mystery writer.

"That's amazing! I'm looking up your name on Amazon now. There it is. Four books! I'm ordering them!"

"Oh, no. Let them be my gift to you!"

"I can't accept gifts in my job. But it's been great to talk to a real author. And to read the books of one I've actually met! Tell me, do you think you will have snow in North Carolina this winter?"

"I can't be sure, but it's possible. It's been great to talk to someone from India. Say hello to your wife and daughter for me."

"I will. God bless you!"

"And you as well, Chandu."

There I was, all ready to be an outraged customer that day, but Chandu charmed the anger right out of me. Of course, it didn't hurt that I got a replacement Kindle, but I do believe that, even if he hadn't been able to help me, he would have established a bond across the miles with his youthful enthusiasm and friendliness.

It has snowed a couple of times since I had that conversation with my friend, and each time it did, I thought of him.

Wish you could be here to see this, Chandu.

—Ellen Edwards Kennedy—

15

I Can Do This

*But I learned that there's a certain character that can
be built from embarrassing yourself endlessly.*
~Christian Bale

Recently divorced and jobless, I needed to find work. I picked up a newspaper, flipped to the want ads, and groaned. I hadn't been in the workforce for years. What could I be qualified to do? I began to highlight the possibilities.

I crossed out more ads than I highlighted before I found this: Waitress Wanted – Day Shift. "Really?" I spoke out loud. I giggled. "Why not?" I sat back, smiled and wondered whether I'd have a uniform.

I dressed quickly in a dark blue pencil skirt and white, button-down blouse. I swept my long, blond hair into a high ponytail. I slipped my black flats on my feet, paused at the mirror, and pinched each cheek for a little color. "I can do this," I said to the mirror.

When I got to the restaurant, the owner asked, "Have you had any experience?"

"Oh, yes," I beamed before I spouted a list of establishments where I'd worked as a teenager. It wasn't really a lie; well, maybe a little.

"Great! I think we can use you. Can you start in a few days?"

"Yes, yes!" I answered with almost too much enthusiasm.

On my first day, the owner placed me in a back room. She explained it would be a little slower at lunch. This way, I could more or less break into a routine of sorts. I busied myself. I filled salt and pepper shakers and took note of how the other waitresses set the tables.

I looked up from the prep station to see what looked like a "herd" of men coming to my station. Panic set in. There were ten of them. I watched them take their seats and settle in before I calmed myself. "I can do this," I repeated several times to myself. I picked up menus. My hands shook as I headed toward the table.

"Hi, y'all. My name's Flo. I'm new, and I'd really appreciate it if y'all would order the fish special to make it really easy on me." I have no clue why I put on a silly accent and pretended to be a waitress I'd seen on a television comedy, but all the men laughed, and this put me at ease. Besides, they all ordered the fish.

Several rounds of drinks passed through the gentlemen's hands before the food was ready. I'd watched some of the other waitresses pile at least three plates on an arm. It didn't look so hard. When my order came up, I confidently placed three plates on one arm and headed through the swinging kitchen door.

Plate one came off, nice and easy. Plate two, the same. Plate three, however, teetered before it fell directly onto the lap in seat number three. Yep, you can see it, can't you? Fish, fries and creamy coleslaw ran right down the front of the gentleman's trousers.

"Oh, no, I'm so sorry!" I yelled. "Here, let me help you." I grabbed napkins from the table and started to frantically wipe the front of his trousers before I realized what I was doing. The entire table of men snickered and then broke into raucous laughter. I know I turned red from the top of my forehead to the tip of my toes before I made it back to the kitchen.

Behind the kitchen door, the entire staff stomped their feet, held their stomachs and reeled with laughter. I leaned against the wall and broke into tears before I then fell into hiccupping laughter. I composed myself and once again said, "I can do this."

I walked calmly to the table, apologized and offered to pay the cleaning bill for the trousers. I also brought out the remainder of the order without incident. The gentlemen's laughter quieted down, and they ordered a few more drinks and went about their conversation as if nothing had happened. I retreated to the kitchen and continued to scoff with the staff about my ineptness at plate handling.

After I presented the bills, I continued to apologize, ask for forgiveness and smile. When the men left, every plate had a napkin with a smiley face drawn on it and a twenty-dollar tip. "Yep," I said to myself, "I can do this."

— Alice Klies —

The Biggest Blessing

*Better to lose count while naming your blessings than
to lose your blessings to counting your troubles.*
~Maltbie D. Babcock

"Is he sick?" the lady supervising the pumpkin patch's corn pit asked me. Considering that I was holding my almost two-year-old in my arms while both of us were covered in vomit, her question was valid.

I shook my head. "No, he's had chemo," I replied. "It's messed with his system, and sometimes this just happens."

It was nearly a year ago when we learned that our then nine-month-old had a rare form of cancer on his adrenal gland. After the tumor was surgically removed, he embarked on a brutal chemotherapy protocol that left us practically living at the hospital for a while. If he wasn't in for treatment, he was in for complications.

I studied my baby. One of the results of the surgery and treatment was adrenal insufficiency. This left him dependent on steroids that we gave him daily and put him at risk of an adrenal crisis, which would be life-threatening and could be coupled with vomiting. Thankfully, however, this was obviously not an adrenal crisis. He was happy and alert after losing his lunch, so that was one blessing in all this mess. No, this vomiting episode was likely due to me placing him in the corn pit moments before. I had thought he would enjoy it, but instead he had become hysterical.

Although I quickly picked him up again, it was too little too late.

Seconds later, he threw up on me. Thankfully, he managed to throw up *only* on me. As covered as I was, I don't know how he managed to spare the corn pit and everyone around us, but he did. So, that was the second blessing of the day.

"Would you like a towel?" the sympathetic employee asked.

"That would be wonderful," I replied. "My husband went to find some paper towels, but I'm going to need a lot."

The sweet lady returned in a few minutes with a dampened kitchen towel. "You can just throw it away when you're done," she told me kindly. The cloth fibers of the towel worked so much better than the paper products my husband had found, making it blessing number three. After some scrubbing, I was able to remove most of the goop from my clothes. Fortunately, we had a change of clothes for my son, blessing number four, so we returned to the car to change him and head home.

As we drove home, I thought about all the little blessings in this admittedly unpleasant situation: the kindness of strangers, that it had happened at the end instead of the beginning of the event, and that it wasn't a health crisis for him. We had truly experienced so many blessings.

But then I realized that all these blessings paled in comparison to the biggest blessing of that day: Our baby was here, with us, and able to vomit all over me. So many parents who have had a child diagnosed with cancer would give anything to change places with me, so misery at the unfortunate turn of events wasn't even an option. He was alive, his cancer was in remission, and despite the struggles he would continue to have, he was doing well.

His first pumpkin-patch experience might not have gone exactly as I had envisioned, but we had an amazing time together as a family. With that thought, I rolled my window down a little and thanked God for the vomit.

—Elizabeth Sowder—

Basic Life Training

I could not imagine that the future I was walking
toward could compare in any way to
the past I was leaving behind.
~Nelson Mandela

The first time I realized the benefit of being a child of divorce, I was in basic training. Each flight had two training instructors; we called them TIs. For the first few days, our TIs shared responsibilities.

On our third day, duty assignments were handed out. Before I left for basic training, my enlisted friends had warned me, "Volunteer early. You don't want to be the last man standing. You'll get a job no one wants." Not wanting bathroom duty, I volunteered when the TI asked who had marching band or color guard experience.

My clever volunteering landed me at the front of the flight, by myself, carrying a flag on a large pole. I had tried out for flag team in high school but I sucked at carrying and twirling a flag. Now, to my chagrin, I would be marching everywhere with a flapping flag on a tall pole.

Our older TI had lots of rules. Her presentation was rigid. She sneered at my blue-tinged glasses and mocked my squad leader's nicotine-withdrawal symptoms.

Our younger TI was less wordy but seemed to be on the verge of exploding in anger. She conveyed expectations with a mere look.

The two TIs constantly conferred, as if they hadn't worked together before. I stayed on alert, trying to figure out what their combined next move would be.

Before the end of our first week, the older TI had a medical emergency. The younger TI snarled and spat at us. "I'm not going to get a break for a couple of weeks. I don't even get to go home to my family, so you'd all better get used to it."

During my first training as a unit guide, I prayed, "God, please help me do this and help me graduate with this flight. I don't think I can stand repeating any of this." By the end of that first night, my shoulders and forearms ached, and my back felt like one giant knot. The shorter practice pole didn't even have a flag on it, so I knew things would only get worse.

The next day, as we marched up to the chow hall, I could see the other guides lined up near the door. I had not received that directive, so I maintained my position at the front of the flight. I heard our TI conferring with other TIs. After a pause, she came up to me and whispered, "From now on, when we get to the chow hall, after I call the flight to a halt, wait for a break and then march up to that wall near the door. When the duty sergeant gives you the signal to proceed, call our flight to attention. You will lead everyone in the door."

I marched forward and waited. On cue, I called the flight to attention. As our first squad approached, I stepped in front of them and began marching toward the door, wondering where I was supposed to put the full-sized pole. It was too tall to fit through the doorway, so I tilted it over my shoulder.

"Airman," I recognized the voice of the duty sergeant. "What the [bleep] do you think you are doing?"

I tried to turn around, but the flagpole prevented a proper address. He ordered our entire flight back into formation and then dressed down my TI, who humbly asked where he wanted the flags kept. Then, he looked at me.

"Why are you still standing there? Get to the back of the line."

I took my pole and stood behind the last guide.

When the duty sergeant signaled again, I placed the flag behind the door and led our flight through the entryway with a quiet dignity, even though the rocks in my stomach were shouting more than the muscles in my back.

Our TI came up behind me at our table and quietly snarled in my ear, "If you ever embarrass me again…" Her Smokey Bear training-instructor hat drilled into my temple, and my glasses skewed, grinding the nose pad against the bridge of my nose. She didn't need to finish her sentence. My imagination filled in all manner of woes.

For the next two weeks, I was the star guide, but in week three the older TI returned. I was eager to demonstrate my knowledge of the rules. We marched to the chow hall that morning. When the flight entering the chow hall passed by, I started toward the door.

"Airman! Halt!"

I halted. I heard her hat being pulled off her head and hitting her thigh. I heard the hat being slapped back on her head, and then the sound of her hard-soled shoes clicking steadily across the blacktop toward me. She appeared in front of my face, her wide hat bill two inches from my eyes.

"What the hell do you think you are doing?"

"Ma'am. Standing by the door, ma'am."

"Standing by the door." Sarcasm dripped from her lips. She looked around at the other TIs and huffed. Then, she snarled, "Are you tired or something?"

"Ma'am. No, ma'am."

"Are you in a hurry?"

"Ma'am. No, ma'am."

Her voice echoed off the cement overhang. "Then get back with your flight where you belong!"

"Ma'am. Yes, ma'am." I about-faced and marched back into position.

For the next twenty days, our instructors alternated every two or three days, only overlapping for an hour or two to pass along informa-tion. If the younger TI was with us, I stood by the door. If the older TI was with us, I stood with the flight. All was well.

Then one day, late in week five, both instructors were marching with us to the chow hall. My teeth tasted metallic. Little bright spots flashed in front of my eyes. I prayed, "God, what do I do now?" Then an idea formed: I would just follow the rule of the TI calling the orders. The younger instructor's voice came through loud and clear. I halted with the flight and then marched toward the door.

Near the door, I did an about-face as required and stood facing our flight. I could see the older TI's mouth drop open. The four squad leaders stood at ease, smirking. I looked over their heads. The older TI turned to the younger TI.

"What in God's name is she doing?"

The younger TI looked in my direction, one eyebrow tilted down.

"I always have her stand there." She turned to the older TI. "What do you have her do?"

I could see realization dawn on their faces. Then both heads slowly turned my way. The squad leaders appeared to be stifling a chuckle. I focused on a cloud hovering in the blue sky behind our flight and waited for the duty sergeant's signal.

Inside the dining hall, my squad leader sauntered to the table and slid into the chair next to me. "Well, slick, how did you manage that one?"

"Easy. I had divorced parents. The rules were different at each house. I've had to learn to play by two sets of rules since I was ten."

— Debbie Maselli —

Chapter 3

Reframe It

18

Selective Memories

Stay positive. The only difference between a good day
and a bad day is your attitude.
~Dennis S. Brown

M y daughter Heidi ran around the backyard in the summer sunshine, being her usual goofy three-year-old self. She spied the large gallon glass jar on the patio that was filled with water and tea bags, brewing sun tea. She went over and sat down on the top of the closed lid. It seemed like a nice little stool, just her size. But the hot jar immediately collapsed into a thousand shards of glass.

Heidi screamed as she hit the cement. She stood up and displayed a small but deep cut on the back of her thigh. Blood poured out of the cut. We were off to the emergency room in a matter of minutes. I tried to calm Heidi as she sat crying softly while we waited for help. After a long wait, we were ushered into a small room, and Dr. Anderson came in. He was very calm and friendly. He talked about his grandchildren and told Heidi a silly joke as he examined her injury. He said the cut was pretty deep but not too bad. He put Heidi at ease, and she seemed to hardly notice when he gave her a shot and stitched her up.

After he bandaged Heidi's leg, he left for a minute and returned with a clean rubber surgical glove. He blew it up like a balloon, tied it, and used a marker to draw a chicken face on it, like the glove was a chicken head and the thumb of the glove was the chicken's beak. Heidi laughed and played with her new chicken toy for the next few days until it finally deflated.

Fast forward thirty years. Beautiful adult Heidi and the family were sharing memories at a holiday dinner, and we talked about the sun-tea jar accident. I shared what I knew to be the truth: broken glass, Heidi screaming, blood, long waiting-room wait, etc. At this point, Heidi looked at me, genuinely surprised.

"Oh, Mom," she said, "that's not what happened at all."

And she told us her memory of what had transpired. It was much more pleasant, with a quick crash and driving straight to the emergency room. Then she spoke for a good while about Dr. Anderson — how funny and kind he was — and told us all about that silly chicken-head glove. She said she looked back fondly on that day.

I thought about Heidi's words for days. She somehow had the ability to sort out and sift down the unpleasant elements and only remember the good parts of what happened. To hear Heidi tell it, one would think it was a pleasant visit to sweet grandpa Dr. Anderson, not a bloody accident.

Then, I realized that the ability to filter out the negative things in our lives is a good thing and something that I now try to do. The past is the past. Why rehearse the uncomfortable and downright hard parts over and over? What is the benefit?

I caught myself looking back at my own childhood and thought about several incidents that could be viewed as less than happy, but as a young child I didn't dwell on those things. Instead, I chose to remember the sweet and good things, just like Heidi did. Maybe all children naturally do that, but most of us have lost that ability over time.

So now I try to live in the moment and enjoy the good, get through the bad quickly, and not dwell on it. Heidi taught me that there's always something good in everything, and that's what we should focus on. And a heartfelt thank-you to all the Dr. Andersons out there who are so good at what they do. Their kindness to children will not soon be forgotten.

— Laura McKenzie —

19

My Photo-a-Day Transformation

Greet each day with your eyes open to beauty, your mind
open to change, and your heart open to love.
~Paula Finn

Several years ago, I went through a bad stretch. I was beaten down by loneliness and marriage problems, and our house was constantly going through construction. To top it all off, my epilepsy became so severe that I spent a life-threatening week in the hospital, part of the time in a coma.

After a miraculous escape from death, it dawned on me: My number should have been called, but I was still here. There must be a reason. I needed to set my life on a better trajectory. But what could I do? Plenty of things had to change, but most of the pieces were out of my control.

Then, a thought flashed through my mind.

The only thing I had control over was my response to situations. It was my choice whether I saw the troubles as defeats or challenges. Whether I saw the issues as shameful or as opportunities for transformation.

Instead of letting all the failures beat me up, I could celebrate the good things. I could accept my life as a work in progress and focus on the joyful moments, no matter how small, rather than self-criticize the painful ones. But how?

I'd always enjoyed photography, but in the mess of life, I had pushed it aside.

I brought my camera back out and decided to capture one special moment every day with a photo. By the end of the year, I would have 365 good memories recorded.

That was the plan. In the end, there were plenty of days when I didn't get a photo, but many days when I did. And as I looked through the growing number of pictures, new thought patterns began to emerge. I had proof of joyful moments. I had photos of the people and things I truly valued.

The photos helped draw me out of a well of negativity. My problems were real, but they weren't all-encompassing. I had been so focused on things not working and not happening in the correct order and time that I forgot how many good things were occurring all around me. The photo project helped me see that and made me realize that I wanted to accomplish more.

There were still times when the days felt hopeless, but I gradually picked up on lighthearted strands, like golden threads woven through a plain cloth. And the more I looked for them, the more prevalent they seemed to become.

In the photos, I saw inside jokes, sunrises, new recipe attempts, impromptu picnics, an animal rescue, family gatherings, and budding friendships. I watched as we finally installed the kitchen in our house. Things were improving. And the photos encouraged me to focus on the positive.

And it worked. At the end of the year, I arranged the photos in an online photo book and had it printed. I kept the book beside my desk and regularly paged through it. It reminded me of all the things I had to be grateful for. It also taught me that sometimes life moves at a slower pace and in a different order than I like — and that's okay. Things will eventually get where they need to be.

The photo book is now a family tradition. My husband contributes, and friends sometimes pass photos along as well. These days, "Get a picture for the photo book!" is a regular phrase for us. We're currently working on the third edition.

Now, our house is almost fixed, our marriage is going strong, and I'm working toward the career I used to dream about but didn't pursue. The daily photos didn't make that all happen, but they did give me a bright light to focus on when all other things were dark. And, one photo at a time, that made all the difference.

—Angela M. Adams—

20

Volunteering to Be Happy

You can focus on things that are barriers or you can
focus on scaling the wall or redefining the problem.
~Tim Cook, CEO of Apple

My friend Karen was having a problem with an unwanted obligation. She and her husband David were acquainted with an elderly lady, Rose, who fell ill and had no one to help her. Karen and David weren't related to Rose, but since there was no one else, they stepped in and acted like family.

Rose was difficult. She would take them out for dinner but then restrict what they were allowed to order. She would complain about everything they did for her even though they were just trying to help.

Karen and David helped Rose for a couple of years, moving her into an assisted-living facility, overseeing her medical care, taking her out for meals, and then moving her again, this time into a nursing home. Eventually, they were driving two hours each way to tend to Rose's needs, and it was cutting into their workdays and time with their children and grandchildren.

Karen and David are the nicest people you've ever met, so generous with their time and money, but even they felt increasingly overwhelmed. They weren't resentful, but they did feel that this obligation had taken over their lives. After all, Rose was just an acquaintance. How did they get stuck with this?

One day, Karen was telling me how hard this was. I asked her if she did any volunteer work. She said that she would like to, but she didn't have time. I suggested that she view caring for Rose as her volunteer work.

It was like a light bulb went on. Karen's attitude was transformed instantly. She didn't need to do any less for Rose, but now that she was "volunteering," her perception of the work shifted. Karen told David what I said that night — that this was their "volunteer work" — and she called me back to say that this changed everything for him, too.

For the rest of Rose's life, Karen and David happily did their "volunteer work."

We talk a lot about volunteering at Chicken Soup for the Soul. We've published a couple of books specifically on the topic, and we have stories about volunteering sprinkled throughout all our books, probably because our writers are a nice bunch of people, but also because volunteering makes us *feel* good, and we're all about stories that make us feel good.

The biggest *beneficiary* of volunteering is usually the person *doing* the volunteering, not the *recipient* of the work. Therapists often recommend that people who are depressed or even suicidal take up volunteer work as a way of showing themselves that they add value to society, that what they do makes a difference.

So, there's real volunteering — and then there's the type I'm talking about when we redefine a slightly onerous commitment that we've made as "volunteering." That way, a task that we feel *forced* to do can turn into *voluntary* volunteering.

Here's my own example, and this is what led me to give that advice to Karen. For almost twenty-five years — a quarter-century! — I served as the treasurer for my neighborhood tax district, which basically meant that I ran it. I carved out many hours each month to serve as the tax assessor, tax collector, bill payer, and tax-return preparer. I also managed the garbage collection and some other services for the whole neighborhood. There were nineteen homes, and while almost everyone was wonderful, there were always a few people who were difficult.

After many years, someone asked me if I did volunteer work, and I said, "No, because I am so busy with work and our four grown kids and a house and running my neighborhood association that I don't have time to do volunteer work." And then I realized, "Oh! Running the association *is* my volunteer work." And that changed everything.

After that revelation, when I got aggravated over someone complaining about the snowplowing, or a tree falling across the road, or my unpleasant neighbor Anger Management Guy not paying his neighborhood taxes, I reminded myself that this was my volunteer work, and it seemed much more palatable.

That almost always worked, except when it didn't. One winter, we got something like six feet of snow in one month, plus lots of freezing rain. Our two roads were covered with black ice, and you had to hold onto your car to get your mail from the mailbox without falling.

One woman called and complained there was ice in her parking area. *Duh.* Another neighbor refused to leave his driveway gate open and then complained when he wasn't plowed first. He had me up at 5:00 in the morning texting the snowplow guy. And then there was Mrs. Anger Management Guy, who complained that the plow was pushing snow onto the landscaping on the edge of her driveway. As if six feet of snow could be miraculously transported into space instead of *pushed* to the side of her driveway!

I was going crazy that winter. My colleagues at work would hear me on the phone fielding complaints and talking to the snowplow guy. Ernest Hemingway said that all poets are crazy; I get it now! I had to express my angst, and I turned to poetry! Despite the fact that I had *never, ever* voluntarily written a poem, I sat down and composed eight haikus—in classic five-syllable seven-syllable five-syllable format — about the snowplowing situation, some less polite than others, and e-mailed them off to my friends within the neighborhood. Here are four of them:

> one more dumb complaint
> about snow, ice, and slipping
> and there will be blood

> paternalistic
> society not the plan
> so let's grow up now

shrubs and lights you put
along driveway go under
snow as you designed

only one person
can go first in the real world
despite what you wish

My "good" neighbors wrote back that they were laughing out loud. They all knew who the "bad" neighbors were. For me, it was a way of venting, but it was also a creative way to redefine and refocus my frustration. After all, our mothers always said, "Use your words."

I've discovered that with words and thoughts, almost anything can be redefined, turned upside down and inside out, and re-examined in a new light.

When my kids were teenagers, they sometimes accused me of "rationalizing" things. But I don't think it's *rationalizing* to look for a better way to deal with difficult circumstances, to *redefine* them into something more palatable, even something exciting and good. That just seems *rational* to me.

It worked for me, and it worked for Karen and David.

— Amy Newmark —

21

Rainy Days and Mondays

Since we cannot change reality,
let us change the eyes which see reality.
~Nikos Kazantzakis

The more I prayed, the harder it rained. As my husband Bill and I traveled to what was supposed to be our romantic anniversary getaway, an unexpected storm surged around us. Our discouragement increased as each raindrop fell.

When Bill and I married, we made a promise to celebrate our wedding anniversary each year with a short vacation. We did alright for the first few years, enjoying some of our favorite destinations. Then, life got in the way. Family responsibilities, financial issues and, most recently, Covid were among the reasons that stopped us. This year, we decided not to allow any more excuses to keep us from our celebration. So, we mulled it over and decided that an early autumn overnighter at a peaceful shore destination would be perfect.

The Manor, an historic hotel, had long been a yearned-for destination with its vast array of amenities, including Olympic-size pool, spa, yoga studio and award-winning restaurant. Nestled atop a hill overlooking the Atlantic Ocean, it sat within walking distance of a nearby town full of the kitschy type of tourist shops we loved. At the other end of the road was a majestic lighthouse where sightseers could climb the winding staircase to the observation deck. This trip promised to be fantastic — until the skies opened, and the rain poured down.

"Well," I told Bill as we entered The Manor, "this trip won't be a complete wash-out. There's plenty to do right here until the storm passes."

The indoor pool would be our first destination. We slipped into our bathing suits and took the quick walk down the hall to the pool. Bill and I looked at each other. Something seemed strange. Why were there sheets of brown paper covering the glass entry door? I yanked on the door handle. Locked. I peeked into the nearby laundry room and asked one of the staff members, "Excuse me. Do you know why the pool door is locked?"

"Sorry," the laundress answered. "It's under renovation right now." Ugh.

"Let's go back to the room and get dressed," Bill suggested. "We'll get a drink at the bar and chill until dinner."

Well, that sounded like a good idea... until we got to the bar. The sign outside read: *Closed on Mondays*. I felt a tear puddle in my eye. This wasn't working out according to plan.

"Relax," Bill said. "We're on vacation. We'll have an early dinner and figure out our next move then."

"At this rate," I grumbled, "the restaurant will be closed, too."

"Pessimist," Bill scoffed.

So, we followed the arrows that led from the bar to the hotel restaurant where we were greeted by another sign: *Closed on Mondays*. Oh, this just couldn't be possible. Was nothing in this place open? Fueled by frustration, I marched to the concierge desk. "Is anything open on Mondays around here?" I asked.

The concierge smiled. "Yes. All the shops and restaurants in town are open. Plus, there is a lovely winery down the road a bit." She lifted her wrist and checked her watch. "If you leave now, you'll get there just in time for their last wine tasting. Our hotel shuttle can take you there."

Bill and I looked at each other again. This time, we were smiling.

After a sampling of wine and snacks on the enclosed porch of the winery, we were ready for some more serious eating. Certainly, one of the restaurants in town would fit the bill. As if on cue, the winery bartender approached us as he readied to close for the evening. "Would you like me to call the hotel shuttle to take you into town?"

Within minutes, we arrived outside the door of a quaint restaurant where we both enjoyed our dinner. As we contemplated dessert, the flash of a neon sign struck my attention. "Homemade ice cream," it read. "Thirty flavors."

We dodged raindrops as we ran to the corner ice-cream shop where I did something I hadn't done in years. I ordered a large cone and ate the whole thing. That night, as the shuttle brought us back to The Manor, Bill turned to me. "Well, things didn't go as expected." He patted my hand. "But tomorrow we can still climb to the top of the lighthouse. I know how much you want to do that."

Now, I was looking forward to that adventure because the view of the ocean is reported to be quite amazing... a panorama that's really something to see. Plus, I had been anticipating the challenge of climbing to the lofty heights necessary for a complete 360-degree view. Truly, I couldn't wait.

The following morning, as we approached the lighthouse, I understood all the hoopla about this place. It was a majestic structure, indeed; of course, the view from its observation deck would be fantastic. With my breath catching in my throat, I sprinted from the parking lot to the metal fencing surrounding the lighthouse. I yanked on the gate, ignoring the sign posted against its steel post: CLOSED FOR RENOVATIONS. No! It couldn't be. I turned toward my husband as he gingerly kept his distance. "Oh, you have got to be kidding me!"

"Look," Bill said in an attempt to distract me. He pointed toward a clearing in the pines that surrounded the shore. "The beach is still open. We can walk on the beach."

Well, the atmosphere was cold and gray, and the interminable drizzle present since the night before continued to float downward, but it was true... the beach was still walkable. So, we continued down the path toward the place where the pines gave way to sand. There, we encountered four women artists, self-named The Graphite Grannies, creating pencil sketches of the lighthouse and scenery. They were fascinating to watch. Their concentration, talent and commitment were unhindered by age or the elements.

Beyond them moved pockets of tourists, some climbing large

boulders for a better vantage point while those below gathered oddly shaped stones and rocks as souvenirs. I instinctively followed their lead, carefully scaling slippery stones until I reached the highest point possible to reveal the breathtaking vista. I stood there for a long time taking it all in, and after Bill finally succeeded in coaxing me down from my perch, we gathered a few special stones and shells of our own before returning to our car.

As we drove the highway toward home, Bill turned to me. "This trip certainly didn't go according to plan, did it?"

I thought about the past forty-eight hours. True, this trip hadn't gone as planned. Yet we had enjoyed so much. The snafu at the hotel pool had set in motion an early evening visit to a winery where we drank blueberry port and ate chocolate as we looked out at acres of cool, green grape arbors. A cozy dinner in town followed where we enjoyed fresh seafood straight from the fisherman's boat and, afterward ran giggling through the raindrops to the shop where we gorged on homemade pumpkin ice cream covered in bits of broken Oreo cookies. The next day, refreshed by the type of peaceful sleep one can only get in a quiet hotel detached from the cares of home, we were inspired by four well-seasoned artists after which we climbed rocks and gathered shells as the moist salt air refreshed our faces.

"No," I smiled back, "this trip didn't go as planned. It went much better."

It went so much better, in fact, that we decided to return to The Manor again next year. I'm hoping that lots of things will go wrong!

— Monica A. Andermann —

22

Worth the Time

In the end, all that really matters is the time
we spent with the people we love.
~Author Unknown

"Do you need some help?" asked my son as he gently stepped over boxes and bubble wrap.

I grunted sarcastically to myself. Did I need some help? That was an understatement. I looked at the sprawling mess around me. The floor was covered with piles of lights, ornaments, fake snow, and half-empty totes. "I need an army," I replied as I tried to gather my hair back into a worn ponytail holder.

"Well, I will just have to do," he said as he grinned at me. "Where should I start?"

"Aren't you studying for your college exams?" I asked. "I don't want to pull you away from schoolwork."

"I need a break anyway. So, what do we tackle first?" he said as he rubbed his hands together.

I looked at the piles I had strewn everywhere. Who was I kidding? I couldn't even figure out a direction to go, much less find one for him. Noting my hesitation, he offered an idea.

"Why don't we work on the villages together? Then you could teach me how to do them," he said as he moved toward my collection of ceramic houses laid out across several tables. I stared blankly at him as if I was suspended in time, unmoving, my brain stuck in fatigue and fog. "Mom, is that okay? Should we start there?"

I snapped out of my exhausted trance. "Yes, of course. We should start there."

I joined him across the room and tried to begin making sense of the mess as I showed him how to set up each house. Setting up fifty-three ceramic houses had at one point sounded like a good idea, but my faith was starting to waver. It was always so beautiful when it was set up, but the work each year was getting harder for me.

Not to mention I was still struggling with remembering how to do it in the first place. For the past two years, I had been sick over Christmas, and I was out of practice. This was the first time in a long time I was attempting to put up all the decorations. I was already drained and shaming myself that it was taking me so long to get it done. But it was a box I was determined to check no matter how hard it was.

My son and I spent the next few hours meticulously arranging each little town section and setting up the cords that would power it all. I taught him all my tips and tricks for setting up villages. I told him the story of each little ceramic person who went into the village and why I put them where I put them. I told him the family stories about how the village began and how it grew into this mammoth collection. I even showed him how to make a few mistakes and how to fix them.

As we crept closer to the finish line, I realized I still had to do the extra lights and I sighed. One of the finishing touches included placing and taping down extra lights around the village floor so that the whole village would glow in a soft white light after the snow was placed on top. As we finished one table and started the second, I could feel the weariness of nine hours on my feet washing over me. I looked down at the lights in my hand and began grumbling.

"I am so tired, but I have to finish this tonight," I said. "I have to work tomorrow, and I don't have any more time this week to do it. And I can't leave the house looking like this," I said as I gestured at the explosion of decorations behind me.

"I understand," my son said. "Maybe we could just skip putting on the extra lights and just finish it up. I think it would still be very pretty."

I looked around the room once more and decided he was right.

I had to choose. "Okay," I said reluctantly. "We will leave them off."

We finished up the rest of the village and cleaned up the disaster I had spent several days creating. When we were done, I collapsed on my old recliner sporting a new heating pad and rubbed my sore feet. Later, as I headed to bed, I walked by the multiple displays of houses, looking back and forth from one table to another, comparing the one with lights under the snow to the one without. It just wasn't the same. I shook my head as I continued to my room, disappointed in myself for being too tired to finish the setup properly.

The next day, I popped my head into my son's room to say good morning. We chatted for a few minutes about our plans for the day. As I was heading out the door for more coffee, I paused and mentioned the lights. "I looked at them before I went to bed last night. I wish I had pushed through and finished those other lights. It is pretty but could have been so much better. It would have been worth it to have finished the job."

He glanced at me for a moment, smiled, and then turned his head back to his computer. "Our time was worth more," he said matter-of-factly without looking back. "And I got to spend time with you."

The student had taught the teacher. How I wish I could see the world through those eyes.

While I was shaming myself for an uncompleted task, for a box of efficiency not checked, my son was looking at the positive. While I was worried about villages and lights, he was appreciating the time spent together. While I was spending time staring at a half-empty glass and seeing what was missing, he was filling his up with what was already there.

It didn't matter to him if the result was perfect; it was still a win because our time together was more important. Taking time to rest and take care of ourselves was more important. I wonder what my life would be like if I looked at everything for its real worth in this short life. What could be possible if I saw things from the positive side and measured by love and time instead of checks on the to-do list? I wonder what my stress level would look like if I could see the positive instead of the deficiency.

Thanks to my son, now I see it every time I walk by those houses. I don't see the dark spots anymore; I see the light that came from the time we spent together setting it up. Instead of seeing what was missing or imperfect, I now can see what was gained. He was right... it was completely worth it.

— Shannon Leach —

23

The Student Was Ready

Attitude is the paintbrush with which
we color the world.
~Ancient Proverb

I t had been a hard year. Illness and loss plagued me. Sleep, when I could manage it, was a welcome respite. However, I'd wake up each morning, cautiously open one eye, and reality would strike. Nothing had changed. All my worries, sadness, and concerns from yesterday were still alive and well. I'd feel a sense of foreboding, a tightness in my chest, and a sinking sensation in the pit of my stomach. Sadly, I thought, stuff happens; change is a constant. Looking back ten years, I could never have imagined this is where I'd be.

I don't know exactly how it happened, but one morning something in me lightened a tiny bit. It was just enough for me to peek through my curtain of despondency and remember the wisdom that a friend, a yoga teacher, had shared with me several years before.

She hated her day job—truly hated it, more than the benign, fleeting, run-of-the-mill Monday morning blues that many of us fall prey to. She felt mistreated by her boss. Her efforts to get help from the company went unheeded. The outlook for her in her career was bleak.

She lived in New York City and walked eighteen blocks to work every morning. She loved walking around the city, but her morning walks often felt like drudgery. Inevitably, the thought, *I hate this job*, would pop into her head. It would appear, subside, and return numerous times along the way.

One day, on her way to work, she had a flash of awareness. Despite her favorite music piped in through her earphones, she was dwelling in negative thinking about her hatred of her job. She realized she wasn't at work, and that her job was only a portion of her life. Teaching yoga in the evenings brought her joy. Many things brought her joy. Her walk to work could bring her joy, too, if she allowed it. She made a conscious decision to change her inner narrative, to treat her morning commute like any other walk. As ridiculous as it might seem, whenever *I hate my job* popped up, she replaced the thought with *I love my job*.

She said that, at first, it was almost painful. She felt like a liar, betraying herself, not acknowledging the truth. But she persevered. Each day, it got easier. It was never truly easy but less difficult. It became a game she played with herself. Sure enough, when she arrived at work, she felt lighter, less negative, and actually believed on some level that she didn't hate her job. Her job hadn't improved and, in fact, it never did. But her relationship to it did. And her walk was delightful.

We've all heard the saying that when the student is ready, the teacher will appear. When I was at the height of my turmoil, engulfed in sadness, grief, anxiety, it wasn't possible to simply turn a switch and change my thoughts. But when it lifted that little bit, just enough, I was able to remember my friend's wisdom. I was ready to try it for myself.

When I got out of bed, buoyed by her experience, I knew I had a choice. I made a conscious decision to embrace the day. I would resist my urge to immediately wallow in my usual painful thoughts. It truly was a new day. I could decide to intentionally view it as such.

My morning narrative was no longer based in fear and pessimism. Nor did I try to force myself into accepting some fantasy phrase that felt outlandish and insincere. Mine was simple: *I love life*. That I could accept. That I did believe. That was my wish for my present and for the future.

They say, *Fake it 'til you make it*. The truth is, when I get up in the morning and choose to look on the bright side, to see the beauty and hope and possibility, when I'm thankful for another day to be alive, it's not faking at all. I pay attention and enjoy my delicious breakfast, look out the window and appreciate the weather, whatever it is. I do love life. It is true. My grief and loss are equally true. They're both real, and they can coexist.

Experts say we have thousands of thoughts each day, and a great percentage of them are the same. If I'm going to have thousands, a few of them can be lovely. I'm not suggesting that I can tame all my thoughts and emotions. I can't change the course of history or make sadness disappear. But my comfort in the midst of pain has been enhanced. Choosing to look on the bright side can't take away grief, illness and loss, but it most definitely helps me to navigate them with greater grace, balance and ease.

There's another thing my yogi friend taught me. She said one of the most important yoga poses of all is the one where you raise the corners of your mouth toward your ears. I'm thankful for her wisdom. When I think of her, I most definitely smile.

— Judith Shapiro —

24

A Gift of the World

Happiness is not by chance but by choice.
~Jim Rohn

We began the bus trips when I was around seven years old. Back then, we lived at our grandparents' house in Oceanside, California. Finances were tight since my father had retired from the Air Force and had yet to find steady employment. In addition, we were struggling to find an affordable place to call our own.

I suppose it would have been easy to yield to frustration. But my mom had other ideas, using the situation to give my brother Jess and me fond memories that would affect our perspective forever. However, I only appreciated the full extent of her wisdom many years later.

As it was, once or twice a week, my mom would lead Jess and me up the slope from our grandparents' house to the nearest bus stop, and from there we would go on to "see the world." The public transportation system around the area was remarkably extensive. For a very low fee, it was possible to purchase a ticket that allowed riders to hop aboard all the buses they wanted throughout an entire day. My mom studied this system well, and she would guide us to a wide variety of destinations.

Among our most frequented points of interest was the mall in Carlsbad. There was a large, glass clock tower that stood at its very heart. It featured gears and other mechanisms that rolled rubber balls along rails, bouncing them onto drums and then ramps, and sending them back up in little elevators to make the whole journey again. The sight always drew a small crowd throughout the day, mostly children.

We would window-shop at the mall and in the surrounding neighborhood. We weren't there to buy. The goal was to enjoy the sights and do some people-watching too.

On other adventures, we would take the bus all the way to Strand Beach, where we collected sand dollars and shells for souvenirs. We would watch ships sail past in the distance and often heard helicopters or other aircraft soar overhead on their way to the naval base at Camp Pendleton.

Every trip we took was a grand expedition. I was grateful to my mom for making that tough period so much fun. Eventually, my father got a steady job at the DMV, and we found a nice home in the countryside.

My mom did more than distract Jess and me from our troubles. She instilled in us an enthusiasm for keeping our eyes open and appreciating a world that was ours without having to really pay anything. And she showed us that regardless of where we were, and what we were going through, there was something we could smile about somewhere.

— Joyce Jacobo —

The Great Coat Switch

The most important thing you'll
ever wear is your attitude.
~Jeff Moore

My husband and I sat at a beautiful restaurant on the Willamette River, savoring a delicious linguini and watching the Christmas boats go by. Most of the boats were owned by Portlanders and decked out for the season with lights in various themes from the Grinch to Santa and his reindeer. Every year they plied the Willamette and Columbia Rivers for several evenings during the holidays, and that night we had ringside seats.

"Isn't this the best evening ever?" I grasped my husband's hand across the table. "I'm enjoying every minute." We seldom ate out, and the sight of the festive boats added a touch of magic.

Smiling and chatting, we stretched dinner out to nearly two hours, with drinks rare for us, followed by a house salad, sesame crusted ahi, and a shared chocolate mousse. I almost danced to the coat rack to get my coat. A black hooded wool carcoat, it had been given to me by my daughter who bought it when she lived in Boston. It was a bit large on her and fit me perfectly, so she'd passed it on. It made me smile every time I wore it. In a cold snap like we were having that night, it was heaven to slip on.

I reached for the only black coat on the rack and, paying no real attention to it, put it on. Wait, what? It reached below my calves, not mid-thigh. And I guessed it to be a size 16, not an 8. I pawed through the collection on the rack again thinking I must have somehow missed mine. It wasn't there.

Blinking back tears, I told myself that as soon as the owner of this long black coat I now wore put on mine, she would discover her mistake and take it back to the restaurant. Meanwhile, I'd need to wear hers to go out into the freezing cold night. I left my phone number with the hostess and explained that when the owner returned my coat taken by accident, I'd return hers.

I was confident I'd get a call that evening. I didn't. The next morning, surely. No call. I checked with the restaurant and was surprised no one had brought back my coat and asked for theirs.

My daughter didn't help my spirits when she said the owner of the coat probably put mine over one arm and went to a couple of parties. By the time she put it on, she had no idea where she had left hers.

I was sick at heart. I loved that coat. It had sentimental value plus it fit me perfectly and was so warm. With misty eyes I hung the long, too-big coat in the hall closet and continued to wait for a call that never came.

A few months later, on another freezing cold evening, my husband and I were getting ready to go to friends' for dinner. I pulled the coat off its hanger, pouting for the hundredth time about my lost carcoat. I'm usually good at silver linings, but I could think of no silver lining for this situation.

My friend Penny greeted me as soon as we walked in the door. "What a great coat!" she exclaimed.

Missy, the hostess, joined her. "It really is. Very classic."

I arched an eyebrow. "You're kidding. It's four sizes too big." I nearly launched into my story of the coat switch.

"If you don't want it, I'll take it," Missy quipped.

"Seriously, I'll flip you for it," Penny said.

I looked at the coat more carefully as I added it to the pile on the bed in the guest room. For the first time I looked at the label and realized it was an expensive garment. I frowned. Did I need an attitude adjustment? What if I were positive instead of negative about my unplanned acquisition? What benefit might there be in having this long coat?

It's amazing what a positive attitude can do. Instead of grumbling, I asked myself what I needed to do with this coat in order to enjoy it. A woman I knew from church did alterations. I asked her to look at the coat, and the price she quoted to alter it was much less than I expected. She measured and pinned, and within weeks called me to pick it up. The alteration must have been a huge job, mostly a favor. I thanked her over and over until she told me to stop.

The following week the temperature dropped from the forties to the low twenties, bitter cold for Portland, Oregon, and unexpected in early spring. Those who experience blizzards on the Great Plains probably think nothing of that temperature, but I had plenty of sympathy from fellow Portlanders bundled up around me. My husband and I were going to meet friends at their floating home.

As I gathered my long, black wool coat to step into the car, I remembered another cold evening that ended with a disappointment that I clung to for a long time. Happily, my friends helped me see the situation differently. I still wish I had the carcoat that my daughter gave me, but my long coat, paired with tall boots, is nearly as warm. It is, as Missy said, a classic black coat that I can wear many places. Both my attitude and the coat needed alteration. Now I wear it often with pleasure.

I realize a switched coat is trivial compared to the concerns many people face, struggling to find shelter and food for their families. But the experience offered an important lesson. Now, when faced with disappointment, I ask myself how I might look at the situation differently. How might a loss also be a gain when approached with a positive attitude?

— Samantha Ducloux Waltz —

Chapter
4

Surprise Yourself

Destination Unknown

And think not you can, direct the course of love,
For love, if it finds you worthy, directs your course.
~D. H. Lawrence

The Sunday *New York Times* wedding page depressed me with all its stories of lucky love. One bride met her future husband while walking along the very street where I lived in Manhattan. She was crying because she'd just broken up with her boyfriend. A handsome man inquired into her distress and *presto!* her singlehood ended after five minutes. Why didn't anything like that ever happen to me?

As a thirty-eight-year-old female physician in the pre-Internet mid-1990s, statistics weren't on my side. *Newsweek* had famously published an article stating that a woman like me, never married and with a lot of education, was "more likely to be killed by a terrorist" than find a mate. The magazine ended up retracting the article, but it felt true to me. I'd tried singles events, trips, and personal ads without success.

Living across the street from Lincoln Center, I often attended concerts and films there. One weekend, I bought tickets to their Danish film festival. The first night's movie was about Norwegian writer Knut Hamsun, winner of the 1920 Nobel Prize in Literature. The subtitles were hard to read. Luckily, the Danish woman seated next to me kindly whispered what was going on whenever I became lost.

At the end of the movie, an emcee announced, "We have here with us today the star of the movie, Ghita Norby!" My interpreter stood up, looking nothing like the old lady she portrayed in the movie. A swarm of admirers gathered around her — and me — pushing us into the next room for an after-party. Ghita graciously chatted with me.

"Susan, we have a lack of doctors in Denmark, especially your specialty of Rehabilitation Medicine. It's an egalitarian country where guys aren't intimidated by highly educated women. There are lots of nice, single men in your age group because it's a shy culture where people have trouble connecting. Please consider coming to Denmark!" she said.

"But your language is so hard!" I replied. "There are guttural sounds I can't even hear correctly let alone pronounce."

Ghita laughed. "Don't worry. Everyone speaks English in Denmark."

The next night, the Danish movie *Portland* was showing. This time, I deliberately snuck into the after-party and bumped into Florence, the wife of *Portland's* director, Niels Arden Oplev. Florence hailed from NYC and was close to my age. "You must come to Denmark!" she said, motioning for her husband to come over. He, too, encouraged me. "Danish humor and bluntness are similar to the New York vibe," he said. "But it's an introverted culture, and they greatly appreciate extroverts like you. Plus, you have dark hair and the kind of look that Danes find exotic."

Florence said, "We have a great expat community. Come join us!"

The gentle friendliness and humility of Ghita and Niels, despite their fame, impressed me, but I didn't seriously consider leaving my country.

A few months later, Ola Andersson, the chair of the Young Physicians section in Malmö, Sweden, sent me an e-mail in my capacity as Young Physicians chair of NY County Medical Society. He was coming to New York for three weeks and wondered if any local doctors his age might have time to get together. I offered to show him around the Big Apple.

Ola was a few years younger than I and about to get married. He had a lot of unused vacation time, so he was traveling by himself. We had a wonderful time together for three weeks, almost like a platonic honeymoon. Yet again, I felt taunted by fate. Why couldn't we have met before he became engaged? On the last day of his trip, Ola said,

"Susan, many Scandinavian men would like you. Denmark is the place for you — the best weather and the happiest people in Scandinavia."

With Ola's words ringing in my ears, I bought a map of Denmark and sat perusing it on my late lunch break. Alone in a cafe at 4:00 p.m., I was shocked when a tall man in his fifties strode in and beelined straight for my table.

"You're looking at a map of Denmark!" he exclaimed. "I'm Danish! I don't know why I had the urge to pop into this cafe. I come in and see just one customer reading a map of my country. What's your interest in Denmark?" After telling my story, Jens said, "I own many rental properties in Copenhagen. If you come to Denmark, I'll rent you something cheap. We need doctors like you in Denmark."

A few weeks later, I ran into my friend Henri, a physician and classical pianist. Henri was excited to hear about my new interest in Denmark. "My friend Thorkil's father was the last rehabilitation-medicine physician in Denmark before he died. Thorkil could arrange for you to work as a volunteer physician at his father's hospital. You should go!"

After so many portentous signs, I took the plunge. Thorkil arranged for me to volunteer at Rigshospitalet in Copenhagen for two weeks in June.

The relaxed pace of medicine, the uncrowded city, the clean public transportation and the lack of crime made me feel like moving there immediately. Danish doctors were horrified at my long hours and small amount of vacation time. Everyone thought I'd have a booming social life in Copenhagen.

The hospital offered me a dream job. All I needed to do was pass a simple oral and written test in Danish.

Given my massive student-loan debt, I couldn't afford to be unemployed for any length of time. I'd have to learn Danish while working. At that time, there were no Danish classes in New York nor any instructional tapes in Danish. No one at the Danish Embassy or Danish Seamen's Church in Brooklyn was willing to teach me Danish.

In desperation, I took out an ad in the only Danish-American newspaper, *The Danish Pioneer*, begging to be taught Danish. Based in Illinois, it had a circulation of just 3,000, almost all Midwesterners.

Chris Steffensen, the editor, charged me half the usual rate because he was certain I was wasting my money.

Only one person answered the ad: Niels Jensen, a Danish engineer living in New Jersey. The day he showed up at my door, I knew he was the one. He felt the same about me. We eventually married and had a beautiful daughter. Niels's career was in the USA, so we remained stateside.

A series of synchronistic events, more miraculous than anything I'd read in the *New York Times* wedding section, led me on a circuitous journey to my heart's desire. Sometimes, when it seems luck is passing us by, it just isn't yet our moment. And sometimes, the path we're certain will lead us where we wish to go takes us to a different and better destination.

By the way, I still can't speak a word of Danish.

— Susan Jensen, MD —

Keep on Swinging

It is not the mountain we conquer, but ourselves.
~Edmund Hillary

I was in my eighties when I contracted both pulmonary fibrosis, a disease of the lungs, and prostate cancer, which had metastasized to my bones. Both are debilitating diseases that will one day take their toll. Until then, I knew I had to keep my mind and body moving.

As the years continued to whiz by, my body became weaker and weaker. If I sat on my butt and did nothing, I would, for sure, get even weaker.

So, I went outside, took a normal-size wiffle ball, and tried to throw it over my white picket fence. I fell short by quite a bit. Then, I picked up another ball and threw it. I noticed it went a little farther. I decided to do this every day. I observed that I was able to throw the balls a little harder each time. I had convinced myself that I was limited because of my condition and age and that I could never throw those balls over the fence from where I was standing.

After months of trying to get the ball over the fence, I found that the balls were getting closer and closer to the fence until the day I got one over the fence. From that day on, I got it into my head that I could find the strength to get the ball over the fence. Until then, I had convinced myself that because I was an old geezer with debilitating diseases, I would never be able to get stronger.

Well, this is where the message from the book, *The Little Engine*

That Could, entered the picture. The moral of that story is, "I THINK I CAN, I THINK I CAN!" I will never be able to totally explain how to do all this, but the reality is that the added strength comes from the power of thinking positively. Somehow, it brings about additional adrenaline or whatever.

Making progress, I decided I would go to the batting cage and hit regular-size baseballs starting at 40 mph. Then I went for the 50, 60, 70 and 80 mph speeds. And, believe it or not, I was able to hit those balls. Not only that, but I was eventually able to hit those balls at 90 mph. I have been doing that for the past five years.

I am now ninety years old. My hope is that I will be able to keep doing what I'm calling "90 at 90" — 90 mph at ninety years of age.

Two years ago, Steve Lopez of the *Los Angeles Times* came to the batting cage to interview me and take pictures of me hitting 90 mph balls.

The power of positive thinking will not get rid of my stage 4 prostate cancer or my pulmonary fibrosis or any other ailments I have, but it probably has a lot to do with my hitting the 90 mph balls at the batting cage.

I now see my debilitating diseases as a horse race. For sure, one of them will be taking me down sooner or later. All I know is that I WILL GO DOWN SWINGING! My positive attitude is not going away anytime soon. It's all about MIND OVER MATTER.

My oldest son, a geriatric physician, put it this way, "We still don't understand it, but there are so many ways a positive attitude affects our whole body and our immune system."

As my other son told me, "DAD, DO IT WHILE YOU CAN!"

— Benny Wasserman —

Who Me?

*Character is the ability to follow through
on a resolution long after the emotion
with which it was made has passed.*
~Brian Tracy

I f you had asked me a few years ago how I felt about exercise, I would have told you that while I had a gym membership, working out basically consisted of walking on the treadmill for maybe fifteen minutes, "pretending" to know what I was doing with a few of the machines and weights for another fifteen minutes, and then making my escape. I was even that person who signed up and paid for personal training and then was able to convince the trainer to wrap up early and go to happy hour with me. Yes, that really did happen on a few occasions! Exercise just wasn't my idea of fun.

Fast forward to just a few years ago. I was dealing with some stuff in my personal life, and I needed an outlet for my frustration. I had heard exercise was a good source of endorphins — relieving stress and improving your mood. I knew if I was going to be successful this time around, I needed to be in a group setting. I definitely needed an accountability partner, someone who would keep me going even when I wanted to skip a session.

I made a few phone calls to local circuit training studios. At one of them, the owner, Adria, was very personable. I could tell she would be good at motivating me.

Accountability partner was an understatement when it came to Adria. Not only did I end up with a great trainer, but I also gained a friend.

Even though we had formed a friendship, none of my excuses worked on her. I hoped being my friend meant she'd let me off the hook if I just didn't feel like attending a class. On days when I said I couldn't attend and gave one excuse after another, she pointed out the other time options that were available on the schedule. If I didn't show up for a day or two, I would get a text asking, "What is your workout plan for this week?" She would not let me out of the commitment I made no matter how many times I tried. Because of her commitment to me, I kept my commitment to her. Before long, I was seeing changes in my body, emotions and attitude. I began to look forward to going to the gym.

One day, Adria mentioned that she was just plain tired and needed a day off. Being open six days a week — with classes all morning and afternoon — and being the sole owner and employee of her gym, her only option would be to close. I sympathized with her but was shocked when the next thing out of her mouth was, "I wish you would get certified because you are the only one I'd trust with the keys." I laughed it off, knowing that was impossible. Me? A trainer?

Although she never mentioned it again, I couldn't get her comment out of my head. It was so flattering that she thought that much of me — and trusted me — but there was no way! I hadn't studied for anything in years, not to mention that a large portion of my "day job" was reading. Could I really read about fitness in the evenings?

For days following our conversation, every time the thought popped into my head, I heard the words "No way!" But for some reason I couldn't stop thinking about it.

I decided to do some research to understand what it would take to be a Group Fitness Instructor. I learned it would take three to six months of reading text, analyzing charts, and watching videos, as well as online activities and listening to the provided podcasts. Prior to taking the final certification exam, I would also have to become CPR- and AED-certified.

I sat with it for weeks and then went online and signed up for the American Council on Exercise (ACE) course. At first, I didn't tell anyone about this, but about two months in, I told my family what I had been doing during the evenings when I was home alone. I am so grateful for my son; every time I came up with excuses for why I couldn't do it and why I thought I wouldn't pass, he reminded me of the hours I spent quizzing him with flashcards for his medical exam. I was his biggest cheerleader on his way to becoming a doctor, and now here he was quizzing me with flashcards, cheering me on and keeping me positive.

There were many times when I wanted to give up. It was hard enough that I had to learn about certain muscles and workouts, but why did I also need to memorize the decibel level for the music used for each type of class? And for water aerobics, why did I need to know the temperature of the water? Or even how to advise on buying the correct exercise shoes?

Each time I started a new section, the negative part of my brain would say, "You are just doing this to occasionally give Adria a day off, and you are wasting your time." But the positive side of me said, "So what if that is all you plan to do with this certification? Just do it!" I had made a commitment to myself, and I needed to follow through.

Test day came, and it was no joke. I had to turn on the camera on my computer so the proctor could scan the area around my desk from floor to ceiling to make sure there were no notes around. He watched my every move for the entire three hours. At one point in the middle of the test, he had me adjust my camera because he could not see my eyes. I finally had to tell him, "I am fifty-four years old, and so are my eyes. There are times I need to squint to read the monitor."

Just short of the three-hour mark, I finished the exam. I honestly had no idea how I had done, but as I started to review my answers, I was so exhausted that I decided to just hit submit. It felt like forever watching the hourglass turn, and then suddenly a large YOU PASSED popped up on the screen.

I was so proud of myself. I never gave up, and I proved to myself that I wasn't too old to learn new things. The icing on the cake was presenting a handmade coupon book to Adria at Christmas with coupons for her to use on occasional Saturdays when she is feeling burnt out or just needs a weekend off.

While I set out to become a certified fitness instructor to do something nice for a friend, I can't tell you how good it feels to walk in for my workout and see my certification on the wall.

— D'ette Corona —

29

And So... We Bought a Boat

We cannot direct the wind, but we can adjust the sails.
~attributed to Dolly Parton and others

I had been telling my husband for several years, "You can retire anytime you're ready!" I had no idea that he would make that decision smack dab in the middle of Covid!

The U.S. was seven months into lockdown, all trips were canceled, restaurants were closed, and people were told to forgo any socializing. Wonderful, what would we do now?

When Bob retired in September, we'd had two exciting trips planned. We would be cruising to Japan later that month, and in November we were meeting friends for a scenic train tour through Canada. The cruise was immediately canceled, and our Canadian tour was later canceled when the borders were closed.

Lockdown was traumatic for everyone, but couple that with a newly 24/7 relationship after fifty-odd years of working, and it really took some getting used to! It seems as though most women marry their husbands for dinner but not lunch, too. I had always told mine that when he retired he needed to have a plan. He needed to have something to do — hobbies or interests that would occupy his time. After all, I had a life, too! I lunched with the girls, played mah jong, shopped, and gardened — none of which he would enjoy, and none of which I was willing to give up.

After several months of lockdown and boredom, months of me finding my bored man projects to do, several months of him waking every morning and asking, "What are we doing today?" and me saying "Costco?" (the only place open), I had finally had enough! I was watching my happy-go-lucky husband fall into depression.

Bob had always loved sailing and talked of plans to sail the Caribbean. But then he married me. Marriage, three daughters' weddings, and life in general put his sailing plans on the back burner.

Now it was time to resurrect that dream. In December, our daughter found a boat for sale on Facebook Marketplace. It was a 25-foot Catalina sailboat, and it was only $5,500.

I was so excited when we presented the idea to him. He was anything but!

He was sure the boat had to be awful for that price, and he had no interest in seeing it. I had my daughter make an appointment for the next weekend. We were going to see it no matter what.

To me, from a decorator standpoint, the boat looked doable. Some new cushions inside, new accessories on the shelves, a little elbow grease cleaning up here and there, and it would do nicely. I listened as my husband asked all the pertinent boat questions, and then all eyes were on me. Did I have any questions? Only two: *Why are you selling?* The owner needed a bigger boat! *What is the name of the boat?* (I knew it was a superstition that you never change the name of a boat, and if the name was something crazy, it would never do.)

The name of the boat was "Therapy." Well, that did it for me! I absolutely love telling our friends that Bob's at therapy!

I decorated, and Bob suddenly had a wish list at Amazon. The packages were coming on a daily basis. My retired husband had the biggest smile on his face, a little more pep in his step, and a wife who was breathing a sigh of relief, all because her husband got therapy!

— Kristine Byron —

30

I Know You Can Do It

*If you're having fun, that's when
the best memories are built.*
~Simone Biles

I was going way too fast down the winding road. I hit a bump, and my entire body jerked up and forward. My legs flew up, and my hands left the handlebars for a brief moment. For a split second, I thought I might crash. By some miracle, I stayed on the bike. I slowed down but didn't stop. I kept pedaling.

I was a non-athletic forty-two-year-old kindergarten teacher. I had three teenage children who went to a youth group at our local church. They were doing a fundraiser to go to summer camp. Ryan, my thirteen-year-old son, approached me and said, "Mom, you should ride in our bikeathon." As he told me the details, I laughed out loud.

"What makes you think I could finish a twenty-mile bikeathon?" I asked.

My son looked me straight in the eyes. "I know you can do it."

I almost laughed again, but my son was serious. I promised to think about it. It would take months of training and new equipment, and my bike needed work. I had neither the time nor the desire to do all of that.

I went to kindergarten class the next day and played a familiar counting song. The kids sang with enthusiasm. "Let's do it again, and this time faster. I know you can do it!"

There it was again: "I know you can do it."

I decided to have a discussion with the kids after the song was over. We talked about what that meant. I have often started a discussion with great hopes of teaching five-year-olds something, and they miss the idea completely. This time, they were on point. Sweet little Emma raised her hand and gave me a profound answer.

She said, "Teacher, when I don't know if I can do something, you tell me I can, and so I try. And then I do it."

Diego said that a kid just needed someone to believe they could do it. I agreed that it makes all the difference.

So, I began preparing. I asked my friends for bikeathon pledges. I told my Kinders about it and asked them to give me some tips on how to get ready. Olivia told me to make a peanut-butter-and-jelly sandwich and wear it as a necklace around my neck so I would have something to eat if I got hungry.

Bikeathon Day came on a cool spring morning. I got in one of the vans with Ryan and a dozen other teenagers. Our bikes were loaded on a flatbed truck, and we were shuttled to the starting point on a hill overlooking our valley, about twenty miles away from the church finish line. I sat there nervously, wondering why most teenagers were looking at me and whispering. Then, I realized they were looking at my peanut-butter-and-jelly sandwich hanging on a ribbon around my neck.

"It's my good-luck PB&J," I told them.

We all left together and began to wind down the hill. I started to go faster and faster; that's when I lost control. The bikers around me didn't seem to notice my near crash, so I just kept going. As the bikers spread out, some ahead of me and many behind me, I began to sing my Kinder song to myself.

"I know you can do it."

Finally, I was down on flat land, and I was still alive and pedaling. Now, every mile became a challenge. Our valley was laid out in a grid, so every street was named in numerical order such as 90th, 89th Street, etc. That was daunting at first but gave me hope as the miles disappeared and I was still going.

There were helpers along the way, and I saw that my brother-in-law

Steve was working a stop. He offered me water and didn't notice my sandwich. I pulled open the baggie and took a few bites, which had him laughing.

"This is my good-luck sandwich," I repeated.

Steve chuckled and said, "Well, don't eat too much of it, or your luck may run out. You've got quite a way to go yet."

I saluted Steve and continued on my way. One mile at a time.

"I know you can do it."

The next few miles of road had a few dried grasshoppers on them, a manifestation of our state's current drought. Each mile, they became deeper. Pretty soon, thousands of dead, dried grasshoppers crunched under my bicycle tires.

"Well, you don't see that every day," I said in the sunny, morning air.

Mile after mile I went. I began to feel a certain contentment in the monotonous rhythm and the confidence that I was giving my all to this endeavor. I had passed quite a few bikers, and I couldn't see anyone in front of me anymore. Maybe they had already turned the corner to go back into town. The only bike I saw was Ryan's. He was just ahead, and when he stopped for water, I passed him. We basically stayed together for the rest of the miles. He praised me for doing so well.

"You are my Iron Mommy!" he said.

Finally, we made the big turn and entered back into town. I was slightly ahead of Ryan. I wish I could say that I waited for him, grabbed his hand, and we both floated across the finish line together. But the truth is, I suddenly became very competitive (who knew I had that in me?), and I left Ryan waiting at a crosswalk light and sped ahead.

When I arrived at the finish line, people clapped and looked at me with surprised faces. I looked around for more bikers, but I didn't see any. I asked a helper how many other bikers had already made it back.

"Nobody is back yet! You came in first! Are you sure you rode the whole way?"

I assured him I did as Ryan rolled up behind me.

My son was very good-natured about me leaving him at the light, but I apologized to him.

Ryan was right. He knew I could do it, and I did.

Twenty-five years later, from time to time, he still calls me his Iron Mommy.

—Laura McKenzie—

31

The Move

The secret of change is to focus all of your energy not on fighting the old, but on building the new.
~Socrates

Are my teenage daughters going to be in therapy when they are in their thirties because we moved them 1,400 miles away from everything they had ever known? This was the thought that kept swirling through my mind as we made the move from Rhode Island to Florida. It was something that we had to do for everyone's wellbeing, but when the move was put into motion, fear, anxiety, worry, self-doubt, you name it, came in like a tidal wave.

No one understood why we would uproot our lives and move all the way down to southwest Florida. Rhode Island is a very small state, with devoted citizens. In Rhode Island, many people never leave the town where they grew up.

But there were some negative things happening to our family in Rhode Island, particularly to my daughters. We needed a change.

Many said we wouldn't last two years in Florida. My dad promised my younger daughter a horse if she convinced us to stay. He lived in a rural area of Rhode Island and had a horse at one time, so he was equipped with the barn and open space that were needed. My daughter was taking horseback-riding lessons at the time and loved to be around horses. She even enjoyed mucking out the stalls. This could have thrown a big wrench in the move, but luckily she didn't cause a fuss.

We didn't know anyone in Florida when we moved. In fact, I

remember one night soon after our move when my husband and I were having dinner in the bar area of a local restaurant. We liked to sit at the bar because it allows you to meet more people than sitting at a table for two. From my seat, I could see the front door, people coming in and going out. Coming from Rhode Island, about 90 percent of the time when we were out somewhere, someone we knew would walk in. Seeing someone you know gives you a nice, homey feeling.

This night, I was in a negative spiral as I watched that front door. I turned to my husband and said, "Do you realize we will not know one person who walks through that door? Not one!"

Feeling sorry for myself was an understatement. I was rethinking our decision. However, the universe provides when you need it.

A woman was sitting two stools away from us, reading a book. The stool between us was empty. She overheard my husband and me talking about the upcoming football season at the high school that our daughter was attending. She had made Dance Line and was a cheerleader, so we were excited to see the first game.

It turned out this woman had twin daughters in the rival high school who were also on Dance Line. She was very sweet and gave us the ins and outs of being a football parent: where to sit, how to get season tickets, and more. When we left the restaurant that night, I felt so much happier and realized this was a sign that we were indeed in the right place.

The first football game was more than we could have ever imagined. The half-time show, when the Dance Line came out with the band, was like watching a *Friday Night Lights* kind of movie. The whole town came out to watch the game. We later learned that most of them really came for the half-time show. (The team was not that good!)

Between the band, the Dance Line and Flag Line, there were about six hundred kids on the field. It was incredible! I was sitting in the bleachers crying as I watched this amazing event that included my daughter. It was another validation that this was the right move.

As the girls were excelling in school, we discovered that they had more opportunities in these Florida schools than they would have had in their Rhode Island schools. For me, it was a life-changing event.

Because I carried the weight of everyone's happiness on my shoulders, this caused me to make a decision: either live in my negative head space (which kept me away from the joy of being in the present moment and, held onto long enough, could affect my health), or take a deep dive into the healing journey I had slipped into years ago.

I'm happy to say that the deep dive won out! I began to read more self-help books and, somewhat by accident, found an amazing spiritual community full of beautiful healers.

This made me hungry for more healing to be able to be in better control of my emotions and mind chatter. I was on a mission. When you focus on something, you get more of it. Focusing on your negative mind chatter, limiting beliefs and other people's opinions will get you more of the same. It's like a hamster wheel, going round and round. When you focus on positive change and have positive conversations with yourself, people will come into your life to teach you healing tools that are effective modalities of change.

Since that difficult decision to move and disappoint a lot of people, my life has completely changed. Healing is a lifelong journey and has also become my career of purpose. I do not think I would be in the positive space I am in, as well as helping others to be in that space, if it were not for going against the grain and moving 1,400 miles away from everything we knew.

— Sue Campanella —

32

Graduation

Friendship is the golden thread
that ties the heart of all the world.
~John Evelyn

My whole family flew in from New England. Seattle in the winter is not the best vacation experience, but they weren't visiting me for vacation. They were in Seattle to attend my graduation from graduate school.

The ceremony was to be held in a large church downtown that I had never visited. It was a damp Seattle December afternoon, and I was getting ready. I chose a simple, black dress that would fit nicely under my robe. I even put on a bit of makeup for the occasion. A dress and makeup were very much out of character for me at that time, but so was graduating from grad school.

There were no cell phones, but somehow I heard about the stairs that I'd have to negotiate during my graduation. I decided that I couldn't handle the pressure of steps. Walking across the stage was going to be scary enough.

I called my friend Sally in tears and told her that I was not going. The stairs were the last straw for me. She let me voice my fears. She and I had been through many rough spots during the past two years of graduate school. We took all our classes together. We studied together. We edited each other's work.

Sally was paid by the school to be my notetaker because I write slowly due to cerebral palsy. There was no physical way that I could take notes, listen to the lectures, and participate in class. She knew that I needed a good cry when I called her that day because I was overwhelmed. She knew that it wasn't simply about the stairs. It was more about accessibility and feeling not seen. Everyone knew I had cerebral palsy, but the planners hadn't taken accessibility into account.

Sally knew what to do. "You are walking, damn it!" And she said she'd take care of everything; she would make a plan.

My breathing slowed, and I could feel my body again. At this time in my life, I was not taking any medication to help my body relax, but I knew that I had to sit quietly and let Sally work her plan, whatever that was. She made me promise that I would be at the church in an hour to get into my gown.

Okay, I told myself as I splashed cold water on my tear-stained face and touched up my makeup. *I'm doing this. They're just stupid stairs.*

I arrived at the church and saw the stairs on both sides of the stage. I would walk up on one side, shake everyone's hand, and then walk down the stairs on the other side to leave the stage.

It wasn't just the stairs I worried about; it was the handshake, too. My cerebral palsy mostly affects my right side, giving me limited coordination of my right hand. Not only would I need to walk the stairs and the stage in front of hundreds of people, but I also would need to shake hands with five people while on stage using my spastic hand.

The whole day was falling apart fast, and my tears threatened to return. But I knew that I just had to trust Sally.

When I found her, she rushed over and hugged me. "I have it all worked out," she said. "It's going to be fine. I love you."

I knew that if I said anything, I'd start crying. This day was supposed to be fun, a celebration. But I just wanted out. Runaway brides happen. Would I be the first runaway graduate? She understood and she took me to get my gown and splash more water on my face. In the restroom, we made jokes about everyone falling down the stairs and tripping over their gowns.

"Yeah, at least three of us are going to bite the dust in these gowns. I won't be alone anyway," I joked.

"No, Whittier, you will not be alone. That I can promise you."

We were laughing as we exited the restroom together. I felt better; I had an ally and would make it through the day. I was not alone in my disability.

I can't tell you who spoke or what they said during graduation. I was focused on getting through. When they started calling graduates up in alphabetical order, I began to get nervous about the whole ceremony.

I watched as my classmates glided up the stairs and over the stage as if they were floating. They were so beautiful. I couldn't help but be proud to be part of this amazing class. I let go of worry and just sat in awe of us all.

As my name got closer, I couldn't help but feel the spasms starting. They were about to call my name when I saw two classmates walk to the stairs on both sides of the stage. Four of my friends were waiting by the stairs. My name was called as I was at the bottom of the stage. Kurt and Sally walked me up the stairs. Both gave me hugs at the top and quickly left. I didn't have to shake hands with any of my professors on stage. We were all about the hugs.

My advisor fumbled with my sash as he put it on me, and we laughed. He said, "I'm sorry," as he fumbled. "You're my first-ever graduate!" We laughed and hugged.

"Thank you. It's perfect," I said. It was upside-down and backward, and he was embarrassed. I was happy, and we laughed together. With diploma in hand, I walked to the other side of the stage, and there stood my friends Heidi and Sara to help me down the stairs. My mother was waiting for me at the bottom. I hugged and thanked everyone and felt so supported, like a princess.

Someone even said that I received the loudest cheers, but I was so surrounded by love that I didn't hear them at all. When we gathered for refreshments in the church basement, my professors gravitated toward me. I was surprised and honored to be surrounded by the people who had taught me the skills that I'd use for years to come.

The day that I feared had turned into one of the best days of my life. This is what it means to have the courage to be vulnerable with allies. That day, my people came through. I'm not even sure if they realize the gift they gave me that day, but I will be forever grateful to them.

—Whittier Mikkelsen—

33

Raising the Barre

When you trip in life, make it part of your dance.
~Author Unknown

I'd loved hip-hop dancing since my childhood, and in high school I took classes that focused on jazz and hip-hop. Dance was my favorite class, and I looked forward to going every day. I had met some of my best friends through dance. And this year, my senior year, was going to be the best dance class yet.

As I was walking excitedly over to the first day of dance class, I passed one of my fellow dancers from the previous year.

"Sarah, have you heard?"

"Heard what?"

"We have a new dance teacher. Her name is Ms. Barton, and she is strictly ballet."

Ballet? Well, this ought to be interesting.

I had never taken ballet in my life. I'll admit, I was a bit nervous, but also up for the challenge. I mean, how hard could it be, right?

As I entered the classroom, all the girls were in their black leotards and ballet slippers. I must have missed the memo of the dress requirement, let alone that I was taking a ballet class. I changed into hip-hop–styled clothing that I had in my backpack. It would have to do for now.

We all stood at the barre as Ms. Barton ran us through basic ballet steps — plié, tendu, dégagé and rond de jambe to name a few. She was just how I had imagined a ballet teacher would be: excellent posture

80

with a snobby attitude.

She also assumed all the students in the room already knew some ballet.

"Grand plié," demanded Ms. Barton.

Along with my fellow classmates, I began my grand plié, with one hand on the barre and the other motioning out to the side, slowly bending down with my knees at a horizontal.

I wanted to give myself a pat on the back. But Ms. Barton gave me a stare.

"What is your name?" she asked.

"Sarah. Sarah Brunner," I responded with a smile.

"Class, I would like everyone to watch Miss Sarah do a grand plié." She motioned for me to continue.

Wow, she must think I'm great to ask me to demonstrate in front of the class, I thought, hiding my excitement. I slowly got into position and then performed a grand plié.

Complete silence. All eyes were on me.

"Now, class, this is a prime example of what *not* to do," Ms. Barton said. She raised her voice with an emphasis on the *not*.

Red face. Eyes watering. A wave of pure embarrassment came over me. What had just happened? What should I do? It was completely mortifying.

I participated in the rest of the class to the best of my abilities, but I couldn't believe this teacher had humiliated me. Why was I even there? I didn't want to take ballet. I wanted to take hip-hop.

I spent the rest of the day dwelling on this humiliating moment, wondering if I should quit. But my pride wouldn't allow it. As I lay in bed that night, I knew I was going back. I could do it. I would show that teacher.

I persisted day by day, week by week, and I was proud to say that I was still standing by the end of the semester. I felt like Ms. Barton and I had developed an agreeable relationship. She seemed to tolerate my ballet well enough to not make every dance class dreadful. I'd also like to think she appreciated my hip-hop style — well enough that she asked me to choreograph two hip-hop pieces for our final production.

"20 Barres from the Top" was to be a four-day showcase performed at our high-school theater. It was for our families, friends, other students, and anyone who purchased a ticket. It included twenty dance pieces that were not just ballet. One could expect to see hip-hop, modern, jazz, etc.

As a requirement for class, students had to choose to be in at least six dance pieces of the twenty being performed. Out of the six, I was part of my two hip-hop pieces along with two modern pieces, a jazz piece and, for the last... That's right, folks, a *ballet* piece choreographed by Ms. Barton. I think Ms. Barton was shocked that I chose to be in her closing ballet piece, but something inside me wanted to prove to her that I was good enough.

Our production turned out to be a huge success. We had nearly sold-out shows all four nights. My favorite piece turned out to be our closing ballet piece to Aretha Franklin's "Respect." Though I was not the best ballet dancer out there, I had the best time dancing to it and gave it my all. Kudos to Ms. Barton for choreographing such a fun, lively and exhilarating piece, leaving our audience cheering and giving standing ovations. Underneath her stern look and emotionless facade, I'd like to think I made her a little proud.

On the last day of my senior year, I was clearing out my locker along with a few other classmates in dance class. Ms. Barton was at the front of the room, motioning that she had an announcement to make. She cleared her throat.

"At the end of the semester, I always like to award one student the Ballerina." Ms. Barton held up a ballerina trophy figurine.

Still at my locker, I laughed and whispered to my nearby classmates, "Yep, definitely not me." I continued to pack up.

Ms. Barton said, "This student, you could clearly tell, had no ballet experience. She has shown such a great amount of improvement, and I am truly proud of her... Sarah Brunner."

In shock, I looked up from my locker toward Ms. Barton, who was smiling at me. My fellow classmates clapped and cheered for me. I couldn't believe my ears.

As I walked to the front of the classroom to receive the Ballerina award, a bit teary-eyed, I smiled back at Ms. Barton and said, "Thank you for challenging me."

— S.L. Brunner —

34

The List

You create your thoughts, your thoughts create your
intentions and your intentions create your reality.
~Wayne Dyer

Newly divorced, I had imposed on my friend April's kindness and spare room for too long. I knew I had to find a place of my own, but I was scared.

I stalled for days, paralyzed by the thought of striking out and the "impossibility," repeated by friends and acquaintances, of finding an affordable and decent place in New York City. Everyone offered what they thought was helpful advice: live with a roommate, live with your mother, move to another city.

Any of these alternatives was unthinkable. A roommate would mean even more adjustments than living alone, for the first time in many years. April was supremely easygoing, yet I didn't feel wholly comfortable even staying with her. My mother's studio apartment was barely big enough for her pullout couch. A different city, any city, was even scarier.

April noticed my increasingly sleepless nights. One morning at the kitchen table, as she refilled my coffee cup, she said, "Hey, remember that workshop I went to a few months ago?"

"Right," I said. "What was the subject?" I couldn't help my skeptical tone. "The Law of Subtraction?"

"Come on," she said, smiling in spite of herself. "Now, stay open. The Law of Attraction." She paused and said, "One person talked about her momentous decision to open a pottery shop in a town near her home."

"I'm no good with clay," I said. "But I can type and cook an omelet."

"Please, just listen."

I nodded.

"You know the principle — what you think about comes about. Well, this woman made a list of everything she wanted in a shop: roomy and airy, what she could afford, with space and equipment to give classes, near the main highway and the right supplies, and people who were supportive."

"Wow," I said. "And?"

"She kept reading that list over and over, even though she sometimes thought it was ridiculous. She struggled with negative thoughts but kept at it, seeing herself in her shop. You know what happened?"

I shook my head. It sounded hokey.

"Little by little, as she repeated those ideas, she noticed signs in shop windows of spaces for rent and ads in the paper. People called her with offers, and she felt led to explore different places. Finally, she found the perfect space. Now, she sells her pots and gives classes at Muddy Joy, and several local artists want to exhibit with her."

I was impressed. "So, you think I should make a list?"

"Not that I don't love your company," April said, her hand on my arm, "but you know you've got to take the next step. And what that woman did works."

Well, why not? I thought. *What was to lose — a piece of paper?*

A few days later, in a corner of the local cafe, armed with a venti latte and double order of chocolate-chip muffins, I took out my clipboard. On a fresh piece of paper in bold ink, I wrote: "What I Want in My Apartment." Then I started my list.

The first few things were easy:

1. a studio or one-bedroom
2. within my budget
3. near the local businesses for supplies and contacts for my editing work

4. near friends
5. near the subway stop to go to my mother's

I got bolder:
   6. appliances that weren't too old
   7. a nice building entrance for seeing clients

And more daring:
   8. with warm wood
   9. on a high floor with a nice view
   10. near a park so I could get out easily to run

I took a big gulp of latte. Was I too demanding of the Universe? The practicalities were defensible (within budget, near businesses), but the luxuries (wood, a view, near a park)? Was I overstepping?

To gain confidence, I started reading more about the Law of Attraction. Our self-deprecations don't affect it. It responds to our strong thoughts, visualizations, and convictions. The trick is to kick out our lack of belief and suspicions of futility and just keep seeing — and especially feeling — ourselves in the situation we want.

I read over my list every morning when I got up and every evening before bed. As the readings cautioned, I didn't tell anyone except April, who cheered, and my new boyfriend, who said, "Great!" Every day, I found it easier to visualize myself in the "perfect" place.

My fear had stopped me from taking the first necessary step — contacting a real-estate agent. Now, I was almost eager. On another friend's recommendation, I registered with a Realtor, kept checking in with him, and followed him around to the listings.

The first three places were disappointing — old New York apartment buildings with funereal lobbies, depressingly worn appliances and cabinets, and windows facing right into other apartments. I started to believe those ominous can't-find-a-place clichés.

So, I renewed my efforts for more exposure. I printed multiple copies of my list and put them in my purse and pockets, taped copies to the refrigerator door and bathroom mirror, and added a lunchtime review.

One windy, chilly January afternoon, the Realtor called, and we went out to see another apartment. On the way, he said, "This studio is within your range," and my heart leapt. But then he added, "The lease is only nine months because the building is being sold."

I sighed. "I'll look." How much more uncertain could the future be? And nine months seemed a long way off.

We reached the building, a brownstone with a wrought-iron gate at the entrance. Flower boxes lined either side. He preceded me up the steps, unlocked the outer door, and then opened the first door inside.

I stepped in… and knew! The apartment had warm wood floors throughout, a big window, and a bright kitchenette with new appliances. And it was a block from the subway that went to my mother's, two blocks from the park, and three blocks from a branch of my favorite stationery-supply shop. The manager I knew had even been transferred there!

Okay, the apartment was on the first floor and had no view. But it was also four blocks from my boyfriend's (later husband's) two-bedroom, high-floor doorman apartment, and he had a great view of the park and the river!

My little studio was perfect for my needs at the time. Of course, I had to harness my doubts, envision what I wanted, and enlist a Realtor. Maybe the right place would have shown up anyway, or maybe not.

But I gained more than an apartment. I learned to specify my needs, deserve my desires, and believe and expect fulfillment.

Since then, I have used the Law of Attraction "list method" often, with thrilling results and outcomes. As for my studio, eight months after I moved in and just before my lease was up, my boyfriend asked me to move in with him.

— Noelle Sterne —

Chapter
5

Let It Go

35

Lessons from a Son

*Forgiveness is one of the most beautiful words in the
human vocabulary. How much pain and unhappy
consequences could be avoided if we all learned
the meaning of this word?*
~Billy Graham

It was to have been a pleasant family dinner at a nice restaurant with my husband Trevor, our twenty-two-year-old son Ryan, my husband's father Bob, and me. Since his wife had died five years earlier, Bob went everywhere with us.

"So, Ryan, it looks like you've put on some weight," Bob observed. "How much do you weigh now?"

Ryan shifted in his seat. "Two fifty." He had always struggled with his weight.

Bob gave a low whistle. "Two hundred and fifty pounds. That's a lot of weight for a young fellow like you to be carrying around. Hard on the heart, you know."

"I know."

"You still looking to get married some day?" Bob asked.

"Yes." The single word was clipped, indicating that Ryan would rather be anywhere but here.

"What you need to do is to find yourself an ugly girl. She'll be so grateful that you asked her out that she won't care that you're fat."

I blinked in astonishment. Bob had always been blunt, even rude at times, but this was too much. I started to say something when my husband sent me a pleading look not to get into it with his father.

Tight-lipped, I nodded.

The evening limped by. Bob remarked that I was putting on weight myself. I nodded in acknowledgment, grateful that the focus had moved away from Ryan. I was happy to be the target of Bob's insults if it took his attention away from my son.

On the way home, I asked Trevor to take me home before he dropped off his father. I couldn't bear to be in Bob's company a moment longer than necessary. Ryan helped me out of the car and then climbed into his own car, which he'd left in front of our house.

The following morning, I called Ryan and told him how sorry I was for the previous night. "Your grandfather crossed the line."

"It's okay, Mom," he said. "That's just how Grandpa is. I got over it and moved on." Was he implying that I should do the same?

"Already?" I asked, unable to keep the astonishment from my voice. "But aren't you angry?"

"Being angry won't change Grandpa. And it won't make me feel any better."

He was right. Being angry wouldn't change anything.

I wanted to hug my son and hoped he heard the love in my voice. "You're pretty smart. Did you know that?"

At only twenty-two, he possessed far more emotional and spiritual maturity than I could lay claim to.

"I have my moments," he teased.

After a few more minutes, we hung up. I had a lot to think about. For years, I had tried to turn around my negative thinking. Could it be that forgiveness was the answer to thinking more positively?

My son, only a few years out of his teens, understood the importance of forgiveness. Unknowingly, he had become a role model for me.

— Jane McBride —

The Power of Apology

Anger makes you smaller, while forgiveness
forces you to grow beyond what you were.
~Cheri Carter-Scott

M y wife and I wanted to share our new home with family and friends by hosting a small gathering in the early summer. She had prepared lots of snacks and delectables, while my job was to have the backyard in order. That meant lawn mowed, play structure cleared of cobwebs, and patio furniture cleaned.

There was plenty of space for the kids to run and play. There was just one thing I hadn't counted on: My brother chose to bring his unruly Irish Setter, Max. I knew from past encounters that Max was friendly enough, but like many two-year-olds, he was full of energy and quite rambunctious. Weighing in at just over fifty pounds, he could easily knock over my niece's small boys, never mind my six-month-old granddaughter.

So, when my brother showed up, I asked him to watch Max and keep him outside, relegated to the backyard. I didn't want his dog in the house, running around in the confined space, knocking over the little tykes like bowling balls.

My plan was working out just fine. Max was using up his energy by running back and forth in the backyard and giving the kids plenty of room. Unexpectedly, after supper, those who had been outside started to come in. The weather had changed, and a partly cloudy sky had given way to overcast. What followed was scant precipitation that turned to light drizzle and was threatening to rain. Our backyard fun had suddenly come to an end. The day was nearly spent, but what was to be done with Max?

Perhaps I should have relented and told my brother to bring Max inside. It was an awkward moment. I wasn't keen on his dog running around in the house, and he wasn't happy with driving home with a wet dog. While the rest of the family headed to the rec room, Max looked in from the patio door, barking his displeasure. Eventually, my brother decided to leave rather than force the issue.

In hindsight, I regret not being more accommodating. I joined my family in a lively game of table tennis and thought no more about Max or his owner. A few days passed, and I hadn't heard anything from my brother. I texted him and expressed wishes for him to come out again. His reply came as a surprise—a shock, actually: "Not a chance." No sooner had I read those words than it hit home. Clearly, he was unhappy over the way we had parted. After all, I had left him little choice. *Well, he'll get over it,* I reasoned.

A few weeks later, my astute wife asked me how my brother was doing. "Fine, I guess," was my initial reply. Then, sheepishly, I showed her his last words on my cell phone. Then, I realized that we hadn't communicated at all via phone or text message. Two months had passed, and I should have realized he was put out. My wife suggested I get in touch with my brother.

Like a typical guy, I resisted. I held off, waiting for him to call. But then those nagging thoughts kept invading my thinking. It was my conscience trying to penetrate my stubbornness. *You could have handled that better.* I tried to dismiss it. Pride was getting in the way. Thoughts of why he had to bring his unruly dog in the first place popped into my head.

Several more weeks passed. *Wait a minute!* I took a deep breath and revisited the whole scenario in my head. *What was really happening?* My brother was facing a number of health issues. On top of that, his wife of thirty-five years had passed only a few months earlier. His dog, Max, was his constant companion, the one who kept him going.

I mulled it over in my head, and it dawned on me—finally. I

knew it was me who was at fault. Had I allowed my brother to bring Max inside during the party, we could have kept the dog on a leash, and cleanup would have been easy if he had made a mess. In turn, my brother wouldn't have left in a huff.

"You need to make this right," my wife said one morning over coffee. It had been over two months since the gathering, with still no word from him. Naturally, I was tempted to let it slide, but in the end I knew it was up to me.

How often do we hear stories about some family members who don't talk anymore, don't associate or visit, all because of some minor incident — now relegated to the past — but seeming to hang over them like a dark cloud?

I swallowed my pride. I knew my brother's daily routine and reasoned I could catch him at home around lunchtime. So, I picked up a pizza and headed over to his house unannounced. His car was in the driveway, so unless he was out for a walk, he was bound to be at home. I walked up to the front door and rang the bell. As I stood there, I felt apprehensive. What would he say or do? How would he react to my impromptu presence? Would he scowl, swear, even close the door in my face?

It was the moment of truth. He opened the door, and in his first glance I read apprehension. But then he must have spotted the pizza box in my hands, held out in front like a peace offering. There was a momentary pause as he looked into my eyes.

"Can I come in? Can we talk?" I offered meekly.

Max came bounding up to me, tail wagging, mouth slobbering. Well, I took that as a good sign, and perhaps that softened my brother's stance. He motioned that I could step inside. My next words were that I was sorry for the way I had conducted myself at the party. I told him I could have handled that better and asked him to forgive me. I was genuinely sorry.

A faint smile crossed his lips as he took the pizza box out of my hands. We had lunch together, and what I thought would be a relatively short get-together turned into a one-hour visit. It felt good to reconnect.

Several months later, we had another family function at our house.

Of course, my brother brought Max with him. To my relief, there were no accidents or issues, and the kids enjoyed having their furry friend along. My brother had a good time and left in quite a different frame of mind.

Later, as my wife and I were cleaning up, I hugged her and smiled, basking in a feeling of relief and contentment. I was overjoyed that I had not only reconnected with my brother but averted a potentially worsening situation, all started because of my pride.

My wife smiled, acknowledging my happiness, and handed me a broom so I could sweep up the dog hair.

—Robert Stermscheg—

37

A Fresh Chapter

Forgiveness is about empowering yourself,
rather than empowering your past.
~T.D. Jakes

I hung up the phone and slid limply onto the kitchen chair. "Wow!" I breathed softly, my mind whirling from the unexpected news. *Did that call really just happen?* I shook my head as if to dislodge any cobwebs from my brain so I could think more clearly.

The past, a chapter my mother had crammed into a high-security vault many moons ago after an acrimonious divorce, was trying to make an appearance. At the moment, the shock had me slightly reeling. Out of the clear blue, my brother had received a letter from an uncle on our paternal side, whom we never knew.

Our parents divorced while we were children, and our mother had arbitrarily made the decision to cut all ties with not just our father but his entire family. Now, one of my father's three brothers was reaching out to us.

My brother confessed that he was as surprised as I was. Our uncle's request was to simply "leave the past behind and start again."

"What do you think?" my brother asked. Our parents were now deceased, both having passed before their time.

"He's right," I answered thoughtfully. "He's an innocent party, too." Decades had elapsed, and only now did I realize how many people had been affected by the choice that a single individual had made a long time ago.

"Yes, I think we should meet him," I said. After I spoke the words, plans were put in place.

I admit, I was nervous. The three of us had agreed to meet at a key spot at a mall and then go for a meal. My stomach was doing flips as my brother and I stood waiting by the escalators.

"Will you recognize him?" I whispered. He nodded and said our uncle had provided a photo. Agitated, I glanced at the time. Then, I felt like someone was watching me. When I turned my head slightly, I saw an older man with a headful of white hair and startling blue eyes, which were laser-focused on me. My breath caught. Was that him?

The man approached, and I looked at my brother, whose face broke into a smile. He was already stretching out his hand to greet him. With my heart beating a mile a minute, I stood back for a brief second before I found myself engulfed in a warm, loving hug.

"I would have known you anywhere," my uncle stated. "You are your father's daughter."

I was speechless. His words were genuine and true, and I could see the strong emotion in his eyes and hear it in his voice. My smile was a bit shaky.

"It's good to finally meet you," I stammered. We stood for a moment or two longer, unable to believe this reunion was actually happening.

After we arrived at the restaurant and sat down at a table, my uncle began to talk while we listened attentively. It was fascinating to hear about the grandparents we only had shadowy memories of and to see the photos he had brought with him. I had no idea my father had such a large family.

Tears pricked my eyes when I saw the picture of my father's three brothers. One was the image of Dad but sporting a beard. I traced his face with my fingertip, hardly believing all this was real.

Time flew by as we shared our lives. It was like a door had swung open and a neon welcome sign had been lit up over the top. Despite all the missing years, my uncle displayed no animosity. But, from time to time, those blue eyes would glisten when he stared at our faces as if in disbelief. I cannot imagine what it must've been like for the paternal side of my family to have been banned from our existence simply because one person had unfairly painted them all with the same brush.

My heart ached for the relatives who'd spent these past decades wondering about us, and I was grateful for this uncle of mine making the choice to offer an olive branch. He was clearly willing to forgive and forget.

I don't know how long we sat together, but it felt too soon when we were pushing back our chairs and rising to leave.

"We will not lose touch again," our uncle declared as he firmly gripped my brother's hand before embracing me again.

"Agreed," I affirmed as my brother nodded.

The time had come for a fresh chapter, and we were willing to write it together.

—S.K. Naus—

38

Instant Peace

When you forgive, you in no way change the past —
but you sure do change the future.
~Bernard Meltzer

I was driving down the highway in the right lane when a decrepit panel truck next to me in the center lane suddenly moved over to exit the highway. It was literally driving sideways across my lane. I came within a few feet of hitting it broadside at sixty miles per hour.

There was nothing I could do at that high speed except turn hard to the right, drive side by side with the truck that had forced me off the road, and take the exit as well, albeit on the shoulder.

As I sat behind the ramshackle truck at the bottom of the exit ramp, I noticed that I wasn't angry. Clearly, this had been an inadvertent error. The truck driver didn't even know that he'd almost caused a multi-vehicle accident.

The truck, which was missing its rear doors, was packed from floor to ceiling with what looked like a hodgepodge of someone's possessions. Thus, the driver couldn't see out the rearview mirror. And the truck didn't even have a right-side mirror. My car was invisible to him.

I wondered what the driver was going through with that junky truck most likely filled with everything he owned. He was probably having a bad day.

And that was it. Instant forgiveness.

The old me, the pre–Chicken Soup for the Soul me, would have been upset. But the new me instantly went to a better place — a calm, understanding place!

How did this happen? It's because I've edited hundreds of stories about forgiveness. All the wisdom our writers have shared about the power of forgiveness in their own lives has given me a wonderfully constructive worldview.

One of my favorite stories about the power of forgiveness was by Judythe Guarnera, who was trying to recover from the end of her thirty-year marriage. She joined a divorce support group, but she was stuck — she hadn't found a way to shed her resentment and anger and move forward. Then, an insightful speaker addressed the group and said, "Repeat after me. In my marriage, I did the best I could."

Everyone in the room said it. "In my marriage, I did the best I could."

Next, the speaker told them to say, "My spouse did the best he or she could."

Now, there was silence. No one was willing to say that! The speaker tried to persuade them, saying, "Who would choose to do their worst?"

And she was right. If most of us think about our failed relationships — a marriage, a friendship, a work situation — we know that we did our best. So, why can't we assume that the other people also did their best? They might not have done a good job, but if they were *trying*, if the failure wasn't deliberate, it's a lot harder to be angry.

Judythe realized that her husband probably *had* done his best, just as she had. She says, "It took a while before I could embrace that idea and forgive my husband and myself. He wasn't the best husband for me, and I wasn't the best wife for him. But I had loved him and had really intended to do my best."

When she thought about her past, she saw that it was indeed made up of all her best efforts. And so was her husband's.

Well, that's how I viewed that bad driver, too. He wasn't trying to cause an accident. He was doing his best.

I didn't always have such a constructive attitude. I used to carry around all my resentments and anger like they were little medallions sewn onto a cloak. That cloak sure was heavy, and it got worse every year. Every bad thing from my past was on that cloak, and it was weighing me down.

Of course, those resentments, disappointments, insults, etc., were all things that happened in the past. But I was carrying them into the present, and they were definitely going to be part of my future, too.

I learned from Judythe. All those "wrongs" had been done by people who were mostly trying to do "right." They just happened to fail. It was time to stop being angry. How can you be angry with someone who didn't do it on purpose?

I discovered that I could shrug off that heavy cloak but decided the following: I would acknowledge that a bad thing happened, but I would not continue to react to it. That way, it would stay in the past where it belonged.

It was like I shrugged my shoulders and that heavy cloak fell right off me. And that truck driver who almost ran me off the road? He didn't mean it, so I didn't even get mad at all. Instant forgiveness, instant peace.

Whether it's instant forgiveness for a careless driver, or whether you need to get over a past wrong, forgiveness requires no time, no money, no sweating. It all happens in your head. You can do it in one second. All you have to do is decide.

— Amy Newmark —

39

The Mantra That Gets Me Through

Genuine forgiveness does not deny
anger but faces it head-on.
~Alice Miller

y son, PJ, and I had both experienced a number of stressful months. He had been laid off from his job and subsequently decided to start his own business, which came with challenges. He had to go into debt for a new diesel truck and specialty trailer to transport and deliver various items — from large commercial air conditioners to iron beams — to businesses across the country. Other business expenses included insurance and licensing. He also had to learn Department of Transportation rules, regulations, and laws, and meet deadlines for deliveries that were often hindered by weather conditions or traffic jams.

My own stress arrived after experiencing debilitating hip pain that led me to an orthopedic surgeon. After viewing several X-rays, he said, "Your hips are shot. You're bone on bone on both sides, which means two hip replacements."

I was stunned. Through my sixty-eight years, I'd been blessed with good health and enjoyed physical activities. I'd heard success stories about hip replacements, but my greatest anxiety was that I was now widowed and lived alone. The thought of getting through two major surgeries without my husband seemed daunting. He had always pampered me through bouts of stomach flu or bronchitis, as well as my only surgery—an emergency appendectomy.

Now, I was alone with no family to lean on except my son who lived 300 miles away and was coping with his own stress. And, to boot, I had recently moved to a new town in a new state for a new start since widowhood. I had expected to enjoy my new home, near the beach and quaint communities that offered art and culture, with opportunities to meet new people and create new experiences.

Unfortunately, I had not enjoyed one single beach walk since the move due to my unbearable hip pain. Instead of healing from my husband's death, I was experiencing heightened anxiety.

I informed PJ about the situation and the date set for the first procedure. I would be in the hospital overnight and sent home the next day with a walker and instructions for my recovery.

PJ took a week off from his struggling business to be with me. Due to my good health and stamina, I did well with rehab. The second surgery was scheduled for eight weeks after the first.

A week before the second surgery, my son was driving a route for his business that brought him near to me, so he stopped for a quick visit. I wasn't feeling well when he arrived. I was walking slowly as I tried to go without a walker or cane, drained physically and emotionally from the first surgery but anxious to be done with the second. And my anxiety was again rising and creating emotional overload because I desperately missed my husband's presence and care.

Unfortunately, my son had experienced a bad day regarding a delivery so he was irritable. He said, "Mom, I'm not in the mood for talking." Then he sat down and focused on his cell phone.

I felt hurt and invalidated.

"Well, thanks, PJ. No compassion or care about my feelings. I don't know why God left me with no family that cares."

Without a word, he picked up his bag and headed toward the door.

"Well, just leave," I said, stating the obvious.

"I am," he spewed. "I can't listen to you play the victim!"

I was stunned. Crying and confused, I watched him drive away.

PJ didn't answer my texts or calls. I didn't hear from him before or after the second surgery. I was blessed to receive in-home nursing care and good neighbors who looked in on me. As I began my physical healing, I had to also work more on my emotional healing regarding my husband's death and now my son's absence.

Through recovery, I wrote in my journal about the incident with my son. I contemplated the words I had spoken about his lack of compassion and my having no family who cared, which I knew in my "right mind" was false.

It dawned on me that my harsh words were hurtful to my son and left him feeling unappreciated. I recognized that I had allowed my pain, frustration and anxiety to drive me to speak those hateful words.

I started writing positive quotes and words of love toward my son in my journal. I created a canvas wall hanging that I placed in view to read aloud each morning and throughout the day. It said, "May you be happy, blessed, free, peaceful, loved, loving, forgiven and forgiving."

This became my daily mantra to the universe for my son, myself, and all others.

I couldn't control PJ's response to our situation or any other uncontrollable events in my life such as the death of a spouse or double hip replacement. But daily, I could send positive, caring, loving words into the universe.

My mind and emotions cleared. My body began to heal. I started volunteer work at the Navy base with the USO several times each week. I felt great satisfaction and a feeling of purpose in supporting a new generation of military personnel. And six months following his departure from my apartment, a week before Christmas, I received a text from PJ.

"Hi, Mom. I hope you're okay. I would like to visit next weekend if you have no plans. I love you. And I promise, nothing like this will ever happen again."

No greater smile could ever cover my face as the heaviness left my heart. I sent a response: "I'm doing great! See you then! Love you!"

We never talked about his prolonged absence and silence. It wasn't important. We just savored our time together again. And I continued to recite my daily mantra, which still gets me through.

— Deborah Tainsh —

40

Wendy's and Me

It's one of the greatest gifts you can give yourself,
to forgive. Forgive everybody.
~Maya Angelou

I was fired from Wendy's in high school. After three days, the manager said, "I'm sorry, but we're going to have to let you go. Some people just don't have what it takes to make it in fast food." Apparently, I was flipping the hamburger patties too slowly.

What do you do when you're told that you're not good enough to work at a fast-food restaurant? I felt like I had only one career option: I became a United States Congressman. Really.

I never harbored any ill will toward Wendy's. I kept a positive attitude for two reasons: First, nobody likes a Wendy's double cheeseburger and chocolate Frosty more than I do. Second, Wendy's founder, Dave Thomas, was a hero of mine. It wasn't his rags-to-riches story. What really inspired me was how Thomas went back to high school at age sixty-one and earned his diploma. His fellow students voted him "most likely to succeed" and elected him prom king.

Fast forward many years later. To my pleasant surprise, one of my biggest campaign supporters when I was in Congress was none other than Wendy's. They contributed a thousand dollars for every hour that I worked there. I think that makes me the world's highest-paid fast-food reject!

More importantly, the "setback" taught me two valuable lessons about positive thinking in life.

First, don't hold grudges. Your opponent today may be your biggest ally tomorrow. Second, l learned that setbacks are temporary, and we shouldn't take things personally.

— Ric Keller —

Never Too Late

*Friendship is the only cement that will
ever hold the world together.*
~Woodrow Wilson

I slowly eased my way into the parking space. My heart was rapidly beating as I did a quick scan of the parking lot. Looking through the crowds of shoppers, I looked for a familiar face, but I didn't see her.

I was so nervous, I almost put my car in reverse to go back home. I took a deep breath and tried to control my anxiety. *It's been too long, and I've gone this far,* I convinced myself. There was no turning back. I took another deep breath and shut off the engine.

As I walked toward the restaurant where we were meeting, I remembered the good times we had. I tried not to focus on the argument that kept us apart for almost ten years.

Teresa and I had been good friends for many years. We had a lot of the same interests and could stay up all night chatting on the phone, laughing until our sides hurt. We were always there for each other when we needed to vent, cry or celebrate. We were so close that we could read each other's minds and finish each other's sentences. That all changed when we had a huge disagreement and parted ways.

There wasn't a day that passed when I didn't think of her or miss her. I often thought of reaching out to her to make amends. But then I would think, *If she cared, why hasn't she gotten in touch with me?* One other trait that we had in common was that we were both very stubborn.

It had been Teresa's birthday a month before, and that had prompted me to look for her on social media. She had a common name, but I eventually found her photo, with her famous broad smile and a head full of curls. More photos showed she liked to travel and had grandchildren. Ten years had been good to her.

I had sent her a Facebook message and expressed how much I'd missed her throughout the years and what she meant to me. I mentioned a few silly memories we had had together. I told her that I was grateful that she was there for me when I was going through a hard time. I ended the message by asking her if she would like to meet one day, and I wished her a happy birthday.

When I hadn't heard from her, I figured she didn't feel the same way. But then she finally reached out and said that she missed me as well! We'd arranged to have this lunch.

After forty minutes and my third cup of coffee I decided she wasn't coming after all. She hadn't even called or texted me. Maybe it really was too late to rekindle this friendship.

As I was paying the bill, sad and a bit angry that she hadn't showed up, I heard her familiar voice. "I'm here!" Teresa said, exasperated. She went on to tell me why she was late and how she wasn't able to call.

I stopped her midway. "It's okay. I don't care why you're late. I'm just glad you're here!" We hugged for what seemed an eternity.

We stayed in that restaurant for hours, catching up and reminiscing. It was hard to believe we hadn't seen each other in almost ten years. It felt like old times, as if we had seen each other yesterday. Not once did our disagreement come up. The waitress finally made us pay because they were closing. It was dark outside!

I often think that, if I hadn't taken that leap of faith to forgive Teresa, I would have missed out on a wonderful friendship. I really don't know why it took me so long!

— Dorann Weber —

An Accidental Meeting, Twice

To understand somebody else as a human being,
I think, is about as close to real
forgiveness as one can get.
~David Small

There were screeching tires, a thump, and a crunch as my car was propelled to the middle of the lane. It took only seconds to realize what had happened. My car had been hit by another vehicle as I was starting to exit the underground parking lot in the building down the street from my office.

When I got out to speak with the man who had just hit my car, he asked if I was okay. He looked quite flustered and started to apologize. "I am so sorry, miss. Are you okay?" To be quite truthful, I didn't know what to say. After checking out the damage to my cherished car, I was really annoyed.

Not wanting to get into an argument or any type of conversation with this stranger, I suggested we exchange the relevant insurance information. Neither of us had been injured, and the damage wouldn't prevent us from driving our cars. I told the man my plan was to stop at the police station a few blocks away from my home to file a report and suggested he do the same.

While driving to the police station, I kept thinking about how it was just my luck that some jerk decided to speed down the lane behind the building where I parked my car. I expressed my annoyance about the entire episode to the police officer who filed my report. The officer walked out to the parking lot with me to take a look at the damage to my car. The officer made a slow whistling sound.

"Doesn't look too bad, lady, until you lift that hood. Repairs for this type of damage can be quite expensive. Good thing you have insurance," he said.

Still angry when I went to work the next day, I expressed my annoyance to anyone who would listen. This feeling of resentment toward the man who had hit my car went on for a couple of days. My insurance representative had returned my telephone call to review the "Rules of the Road" related to exiting a parking lot. As drivers in the traffic lane have the right of way, I was considered to be at fault. The man who hit me would be able to have his insurance provider file a claim against my policy for the damage to his car, resulting in an increase to my insurance premium.

I tried to explain to the insurance representative that the speed in the lane was 20 miles per hour, and the guy who hit me had been speeding. He had been barreling down the lane, and I clearly heard the screech of his brakes as he tried to slow down to avoid hitting the nose of my car. The insurance representative told me if there had been a witness to prove the person who hit my car was speeding in the lane, we could have him charged by the police. Only then could we file a claim against his insurance policy. As I didn't have a witness, the other party was free to file a claim against my policy.

I hung up the phone, feeling angrier than before. I was being punished for another person's careless actions.

My insurance agent called me again the next day with good news. The man who had hit my car had consulted with his own insurance agent and had made the decision not to file a claim. He planned to personally pay for the repairs to his own vehicle. Apparently, he had told his agent that he didn't want me to be penalized for the accident.

I was stunned. For the past three days, I had let my anger simmer to the point of resentment. Ironically, the way I had been feeling didn't harm the man who had offended me. He wasn't even aware of how I felt, so my resentment wasn't causing him any inner turmoil. The only person my feelings were hurting was me. Now I felt ashamed for all the negative thoughts I'd been having about this man. It was more likely he was a very decent person who had simply made a mistake.

A week later, I walked into the elevator heading to my office on the nineteenth floor of the building where I worked. I didn't pay any attention to the other people in the elevator until I heard a male voice say, "Well, hello, miss. How's your poor car doing?" I turned around to face the man who had hit my car. He worked in the same building. We had a short, pleasant conversation about the damage to both of our vehicles. Before exiting the elevator, he apologized for causing the accident, and I responded with my appreciation for his apology.

Feeling gratified after that chance meeting, I strode into my office with a bounce in my step and a smile on my face. Forgiveness had provided me with a fresh start and a new outlook to my day.

—Kathy Dickie—

Count Your Blessings

From Grief to Gratitude
in Five Seconds

*Perspective changes everything. What you take for
granted someone else considers a luxury. Spend a little
extra time being grateful for what you have today.*
~Mel Robbins

M el Robbins had me captivated. Was it really possible to take
control of our thoughts? I was reeling from the recent loss of
my mother and brother. I felt I had no control over the waves
of grief that would hit me like a tidal wave.

Then I happened upon a YouTube video of motivational speaker
Mel Robbins, and the first words she spoke were, "When you understand the power of a five-second decision, and you understand that
you always have a decision to go from autopilot to decision maker,
everything in your life will change."

I remember thinking, *Really, Mel? Everything? Even grief?* But I
was in a deep, dark place that was scary and all too familiar to me, so
I knew I had to give Mel's "5 Second Rule" a try.

The next morning I awoke with the heavy heartache of the days
before, but I caught myself. I did the five-second countdown and
then thought of five things I was grateful for about the person I was
mourning:

1) The way my brother would call me "Kimbly" with sweet

tenderness in his voice.

2) The gift of getting to spend the last year and a half of my brother's life with him.

3) Our daily walks and talks with Mom in the nursing home.

4) The way my brother listened to me intently, like my thoughts and feelings really mattered.

5) The last time I saw him alive, when he gave me one of his comforting bear hugs, smiled a great big smile, and said, "I'm so happy you're back home where you belong. I love you, Kimbly!"

In that moment, my eyes filled with tears, but they weren't tears of sorrow; they were tears of thankfulness. I still felt the sadness of the loss of my brother, but there was something very healing about shifting the sadness to thankfulness. Over the next several days, I practiced this exercise every time the grief crept in. I always came out on the other side, stronger and more content. I began to realize how much power gratitude has.

Not only did this little exercise pull me out of the vortex of grief and sorrow, but it also made me feel empowered. This little exercise worked every time. I would feel the dark grief of losing my mom, my best friend, and 5-4-3-2-1, I would make a list of the things I was grateful for:

1) My mother's amazing sense of humor and how she could always make me smile.

2) The silly song with thirteen verses we wrote together when I was sixteen.

3) The many, many stories we wrote together over the years.

4) My mother's unwavering belief in me.

5) Her example of faith and resilience after all she had endured throughout her life.

How could I think of those things I was thankful for and not smile? These little exercises were reminders of how fortunate I was to have these people in my life. I would never wish those people out of my life to avoid the grief. I would rather take whatever precious time I had with them and deal with sadness when they leave. As they say, grief is the price we pay for love.

It has now been a few years since the loss of my mother and brother. Although the bouts of grief don't hit me as often, they still occur, and I still use this little five-second exercise. There truly is emotional healing when you learn to turn your grief into gratitude.

—Kim Carney—

44

Gratitude Is a Choice

I am happy because I'm grateful. I choose to be
grateful. That gratitude allows me to be happy.
~Will Arnett

One hand gripped the steering wheel. With the other, I wiped tears that welled up and blurred my vision.

It had been a couple of months since the doctor sat beside me in the emergency department waiting room and said, "Sorry, there was nothing we could do; he is gone."

Why me? Why now? I am only thirty-six years old. I should not be driving to the cemetery to visit my husband's grave. Al and I, Al and I, ran through my head day and night. *I don't know who I am without him. I need him.* Our sons were nine and six years old and needed their father.

On garbage day, tears streamed down my face as I carried trash bags to the curb. I did not mind taking out the garbage, but I was sad and angry that nothing was the same. Every Friday, Al took the garbage to the curb when he left for work.

At the arena, I watched my boys play hockey, but I didn't really see the game. I resented the moms and dads who watched their children together.

Each day, I went through the motions of being a mom. It took enormous effort to smile, make a meal, grocery shop, and go to work. Anger and resentment consumed me. I woke up angry, and I went to bed angry.

Then, one morning, I stood in the kitchen and looked around

at the home that Al and I had created. I listened as the boys stirred in their beds. Sun streamed in the windows. I thought, *I can live the rest of my life with anger and bitterness, or I can cherish the memories and live my life the best I can.*

Until that moment, I had not considered that it was a choice. But I suddenly realized that I could choose how I responded to the death of my husband of fourteen years. I could choose how I showed up for my boys and what I passed on to them.

That thought changed my path, but it was not an easy journey. I had to be intentional about each action and thought because sadness and bitterness were lurking close by, quickly summoned by an older couple holding hands, the smell of peppermint gum, a man with a beard, or a song on the radio.

As I struggled through each day searching for the positive moments, I read about a gratitude journal. Writing about five things I was grateful for before bed each night would give me something concrete to strive for.

I bought a lovely hardcover notebook, the kind I always admired. It sat on my bedside table, and I made a commitment to write in it each night before going to sleep. It was a challenge to think of five things every night. Often, I was grateful that my sons were finally asleep. The bedtime routine had become onerous. The grief, anger, and sadness they held in all day overflowed at the end of the day.

I was grateful to make it through the day, meetings at work, grocery shopping, and hockey practice, pretending to be okay when I wasn't. Sometimes, I wrote something without feeling it, just so I could close my eyes and go to sleep.

Over time, it became easier. I started to notice things during the day and make a mental note to include it in my journal: the birds sang, the boys laughed, a friend stopped by or called, someone asked how I was doing and really wanted to know.

The more I practiced gratitude, the more grateful I became. I still felt sad, angry and all the other feelings that came with grief, but now there were moments of joy and hope. One day at a time, I taught myself to be grateful, to count my blessings. I realized that feelings weren't exclusive. Joy and sadness co-existed, and all my feelings were okay.

The practice of gratitude didn't erase the heartache or difficulties; however, it provided a glimpse of joy and hope amid the pain and grief. Knowing that I had a choice in how I responded changed my perspective and inspired me to keep going, to move forward and envision a better future for my family.

Over time, the gratitude became more automatic. I easily recognized the positives in each situation and circumstance. I had hope and the desire to live life to the fullest. I was grateful for the love that Al and I had shared in the time we had together. I could cherish the memories and share them with others, especially my sons.

Twenty-eight years later, gratitude comes easily for me. My daily practice of recording what I am grateful for is now done on an app on my phone. In the worst of times, I am often surprised by a thought of appreciation and hope. There is always something to be thankful for. I shudder to think about what my life could have been like had I not made the choice to be grateful.

— Rose Couse —

45

Radical Cake Acceptance

Gratitude is riches. Complaint is poverty.
~Doris Day

I'm processing books in the circulation office of the library where I work when I hear a sudden outcry.

"Oh, no!"

"This is dreadful."

"This is just terrible!"

What catastrophe are my coworkers reacting to? Have the library's computers crashed again? Has a letter from an irate patron just been posted on the bulletin board? Is there another new book by James Patterson?

Nope. They're talking about cake.

One of our patrons has baked us a chocolate cake, which sits invitingly on the counter in the circulation office. I continue to eavesdrop as my coworkers respond to this thoughtful gift.

"Oh, my God!"

"Uh-oh."

"This is just evil."

You'd think that eating chocolate cake was the worst possible kind of calamity.

"This is treacherous."

"I'm in trouble now."

"Oh, dear. Oh, dear. Oh, dear."

I begin to wonder, *Isn't anybody going to say anything positive?*

Like: "Chocolate cake? How cool is that?" Or "I love cake. I'm having a nice, big slice."

Not a chance. By afternoon's end, not a single library worker has had anything nice to say about this unexpected treat. We've gobbled it down. But have we enjoyed it?

You sure wouldn't think so, listening to us.

Last week, I helped celebrate my pal Lucy's fortieth birthday. As we all sang "Happy Birthday," Lucy's husband brought out a beautiful layer cake he'd made from scratch, lavishly decorated by Olivia, their seven-year-old daughter.

Although I avoid sweets, I always make an exception for birthday cake. To turn down birthday cake isn't merely rude; it's bad karma.

So, I had some. I enjoyed it, too. But my pleasure was undercut by the guilt I felt about consuming all those empty calories.

Lucy's other friends also said yes to cake, invariably adding, "Just a small slice for me, thanks" or "Just a tiny taste."

But the kids at the party, a gaggle of little girls Olivia's age, had a totally different response. Drawn to that cake like moths to a flame, each child claimed as large a piece as she could get her hands on and then happily made short work of it.

Seeing cake, they weren't alarmed. They were thrilled. They were quite a sight, those little girls, beaming, with huge chunks of cake on their plates.

And yet, sometime between now and adulthood, they, too, will stop being delighted by cake and learn to fear it. Rather than taking a big piece and loving it, they'll ask for a tiny slice and beat themselves up about eating it.

Is there a scientific name for this crazy cake phobia? The terror that strikes the hearts of otherwise sane and mature people when offered a delicious dessert? Yes, cake has zero nutritional value. Still, shouldn't a grown-up be able to simply enjoy a piece from time to time?

Listening to my coworkers kvetch about our cake, and remembering how much those little girls loved eating theirs, I resolve that I will try to shed my own fear of delicious pastry and get back in touch with my inner seven-year-old.

Call it Radical Cake Acceptance.

When it comes to cake, I'm going to give myself just two options: either smile and say "No, thanks," or have a piece and totally enjoy it, without ambivalence or guilt, the way I did when I was a kid.

"Cake is not the enemy" is my brand-new mantra. (You can try it, too. Just repeat after me: "Cake is not dreadful. Cake is delicious.")

Is this an impossible dream?

Invite me to your next birthday party, and let's find out.

— Roz Warren —

46

A Blue-Dress Day

Happiness resides not in possessions, and not in gold;
happiness dwells in the soul.
~Democritus

"**W**hy are you wearing your red dress?" asked Sherry, a girl in my sixth-grade class. The look on my face must have indicated that I didn't understand the question. She asked again. "Your red dress... Why are you wearing it? Today is a blue-dress day."

I rarely noticed what other people wore, so it never occurred to me that anyone would notice I had only two school dresses: a red dress with little yellow flowers and a blue one with navy trim around the neck. I had play clothes and two nice dresses for church, but just the two school dresses. Dresses were required attire back in the 1960s.

The red dress was my favorite, so I wore it on Mondays and Tuesdays. I put on the blue one on Wednesdays and Thursdays, then back to red each Friday.

"Oh," I stammered. "I, uh, dropped chili on it yesterday at lunch. I, uh, can't wear it until Mama washes it."

There was no judgment in Sherry's question, just curiosity. For the first time in my life, though, I wondered, "Do my friends feel sorry for me? Am I poor?"

After school, I hung my red dress in the closet I shared with my older sister, Debra. I put on play clothes and went outside to sulk. I climbed to the lowest branch of a scrawny oak and stared at my house.

The size and shape of a single-wide trailer, the white house with maroon shutters was the biggest house I'd ever lived in. My mother had bought it six months earlier, shortly after my father died from a heart attack.

I made friends in our new town and visited their homes. Sherry lived in a brand-new, red-brick house. She had her own piano in the living room and practiced every day. Another friend lived in a huge, old house with more rooms than I could count. Her family's tobacco fields seemed to go on forever. Both friends had their own bedrooms with white, frilly curtains to match white chenille bedspreads.

I shared a small bedroom with Debra. She chose the navy bedspreads for our bunk beds. When one of us had a friend for a sleepover, the other slept with Mama.

My friends usually asked to come home with me rather than me going to their houses — probably because they were crazy about my mom. She would bake a chocolate cake or a peach cobbler. After supper, she played board games with us around the kitchen table or joined us outside for a game of croquet.

The parents of my friends were nice, but they never played with us. They barely spoke to us. And they didn't sing. Mama was always singing a hymn or some old ballad in her rich alto voice.

Until the day when Sherry asked about my red dress, I had never compared my clothes, my little white house, or my life to anyone else's.

My mother called through the screen door for me to come set the table. I climbed down from my tree and shuffled into the kitchen. Mama was mashing potatoes in a big, green bowl.

I opened a cabinet door and reached for five dinner plates. "Mama, are we poor?" I asked.

I thought my question might make her feel bad. Instead, she asked, "What do you mean by 'poor'?"

"You know, not enough money. Not enough food or clothes. No place to live."

"We don't have a lot of extra money," she answered, "but we get by. We live in a warm house and have clothes to wear, some new and some hand-me-downs from the cousins. As far as enough to eat, I think I can fill you up with fried chicken, mashed potatoes, and the cucumbers and tomatoes I picked from the garden this morning."

Mama reached for a potholder and pulled a pan of golden biscuits from the hot oven. "If you're still hungry, a couple of buttered biscuits ought to do the trick." She gestured toward a brown paper sack on top of the refrigerator. "I bought you something today."

I pulled a hardcover book from the bag and read the title, *Trixie Belden and the Mystery of the Emeralds*. I threw my arms around Mama's waist. The mystery was the latest in the series. I loved the stories about Trixie, her best friend Honey, and all their adventures. Each time a new book came out, Mama scrounged up enough money to buy it.

"I thought you might want to start on it after your homework," she said as she returned my hug. "Right now, finish setting the table and call your sisters before these biscuits get cold."

Pinching the book under my arm, I placed a knife and fork by each plate, and then yelled, "Debra, Mary Faye, Angie, time to eat!"

A minute later, we were around the table, with Mama at one end, me at the other, and my sisters on either side. After the youngest said a prayer, I reached for a juicy chicken leg. Mama spooned a heap of mashed potatoes onto her plate.

"Arlene," she said, "I washed and ironed your blue dress today. You can wear it tomorrow if you want."

I considered the offer. "No, I want to wear the red dress again. Its little yellow flowers make me feel good."

Enough to get by? Oh, I had more than that.

I didn't have a closet full of dresses or a big, rambling house. I didn't have a piano in the living room or white, frilly curtains in my own bedroom, but I was blessed with an amazing mother. She worked hard, played hard, and loved easily. Despite the hard blows of life, Mama chose joy and contentment.

I was rich in every way that mattered.

—Arlene Lassiter Ledbetter—

Simple Secret

For my part, I am almost contented just now, and
very thankful. Gratitude is a divine emotion:
it fills the heart, but not to bursting;
it warms it, but not to fever.
~Charlotte Brontë

I never fully knew the power of positive thinking
I used to operate in the dark
Barely making it by and walking on eggshells
My life was one step forward and two steps back
Recently, I've discovered a simple secret:
Positive thinking
I've started to be thankful for the simple things in life
Food on the table
Close friendships
Being lucky enough to live by a beach
Once my mindset adjusted, my life began to improve
I began noticing the aroma of flowers in my garden
I got involved with my church choir and soaked in the joy of music
Studying the Bible became a pleasure instead of a burden
I pray for enemies instead of wishing them harm
I've even noticed a difference in my writing
I've always been a dreamer of a life I don't currently live
With positive thoughts and gratefulness, I have chosen to live the best
        life I have been given

I remind myself to be thankful for something each day and to look for
    positive things in my life
I may not be living the life I was expecting, but maybe what I was
    expecting was not what I truly desired
What I desire is peace
With that comes simple pleasures and the power of positivity

— Brittany Benko —

48

The Small Things

I awoke this morning with devout thanksgiving
for my friends, the old and the new.
~Ralph Waldo Emerson

I was feeling out of sorts because I lost my job at a home for troubled teens that closed due to budget cuts. So, I signed up for an art class at our community center. That's where I met Rosemary.

When I arrived, the place was packed. There must have been twenty students there. Most of the seats were taken, and the occupants all seemed to know each other. I found one empty table for four at the back.

That's when Rosemary rolled in. She was very thin and wore a scarf around her head. She wheeled herself to "my table," and, I have to admit, I felt a little uncomfortable. I'm not sure why, but I did. Two very elderly women joined us, one using two canes and the other with a walker. I felt like I was back in high school, at the unpopular table.

We were told that the teacher was running late due to car trouble. Rosemary smiled, and her face transformed from a sad, sickly person to a sort of angelic, hairless being. She had no eyebrows or eyelashes and wore no makeup, so her beauty was indeed the real deal.

"Hi, I'm Rosemary, and I'm in a war with breast cancer!" she announced proudly and loudly.

"Hi, I'm Pat," I said.

Carol and Nancy introduced themselves, and there we were.

I didn't know what to say after that. "I'm a crabby, unemployed secretary?" But I was saved by the teacher's arrival.

The course was six weeks long, and the four of us always sat together. By the third week, I viewed Rosemary as a lovely person, not as a cancer patient. She missed the fourth week, and of course I feared the worst. But she came in on week five and seemed okay. Whew.

"I bet ya' thought I died, right?" she chuckled.

I had no words.

Week six marked the end of the class, and Rosemary asked me to join her for coffee at the doughnut shop in town. She pulled a little notebook from her pocket and jotted something down.

"I just had to write something down before I forgot it. My mind is a sieve lately."

We both laughed, partly because who else uses "sieve" these days?

While I was drinking my black coffee and she was eating her second lemon-filled doughnut, I told her about my lost job and how much I missed it and the kids. I'd come to the conclusion that their parents needed direction more than they did. And I shared that my worries about finding another job sometimes kept me up at night.

She smiled and said, "Small things, Pat." I realized again that she had cancer, and I felt a bit selfish.

"Small things?" I asked.

"Yes. I had a lot of sleepless nights when I was diagnosed, and a nurse told me to make a list of things I was grateful for that day instead of worrying. Things like the sun shone that day, and winter was almost over. I don't have to worry about taking care of my hair. There is a two-for-one sale on my favorite brand of ice cream this week. Stuff like that."

"Huh," I said. "Those really are small things."

She laughed and said, "You'd be amazed at how many small things there are to be grateful for, and sometimes big things, too. My last chemo session is coming up, thank goodness. And meeting you! That's what I wrote in my journal, to make sure to tell you how grateful I am that we're friends."

I felt myself tearing up and croaked, "Me, too."

That night, I tried to think about small things instead of worrying about a job. I was surprised at how many I came up with, and I fell asleep in the process. I do it every night now, and it really works.

Rosemary recovered, and we're still friends. And her gift to me was no "small thing."

— Patricia Merewether —

49

Into The Wind

*Gratitude unlocks the fullness of life. It turns what
we have into enough, and more. It turns denial into
acceptance, chaos to order, confusion to clarity.*
~Melody Beattie

It was a beautiful day for a bike ride. I was itching to hop in the
saddle and put in some relaxing miles. I loaded up my bike and
headed out to meet a friend to explore a newly reopened bike
path that I had never ridden before.

As a cyclist for more than twenty-five years, I found that riding my
bike was not only a great physical workout, but also a go-to strategy to
quiet my mind and relieve stress. I felt incredibly blessed to be healthy
enough to go for a ride well into my fifties.

As we meandered along the wooded bike path, we maintained
a relaxed, comfortable pace. A squirrel darted in front of us, but as
experienced cyclists, we easily adjusted our bikes to avoid it.

Riding side by side, we waved to several cyclists passing by. It felt
good to turn the pedals and feel strong and healthy. I felt incredibly
blessed.

As we passed a discarded construction cone at the side of the
path, I suddenly saw a blur of yellow. The next thing I remember, my
bike was no longer underneath me, and I was falling to the pavement.
Apparently, a piece of caution tape had flown off the cone as I passed
and wrapped around the pedal area of my bike.

Keep your head up, I thought, as I seemed to fall in a distorted kind of slow motion and rolled on the pavement. I didn't even know what had happened. I knew I was seriously injured, but I had no idea how much. Thankfully, a quick check of my helmet confirmed I had not hit my head.

A wave of nausea swept over me as I noticed that my wrist looked distorted. Paramedics arrived and, after calming the nausea with IV meds, told me that maybe doctors could simply pop my wrist back into place. It sounded gross, but I figured if that's all there was to it, I could handle it and be on my way.

Unfortunately, it would not be that simple. X-rays showed multiple bone breaks in my wrist and elbow that would require immediate surgery to install screws and plates to stabilize the bones. My right ankle was sprained, my left shoulder was injured, my knees hurt, and I had bruising all over my body. The doctors told me they couldn't even begin to diagnose my other injuries until I healed from the broken bones. Instead of a quick pop of a bone back into place, I was facing months of healing and physical therapy.

I was devastated. How could this have happened on a simple bike path? I had ridden on streets and highways and, in events with thousands of cyclists at a time, had never had an injury. I was angry and frustrated. How would I deal with such a long recovery? What else would I face over time as my other injuries were addressed? The whole experience felt surreal.

As my body slowly healed from the wrist and elbow surgeries, I began physical therapy. I was still angry and upset. Each day, I woke with waves of fear, anger, and uncertainty. My old struggles with depression and anxiety returned. I stopped feeling like myself and descended into a toxic stew of emotions I could not seem to escape. My normal coping skills of going to the gym and riding my bike were unavailable.

Four months later, the doctors were finally able to assess my shoulder. It had a complete tear of the rotator cuff, and the biceps tendon was literally in shreds. Another surgery was required, more painful than the first. More anger, stress, and frustration.

One day, I realized I could not continue with the mindset I had been in since the fall. Everything I knew about stress and the physical body told me that I had to purposefully change how I was thinking about things if I wanted to heal. No one could do it for me — not my doctors, surgeons, or physical therapists. I might not have any control over my injuries, but I absolutely had control over how I thought about them.

Cycling over many years had taught me many life lessons. I thought about how I used to hate riding on windy days, and how I would feel frustrated and hate every minute of pedaling into a strong wind. Over time, I reframed these thoughts and began to enjoy the challenge of cycling on a gusty Oklahoma day. I told myself it would make me stronger and would improve my bike-handling skills. If you're going to ride a bike regularly, you might as well come to terms with the wind. Adversity, like the wind, is just part of life.

Sitting at home with my arm in a sling, I made a decision that changed my life. I decided that no matter how many more surgeries it took, how many hours of physical therapy, how much pain and sleeplessness lay ahead, I was no longer going to fight it. Instead, I would lean into it, release any timeframes or outcomes in my mind, and simply go through the process of healing.

I thought about how much worse it could have been. I could've had a traumatic brain injury, spinal-cord injury, or any number of other things from which I would never recover. I came to see my physical-therapy sessions as a way to be active and participate in my own healing since I couldn't go to the gym yet.

It was like learning how to ride into the wind again. I became grateful for every single day I could get up, move my body, walk, exercise, and heal. I realized that even if I had sustained injuries that would've prevented me from ever riding my bike again, I still had been blessed beyond measure to have been healthy enough to be a cyclist for twenty-six years with no limitations. I made up my mind that I would no longer live in anger and despair but rather gratefulness and a deeper appreciation of the health I had been blessed with my entire life.

I have now had five surgeries. I have been able to occasionally hop on my bike for a short spin. I have not yet fully recovered from the crash. It's going to take some time, but it doesn't matter anymore because I quit fighting it and chose to lean into this experience as a way to get stronger in every way.

Nothing really magical has happened. I still have pain and more recovery ahead, both physically and mentally, but it's okay now. I accept it. I learned that while we can't always control what happens to us, we always have a choice about how we think about it, and that's more important than the actual thing that happened.

I can't wait to go for a long bike ride again. If it's windy, even better.

— Dorian Leigh Quillen —

50

Thankful for Oatmeal

Showing gratitude is one of the simplest yet most powerful things humans can do for each other.
~Randy Pausch

"Good morning, Miss Bolz." A friendly man in his early twenties greeted me as he placed a breakfast tray on the table next to my bed. I struggled to sit up, but after being hospitalized several days for severe breathing difficulties, my body was still very weak.

Now, I was in a convalescent home, and I dreaded staying here until I could gain enough strength to return to my apartment. Most of the other patients in the facility looked as if they were old enough to be my parents. And the two elderly women who were sharing my room kept me up every night with moans and screams. My nerves were shot, and I felt very sleep-deprived.

Fortunately, there was one positive part about my stay at the convalescent home: The food was good. Since I needed to be on medications that had a side effect of stimulating my appetite, I was thankful to have three tasty meals each day.

"You gave me oatmeal again. Thanks for remembering that it's my favorite breakfast!" I told the young man who had brought my tray.

"Well, uh, thanks," he replied, looking surprised. "Actually, we cook oatmeal for all the patients every morning, but nobody has ever told me before that they like it. Everyone on the kitchen staff works very hard to prepare the meals, so it's nice to hear a compliment for a change. Usually, the patients are complaining about the food."

While the young man delivered breakfast trays to the two other women in the room, I wondered what I could do to encourage him and his coworkers. Reaching for a pen on my nightstand, I quickly jotted a compliment about the food on the back of the breakfast menu and waved it in the air.

"Is that for me?" the man asked with a laugh. He read my note and smiled widely. "I'll be sure to show your comments to everyone in the kitchen," he promised before hurrying away to deliver more trays.

As I watched him walk down the hallway, an idea came to me. I decided that I would write a positive and encouraging note to the kitchen staff after every meal. Working on these notes, I soon discovered, got my mind off of my illness and my noisy roommates, at least for a short while. It also gave me something to look forward to besides counting the days until I could go home.

Each morning, afternoon and evening, I enjoyed seeing the surprise and delight on the faces of the employees who picked up my meal trays when they noticed one of my thank-you notes propped on top. I also made it a point to thank each of these staff members by name. They all seemed to greatly appreciate my efforts.

When the day finally arrived for me to be discharged from the convalescent home, the director of food services came to my room to say goodbye. As I sat in a wheelchair next to my bed, he walked over to me and smiled.

"Miss Bolz, we've kept all the notes that you've written about the meals during your stay here," he began. "They're pinned up on the bulletin board downstairs where every staff member can read them. Your comments have touched and encouraged us all. Thank you so much for recognizing our employees and their hard work!"

I nodded and smiled back at him. Being a patient in a convalescent home hadn't been easy for me, but writing the notes of gratitude after every meal had given me something positive to work on during the long, dreary days in bed.

Soon, I'd be heading home to my apartment to continue my recovery there. After that, I couldn't wait to put this illness behind me and resume my normal routine. But one thing, of course, would remain with me from my stay in the convalescent home. I planned to continue writing notes of gratitude whenever I had the opportunity. Taking the time to thank others had become a daily habit for me. And, for that, I was very grateful.

— Carolyn Bolz —

Find a Role Model

51

Liesl's Life Lessons

Life is a succession of lessons which must
be lived to be understood.
~Ralph Waldo Emerson

Being a Jewish Holocaust survivor, Liesl Sondheimer had every reason to believe the world was an ugly place filled with horrific evil. Yet, somehow, she continued to see the beauty surrounding her and to strive each day to make the world a better place. One of my greatest life's blessings was this courageous woman's willingness to take me under her mentoring wing.

Twenty-five years ago, Liesl was silver-haired and wrinkled but still ethereally beautiful when I encountered her shortly after her ninetieth birthday. Back then, I was a television reporter employed at WTLW TV-44 in Lima, Ohio, and she was a local celebrity. While interviewing the well-known lady for a TV feature about the Holocaust, I was honored when she invited me to join her for supper.

As a young woman, Liesl, along with her physician husband and two young daughters, were forced to flee from her beloved Germany during Hitler's regime. Many of her relatives were unable to escape and perished in the concentration camps.

Instead of becoming bitter, my wise mentor embraced forgiveness. It was not the cheap kind of forgiveness that pardons atrocity by denying its existence, but the genuine forgiveness that is a gift to yourself. Once, during an interview, I asked her how she could forgive. She gazed at me intently and firmly said, "You must forgive, or Hitler has won."

Her practical words convinced me of my own need to let go of a few deeply buried hurts. Liesl was like that. She had this uncanny way of teaching you how to improve your own circumstances merely by telling her fascinating stories about choosing courage over fear and positivity over negativity.

My brokenness was probably one of the reasons this humble humanitarian originally reached out to me. Surviving a near-fatal suicide attempt and being confined in a state mental institution as a teen, then later struggling with continued depression and addiction, had left scars on me. These scars were probably only visible to another survivor like Liesl.

Sadly, along my recovery path, I had met some precious people also battling mental illness or addiction who did not survive. Therefore, my compassionate friend with her educational background in social work gently guided me in understanding the lesson of "survivor's guilt." Through her Holocaust experience, she understood firsthand how vital it is to learn to be grateful for the gift of surviving.

Before I met Liesl, triumphing over challenging circumstances left me stuck in the guilt created by contemplating why others were not as fortunate. The Holocaust survivor admitted that this quandary haunted her, too. But she refused to allow this never-to-be-answered question about the past destroy her future and taught me to do the same.

To prevent these tragedies from reoccurring, she believed it was a survivor's moral responsibility to speak up on behalf of those continuing to be marginalized. Even though she forgave, she never forgot about the millions of Holocaust victims. Rather, she passionately shared her personal story to warn others about the dangers of prejudice. She staunchly insisted I had a responsibility to speak up about the challenges I had overcome as well.

That petite, elderly woman bravely shared her message with civic clubs, women's groups, universities, and school classrooms whenever she could. Her story of overcoming impossible odds gave her listeners hope. Liesl was humbled by the amazing support of the Lima community when they packed the Veterans Memorial Civic & Convention Center for the premiere of the biographical documentary about her inspiring journey, "A Simple Matter of God and Country," by Daniel Levy, which won a regional Emmy award.

On a lighter note, my elderly friend adored adventures, especially ones supporting the arts, music, or books. I would occasionally pick her up and whisk her away to an artsy event. Frequently, during these outings, she would relate her wisdom about life.

Once, while driving seventy-five miles to visit the Dayton Art Institute, halfway there Liesl absentmindedly asked, "Did I ever tell you about the time Eleanor Roosevelt stayed at my house?"

"No, I'm sure I would have remembered that," I jokingly replied. We were in heavy traffic on Interstate 75 when she divulged this astonishing revelation. I was so shocked that I'm grateful I kept from hitting the car's brakes and coming to a screeching halt.

Liesl nonchalantly described how, decades earlier, she had invited Eleanor Roosevelt to speak in west-central Ohio simply by sending the former First Lady a letter. Her cause was successful, due to some assistance from an influential friend. This Liesl dissertation was the "You never know—anything can happen if you step out and try" lesson. I needed this motivational message because disappointment and heartbreak had tattered my own Christian faith.

There was also her "Beauty Is Ageless" teaching, which I learned vicariously while watching Liesl shop for clothes. Despite multiple physical ailments, she took time to look her best and never stopped caring about fabric, color, or finding just the right accessory. To celebrate her 100th birthday, I drove her to a mall in a neighboring state where she enthusiastically tried on countless outfits, looking for just the right pieces for her wardrobe.

Most important was the "Love Lesson" Liesl taught me. When I first met school administrator Larry Claypool in 2001, past hurts had left me too afraid to love. When it came to romance, Liesl used to describe me as "a burnt child who was afraid of the fire."

But, at heart, she was a hopeless romantic, which caused her to challenge my initial fears about dating Larry. She asserted that one must sometimes be willing to risk everything to have an opportunity for happiness. My mother gave me the same advice.

The following year, Liesl sat in a church pew attractively attired in a pale pink suit — the same shade of pink that my bridesmaids were wearing. She smiled with satisfaction as Larry and I recited our vows in a candlelit ceremony.

For me, Liesl's legacy of living positively includes the challenge to embrace forgiveness, speak up against injustice, support the arts, step out in faith to follow your dreams, and always look your best.

Personally, though, I will always be most grateful for Liesl's "Love Lesson." After all, it was my husband's protective arms that comforted me when we buried my remarkable 101-year-old friend in the spring of 2009. Even though I miss her terribly, Liesl's life lessons continue to influence me almost daily.

— Christina Ryan Claypool —

52

Mr. Positive

Encouragement is like water to the soul,
it makes everything grow.
~Chris Burkmenn

I couldn't stop smiling because I was so happy. I felt like I was floating on cloud nine. My first children's book had just been published, and the publisher had sent me copies of the book, several bookmarks featuring the book's cover, and a 9x12 poster that announced the book's release.

I was so excited to show my fellow writers that I had arrived thirty minutes early for our monthly writers' meeting at the library. The room where we met was still locked, and as I stood in the dim hallway waiting for the librarian to open the doors, a big teddy bear of a man, wearing a ten-gallon cowboy hat and leather boots, approached me.

He smiled and asked if this was the place where the local writing group met, and I told him it was. He offered me a warm handshake, said howdy with a hearty laugh, and declared he must be in the right place. I had never seen this man before, and he was not a member of our writing group, but we often had visitors who were interested in learning more about writing and publishing.

As we waited in the hallway for the doors to be opened, I think this gentleman sensed that I was about to bubble over with excitement, so he politely asked how I was doing. His simple question opened the floodgates of my joy and enthusiasm.

I told him all about my book, the bookmarks, and the poster. He seemed to enjoy hearing about it. He was so supportive and positive about everything that I said.

I told him about how my children's book came to be, my interactions with the publisher, the book's release, and the recent promotional materials I had received. I showed him the book, handed him a bookmark, and thrust the poster in his face. Then, I proceeded to read the poster to him as if he couldn't decipher the images and wording on his own.

Had I been in my right mind, I might have considered that I could be frightening this stranger with my exuberance, but this huge bear of a man seemed genuinely interested in my book, how it had come to fruition, and the promotional items I had received. He studied the text carefully, thanked me for the bookmark, which he put in his shirt pocket, and held the poster up in the dim light for a better view. He shared my excitement, just as if the book was his own pride and joy.

The more excited I got, the more excited he became. His eyes twinkled as he encouraged me to tell him more, and he kept repeating that you have to stay positive and cherish the happy moments. He was so supportive that he made me feel like I could accomplish anything.

I had floated into that hallway on cloud nine, but after a few minutes of conversing and sharing with this man, I was soaring among the stars and dancing around the moon.

Before long, other members of our writing group started to arrive, and when I saw the librarian approaching to open the door, I decided to run to the restroom before the meeting started.

By the time I returned, the lights were on, and people had taken their seats. At the head of the room, my "hallway gentleman" was standing behind the podium. He was surrounded by huge posters that rested on standing tripods in a semicircle around him. As I stared in amazement, I realized that the posters were each for a different book.

In my excitement, I had forgotten that we were having a guest speaker that evening—and my "hallway gentleman" was the speaker! He was Dusty Richards — the famous Western writer who had authored dozens of books and earned several prominent awards, including multiple Spur Awards and the Western Heritage Wrangler Award.

I had been babbling about my little children's book with a writing superstar!

As I took my seat and struggled to pick my mouth up off the floor, Dusty Richards began talking. He told us to call him Dusty, and he had a "down-home" way of speaking that put everyone at ease. As he spoke, we could sense his passionate zeal for the Western writing genre. He mesmerized everyone with his stories and love of the writing craft. He also explained how several of his novels had been optioned for movies, and said he was currently in talks with another group about turning his latest book into a movie.

When he finished speaking, Dusty indicated he had a long drive to get home and would be leaving before our group's regular meeting. As he carried out the last of his huge posters, he made eye contact with me and gave me a thumbs-up. His expression seemed to say, "Go get 'em," and I remember silently mouthing, "Thank you," as the door closed.

Our writing group continued with its regular business meeting. During the announcements portion, I told the group about my new book. It was a special moment, but nothing like the one I had shared in the hallway.

Sadly, not long after that meeting, I learned Dusty Richards died from injuries sustained in a car accident. It was extremely difficult for me to even think about those sparkling eyes and that hearty laugh being gone forever, but I will never forget him.

Never before or since have I met anyone who truly was so pleased in a stranger's joy and who so heartily celebrated someone else's success. In a matter of minutes, Dusty was unbelievably supportive, encouraging, and kind. He treated me like we were lifetime friends, and even though nothing could be further from the truth, like we were fellow writers and equals. He believed in me and encouraged me to do more.

In the ensuing years, when I have received rejections or events haven't gone my way, I think about that night and how Dusty's bright smile and twinkling eyes lit up that dim hallway. His image always dispels any clouds of doubt or negative thoughts that try to surround me, and I know he'd want me to keep trying and moving ahead.

I was so blessed that night to share a few precious moments with such a talented writer and inspiring role model.

— Billie Holladay Skelley —

53

A Shapeshifting Coyote

Never dare a Coyote.
~Lora Leigh

After finishing my coffee, I stepped into the living room to find Genie transfixed in front of the TV.

I shook my car keys. "I hate to be a killjoy, but you have a doctor's appointment this morning, remember?"

She grimaced. "Do you really think I'd forget I have yet another doctor's appointment to talk even more about cancer?"

I could only imagine how tired she was of dealing with cancer. It's what she'd been doing these past five years, and no end seemed in sight.

Her face softened, and she smiled. She gestured to the TV. "Take a look at this. I was looking for a bit of upbeat news this morning before getting flooded with chemotherapy and, lo and behold, I stumbled across this PBS special on Yellowstone. And there she is."

We'd honeymooned in Yellowstone, a place that had taken our breath away. We always said that, with its massive sky and towering peaks, Yellowstone was what the inside of heaven must look like. To make sure I didn't miss what she was so excited about, she pointed to a coyote stealthily and rhythmically making its way through the sagebrush.

"She's pretty, isn't she?"

I smiled. Genie loved coyotes, which had begun, humorously enough, when she was a kid. She got hooked on Wile E. Coyote cartoons. Genie knew most people considered Wile a goofy bungler, but Genie saw things differently. Yes, the coyote would foolishly careen off sheer cliffs only to land with a thud hundreds of feet below, usually with a boulder on his head. But — and this was the important thing — he'd get right back up, shake himself off, and start after the road runner again. I clearly heard the admiration in her voice when she called the coyote a survivor.

"I'm curious. Why do you think the coyote is a girl?"

She tapped the head of our dog Ruby who was standing diligently by her side. Genie had always said that Ruby shared the same qualities as coyotes.

Just then, I heard Genie's admiration turn to alarm. She pointed madly to the TV screen. A pack of wolves must have caught scent of the coyote and was moving in on him like a well-oiled military machine.

There was no "Ready, set, go!" hollered and no starting flag waved, but the coyote and the wolves took off at a run. The coyote stayed low to the ground, whereas the wolves ran heads-up, probably to get the most speed from their tall legs. As Genie and Ruby tensed beside me, I counted eight, maybe ten, wolves. I assumed there were even more who were close and keeping an eye on things. There was one thing we knew for certain: There was only one coyote.

"They're going to kill him, aren't they?"

Thinking it might help, I tried to explain as dispassionately as I could. "It's all about territory. They don't want strangers straying onto their land."

"There are thousands of empty acres out here. Do they need all of it? Wolves are thugs. They remind me of cancer. Even though it took my breast, it wants more. Where will it stop?"

Both Genie and Ruby tensed because they knew things were about to end badly. My hand went for the remote. "We should get going before this gets messy."

Genie brushed away my hand and maintained control of the remote. "Coyotes are tough. Especially this one. When the wolves zig, she zags. She's giving them a run for the money. She's… scrappy."

That was a word normally reserved for Ruby.

I heard her optimism. Still, I couldn't see how the coyote would get out of this alive. I said, "But the wolves are bigger, faster, and meaner."

Genie's hand rubbed Ruby's head. "Ruby could get out of this mess."

That told me we'd be watching to the end. But, despite how I thought it was going to go, I had to admit there was something inspiring about the coyote.

We saw that a handful of fast wolves were flanking the coyote.

The end was near.

Just then, and like out of so many horror movies, the coyote tripped and tumbled to the ground. I shouted, "Stay down!" I figured it'd be quicker that way.

But Genie begged her to get up and keep running.

Surprisingly, the coyote hopped up and assessed the situation. The wolves had her surrounded. For them, the race was over, so why hurry?

Now that they were grouped together, it was clear to see how much larger the wolves were. It was like a German Shepherd standing next to a Cocker Spaniel. The coyote had no chance, not even from the beginning, and especially now.

But the coyote didn't see things that way and certainly gave no indication of giving up. Time stood still, and an eerie and peculiar feeling settled over the contestants. It became obvious to us that, among all the other things she was, a contrarian was one of them. Much like Ruby — and even more like Genie — the coyote insisted on doing things her way.

The coyote whipped around so she could see the wolves, even those on her flanks. Then, she did something none of the wolves expected: She ran right at them. The wolves flinched, not knowing what to expect, but it was no feint, no clever subterfuge, no quarterback sneak. No, she ran straight into the group of snapping jaws.

Like an underweight running back in a championship game, this tired, little dog found an opening in the wolves' line, and she blasted through. It was, no doubt, the last thing the wolves expected. They stood flat-footed and watched in awe as the coyote ran like the wind, sailing up and over the hill.

The powerful wolves weren't fatigued, probably not even winded.

They could have given chase but didn't. Wolves can cover thirty miles in a day, sometimes at a gallop, but this group closed ranks and exchanged looks.

"That coyote's a nut," I said.

Genie's smile went from ear-to-ear. "They're letting her go out of respect."

"They respect her for being a nut?" I asked.

"Sometimes, that's how you win when the odds are against you," she said as she petted Ruby.

From that point forward, that's how Genie approached breast cancer. There were times when Genie was so beat she could barely stand, and times when we felt the hot, close breath of cancer on our necks.

There were times when we looked out to appraise the situation, only to see gnashing teeth.

There'd been times when things got so bad, I'd start praying.

Genie would always take my hand and say, "That little coyote got out of worse, David."

And off we'd run into a new group of snapping jaws.

— David Weiskircher —

54

Believe It

Believe you can and you're halfway there.
~Theodore Roosevelt

A long time ago, when I was only fifteen years old, I was a high-school football player. I was a fairly serious athlete and I worked out almost every day.

One day, I came to the realization that I wasn't ready for the collegiate level and almost quit. My father was very supportive. He suggested that I join a gym where other top athletes trained. He told me that I was sure to get some advice that could help me get to the next level.

He was right. However, it was not the advice that I was looking for. It was much more than that. I got a lesson that was not just about playing football.

My first few outings at this elite gym were not the best. I realized how much I was lacking. The guys there were all much bigger, stronger, and faster than I was. I was struggling to keep up with it all.

Then, I met this one guy. He was tall, fast, and had done rather well for himself in minor-league baseball and professional football. He was a two-sport athlete who had confidence that seemed like it was just oozing out of him. He impressed everyone at the gym.

One day as I was working out, I'd done well in a football drill. I'd actually beat out a pro player as a high-school player. Everyone was so excited and energized. However, I'd been taught to always be humble and never express any level of pride outwardly. Then, the pro athlete

I'd admired caught me getting water and asked me to sit down with him. He looked at me and sighed.

"Boy, you look like a freight train out there. You've got what it takes to make it, but you have no swagger. You've got no flavor," he explained.

I was confused as I responded, "What's that supposed to mean? I keep my head down, and I do my job. Isn't that what a team player is supposed to do?"

He looked at me and smiled. He even shook his head because he saw just how earnest I was being.

"Look, kid. That Jimmy Stewart stuff will only get you so far in life. You can't just be a cog in the machine living in this world. You've got to be a person who people look up to. You've got to be better than what the world expects of you to succeed. Not only do you have to be better, but you've gotta show better. Do you think that regular people look to other regular people for inspiration? No! Regular people look to people like us for that kind of inspiration. People are inspired by super versions of themselves. It's how the world works. Now, I'm not saying that you have to be super. But you do need to make other people believe that you are. To do that, you've got to have confidence in what you're doing. That starts with how you view yourself."

"How I view myself?"

"Yeah, kid. How you view yourself is important. The reality of it is, if you don't believe that you are the best, then no one else will either. And if your fans and supporters don't believe in you, you're dead in the water. You have to believe it before they do. I want to see you make it. I believe in you, even if you don't. Now, go over there and talk that talk, young man. Let them know just how good you really are," he told me as he patted me on the shoulder and went back to his workout.

I went back and had more confidence and pride in what I was doing. Did I go to the NFL? No. However, it did teach me a valuable lesson. I have to believe in my ability more than anyone. I have to be my biggest fan. I'm an author now. I've written many successful books, and I've gained a great following. It's not because I'm better than anyone else. It's because the belief I have in myself allows others to live through me and be the people they've always wanted to be.

— Weston L. Collins —

Generation Gap

Aging is not "lost youth" but a new stage
of opportunity and strength.
~Betty Friedan

I stood uncomfortably at the nursing-home door.
She was old, and I was young.
Separated by so many years,
a lifetime apart.
How could we possibly have anything in common?

As though she understood,
she spoke first.
She spoke of a girl, just my age,
dealing with pimples and teenage crushes.
She could have been talking about me.
"Your granddaughter?" I asked.
"No," she replied with a smile.

She spoke of a woman,
young and in love.
Of a marriage only heard about in fairy tales,
with children, puppies and childhood pranks.
A family surrounded by laughter and love.
Just the kind I hoped for.
"Your daughter?" I asked.
With a twinkle in her eye, she shook her head.

She spoke of a woman, older now,
full of life, though her body was old.
Who still loved, still laughed, still remembered.
At last, I understood,
and as she smiled, I saw all those people,
reflected in her eyes.

— Elizabeth Anne Brock Springs —

The Meal That Made Me Brave

*You will enrich your life immeasurably if you approach
it with a sense of wonder and discovery, and always
challenge yourself to try new things.*
~Nate Berkus

Uncle Leo may have owned a fast-food franchise, but he was also a man of champagne taste. Even so, he was just as comfortable digging into a box of fried chicken as enjoying an evening of fine dining—which is how he ended up sitting around a table at the city's most exclusive restaurant with four rowdy teenage girls!

Now, I must clarify that Uncle Leo was not a blood relative. He was one of those friends who, over time, became as close as family. He was a grandfather, but with enough joie de vivre and energy to rival any teenager.

As my friends and I entered the weeks leading up to graduation, Uncle Leo came to us with an idea.

"Let's celebrate the end of your high-school days! Get dressed up. We're all going to The Stone House."

My friends and I were in shock! The Stone House was the newest and most-talked-about restaurant in town. Built into an ancient stone home, the dining room was small, with a long waiting list for reservations. They had quickly created a stellar reputation with their impeccable service, innovative menu, and incredible dining experience.

So, on a warm evening in early June, we all gathered at my house to don our best dresses, curl our hair, and apply way too much makeup! My parents took photos as Uncle Leo loaded us into his car and took us to the restaurant.

We entered the lavish dining room — four grinning teenagers linked arm-in-arm with Uncle Leo in the middle. None of us could stop giggling! We felt enormously glamorous and, like most teenagers, a little out of place. Everything was so elegant and refined. It wasn't our usual burgers-and-fries kind of hangout!

As I reviewed the menu, I started to get overwhelmed. Despite my best intentions, I was a picky eater. Eating in restaurants was usually okay, though, because I could pick and choose what I wanted. There was always something I liked.

But this was too much! It was so… fancy! I hardly recognized a thing. Where was the lasagna or the roasted chicken breast? I felt my stomach knotting up. What was I going to eat tonight?

Finally, I saw something I recognized: chicken stir fry. I breathed a sigh of relief. I would be okay.

"So, what have we all chosen?" Uncle Leo asked the table.

"I'm having the chicken stir fry," I boldly proclaimed.

Suddenly, echoes of "Me, too!" rounded the table. All four of us had chosen the chicken stir fry. All four of us had chosen the one thing we recognized, the one thing that felt safe.

It wasn't until years later that I understood the look in Uncle Leo's eyes—that sympathetic look offered to teenagers struggling to be brave in a world not built for them.

"Okay," he said, "let's try something. Let's all order something different. Appetizers and entrees! We can share, but no two people can order the same dish. Let's try things we've never tried before! If you don't like what you ordered, we can just send it back, and I'll get you a chicken stir fry. Deal?"

We all looked at each other, a hint of bravery sparkling amongst us. We dug back into the menus and ordered the strangest, most exotic things we could find.

Our little table buzzed with excitement as the plates began to arrive. We had no idea what we had gotten ourselves into, but there was no turning back now.

The waiter laid a beautiful platter in front of me. My first wild choice: frog legs!

I'd heard of people eating frog legs in movies and on TV. They always made the same joke: "They taste like chicken!" But I'd never actually known anyone who had eaten them in real life.

Suddenly, right there on my plate, lay three sets of frog legs. They were lightly battered, but they were still frighteningly recognizable. I mean, you could literally tell they were legs! They were still joined at the hip and bent at the knee. I half expected them to jump right off my plate.

My stomach took a little lurch. But everyone else was digging into their appetizers, and I had said I would give it a try.

I grabbed one little leg and gave it a nibble. Then, another nibble. And then, a huge bite. It was delicious! Yes, it was a little like chicken, but better. More delicate, more tender. And way more fun! I was eating frog legs, and I was loving them!

I invited everyone at the table to take a bite. There was a mix of reactions, but that was okay! We were into the adventure of it, and there was no holding us back.

Over the next few hours, we indulged in all kinds of delicacies: octopus, bison, swordfish, and even pheasant under glass. Needless to say, no one even thought about the chicken stir fry.

That night forever changed the way I look at a menu.

Now, when I visit a restaurant, the first thing I ask is, "What's the weirdest thing on this menu?" Bonus points if it's something local or a chef's signature creation.

Over the years, I've tried squid-ink black pasta, deep-fried alligator, rabbit rillettes, and even a key lime pie topped with chili-lime roasted crickets. Yes, real crickets! Little fussy-eater me ate bugs and loved them!

Uncle Leo thought he was just giving us a fun night before graduation, but he taught me the power of saying "yes" to new things and gastronomic adventures. He forever changed the way I approach dining, whether silver service or fast food.

And, for the record, I never order the chicken stir fry anymore!

But if they're on the menu, I'll always say "yes" to frog legs. Those things are amazing!

—Allison Lynn Flemming—

57

Moving Forward

Acceptance doesn't mean resignation; it means
understanding that something is what it is
and that there's got to be a way through it.
~Michael J. Fox

When my husband Jim and I got married, I knew we'd have an active lifestyle. After we met, we rode bicycles everywhere. At the beach, he'd perform handstands in the sand and vault over me with ease. He taught me how to play tennis and sparked my passion for running. We participated in competitive road races in Central Park and Boston Common. He always finished ahead of me, but then he'd run back through the bystanders, smiling and cheering me on to the finish line.

We ate healthy. We didn't smoke. And as the years went on, we cross-country skied. Snowshoed. Hiked trails. And climbed mountains.

Then, about seventeen years ago, my husband's gait appeared off. He shuffled a bit, but not all the time. We first noticed it around our son's wedding in 2007.

His speech also appeared soft when he was tired, or if he had to hold meetings at work and talk for long periods of time. His handwriting became harder to read. But his signature had always been small, almost a scribble.

I didn't think anything of these subtle changes. Just someone growing older. Denial? Maybe. Or maybe it was my way of staying in the moment. You know, hanging onto that cup as half full? And it was. My husband still raced after a Frisbee with the best of them at the beach. Snowshoed. Climbed. Worked. Traveled. But eventually, the chronic symptoms concerned us enough to have them checked out.

Little did we know, after a scheduled doctor's appointment and an MRI to rule out a brain tumor, Jim would be diagnosed with Parkinson's disease. A progressive, degenerative disease. No cure. Hearing those words, my cup emptied. I couldn't imagine how this active athlete, an administrative law judge, father of four, and soon-to-be grandfather would have to stop doing the things he loved. I didn't know the future. I was afraid. And my go-to routines for challenges weren't working.

After tearful episodes at home alone, walking the beach, or driving in my car, I realized I had to get a grip. When a colleague in my husband's office shared that her twenty-eight-year-old son was diagnosed with multiple sclerosis, my husband felt he had little to complain about. He was sixty-two when he received his diagnosis. And his unwavering faith allowed him to accept it. But I didn't know how to do that.

When he suggested we go to a movie or out to dinner, I started what-iffing. What if the lines were long? What if you stumbled? What if you had to stop and couldn't start walking again? My husband would always say, "I just have to get out of first gear. I'll be fine." But I'd always suggest alternative plans. Rent a movie. Have people over for dinner. I didn't want to shelter him, but I felt the need to protect.

Our first neurologist's advice always seemed rushed and vague. I have never trusted anyone who answers my questions with a question, as if I should know the answer. If I knew the answer, I wouldn't have asked! So, we networked and found another doctor who took his time and addressed all our concerns.

We learned that exercise was a major tool in slowing down Parkinson's progression. We learned we shouldn't stop athletic activities. Doctor's orders! So, we didn't. But eventually, my husband had to start taking prescription medications for symptom relief as the disease slowly progressed. And I couldn't help wondering how many times we would have to increase it. The meds had positive effects, for sure, but some negative ones as well. Confusion. Fatigue. Dizziness. Low blood pressure. But Jim accepted them all, adjusted, and carried on with his daily routines.

I knew I had to embrace his positive outlook, something he has always had. I needed to get beyond sitting on my couch, sad and despondent, while he was at work. And I needed to rein in my fears when he got home. I wanted to be his rock, not an anchor wearing him down. And I didn't want our four adult children seeing me in a way they'd never seen me before. Lack of focus. Lack of energy. My stomach constantly filled with angst.

I worried about everything. But then, one day, something changed. My husband had just finished his last few repetitions of a physical-therapy routine he completed every morning before work. Without fail. Day after day. Week after week. Month after month. And he was always smiling. So, I asked him that morning before he left the house, "How do you do it? How do you not get depressed having Parkinson's disease?" His response, without hesitation, was, "I may have Parkinson's, but Parkinson's won't have me."

Seeing his genuine grin and hearing his definitive determination to keep moving, I realized exactly what I had been doing. I was letting Parkinson's disease have me. Why did it take me so long to recognize this? Fear of the unknown. I had been analyzing our every move at every moment way too much and missing out on the now. I was grieving what we couldn't do, instead of celebrating what we still could.

From that day forward, I felt we were both on a positive path, mentally and physically, not to a cure, but, with diligence, to a lifestyle we could both accept. His words became a ray of sunshine in my cluster of cloudy days. My go-to routines started working again. And I didn't allow myself to empty my visual cup, even when Jim tripped, fell, and fractured his right knee at our local grocery store. Eight weeks of recovery. And, eventually, retirement.

A challenge? Of course, it was. Yet, as soon as we could, we discussed the topic of exercising again. We didn't want to undermine the ongoing healing process for his knee, but we needed to do something.

I remember saying, "Where there is a will, there is a way." And we found one. My husband decided that scooting on his bottom across our long hallway with his knee immobilizer intact would suffice. He listened to a CD of our daughter Sara singing while playing her guitar and I cheered him on to the finish line as he did his reps. Just like he always did when we participated in road races.

After one of his workouts, my husband said, "You are my best cheerleader. I couldn't have done this without you."

And I said sincerely, smiling, "I definitely couldn't have done it without you."

— Elaine D'Alessandro —

58

The Coolest Guy in the World

Remember, there's no such thing as a small act of kindness.
Every act creates a ripple with no logical end.
~Scott Adams

W e pulled into the parking lot of a fast-food restaurant in our small town. "Do you think Jimmy still works here?" my fourteen-year-old son, Nathan, asked.

"I know he does," I answered. "About a month ago, I saw his picture on the front page of the newspaper. They did a story about him because he's worked at this restaurant for twenty-seven years."

"Twenty-seven years? I didn't even think he was that old!"

"I was surprised, too. He must be in his forties, but he seems much younger."

Nathan grinned. "You're in your forties, and he definitely seems younger than you."

I punched his arm playfully, but I had to admit that he was right. Jimmy was a forty-something-year-old man who'd worked at a burger joint for nearly three decades. He was always smiling and ready to help someone. He and Nathan had formed a friendship when Nathan was little. We'd often grabbed lunch there after I picked him up from preschool, and he'd always looked forward to seeing Jimmy. Back then, Nathan didn't know that Jimmy had special needs. They were just friends.

Even now, I could sense that Nathan was excited to see his old friend. I wasn't a bit surprised when Nathan asked, "Do you think he'll remember me?"

"I'd bet on it, Bud."

We walked inside and immediately heard a voice call out, "Nate the Great! Is that you?"

Nathan's face lit up. Jimmy remembered him.

They exchanged fist bumps, and Jimmy commented on how tall Nathan had grown. "I think you're bigger than me now," Jimmy said. "But you'll always be my little buddy."

"Yeah, we'll always be friends," Nathan said. "I'll never forget when you rescued my favorite Hot Wheels car for me."

Jimmy's constant smile grew even bigger. "Anything for my little buddy."

I could hardly believe Jimmy remembered the incident from a decade ago. Nathan and I had stopped for lunch after preschool. Nathan had dropped his toy car, and it had rolled under the soda machine. I tried to retrieve it, but it was stuck in the electrical cords. When Jimmy came around wiping the tables, Nathan tearfully told him about his lost car. Of course, Jimmy offered to help, but he too was unsuccessful in dislodging the car. Nathan had left in tears.

Two weeks later, we visited the restaurant again. We'd barely gotten through the door when Jimmy ran up to us. "Nate the Great, guess what?" He pulled Nathan's toy car from his pocket. "I got it for you." The manager told me quietly that when Jimmy's dad had come to pick him up from his shift that day, he'd refused to leave until his dad helped him retrieve the car. He'd carefully washed it off and then carried it in his pocket every day until we returned.

"Jimmy, when you gave that car back to him, Nathan thought that you were the coolest guy in the whole world," I said.

Jimmy's face lit up. "And now, Nathan is a big kid, and he's the other coolest guy in the world!"

We talked for a few more minutes and then went to order our food. We'd just sat down when a family with young kids came in. Jimmy called out, "Amazing Adam! Super Sarah! I'm so happy to see you guys!"

I smiled at Nathan. "Jimmy makes friends with all the kids who come in here."

"Yeah, when I was little, I thought I was the only one. The first time I heard him greet another kid with a nickname, I was crushed. I thought I was special, but Jimmy treats everyone that way."

"You're still special to him, Bud. Jimmy just has a gift for making people feel important."

Nathan nodded and took a bite of his hamburger. "I know that now, and I'm glad other kids got to feel the way I did."

I smiled. "Our town is lucky to have Jimmy."

"People might think that Jimmy isn't making a difference in the world because he cleans tables at a fast-food restaurant," Nathan said. "But Jimmy makes more people smile each day than almost anyone else I know. He might do a small job, but he does it in a way that really matters to other people."

I nodded as Jimmy called out a special greeting to yet another child who'd come into the restaurant. The child's face lit up. "You're right, Nate," I said. "Jimmy really is the coolest guy in the world."

And I wanted to be just like him. Simply by being himself, Jimmy had found his purpose in life. He made people, especially kids, feel special. I wanted to do my own small, everyday tasks like Jimmy did.

After lunch, Nathan and I stopped at the grocery store. It wasn't my favorite task, and I usually tried to get in and out as quickly as possible. But in an effort to be more like Jimmy, I smiled at every person whom we passed in the aisles. The shopping didn't take any longer, and when people smiled back, I realized this was the most pleasant grocery trip I'd ever had.

At the checkout, I asked the cashier how she was and really listened as she answered. She shared that her little boy was sick, and I promised to pray for him. Her eyes were damp as she thanked me.

When we got to the car, Nathan asked if I knew the cashier.

"No, I didn't know her," I answered. "I've decided that I want to be like Jimmy and do little things in a big way. Grocery shopping might be a small job, but I want to do it in a way that makes others feel special."

Nathan smiled. "I thought the same thing. When Jimmy said I

was cool like him, I figured I better start treating people like he does."

"Let's try it together, Bud," I said.

Most people might not see Jimmy as a role model, but he influenced Nathan and me in such a positive way. He taught us that, no matter how small our task might be, we can always find a purpose in it. Taking just an extra moment to really see the people around us takes a seemingly unimportant job and turns it into something that blesses other people.

And that can change the whole world.

—Diane Stark—

59

Change Your Mind, Change Your Life

*The greatest discovery of all time is that a person can
change his future by merely changing his attitude.*
~Oprah Winfrey

I was a young business manager when I met and married my husband, who was in the Army. My family loved and supported the military, but I had never actually lived a military life.

I grew up in rural Michigan, far from any military installation. In my imagination, an Army post looked like a scene from the television sitcom, *M*A*S*H*. And when that handsome young man I was dating would go off to train in what the Army calls "the field," I thought they would be practicing military skills during the day and sitting around a campfire at night. I would later learn that they were training night and day, often enduring long, grueling hours.

With my business background, I understood a civilian business reporting structure, but I had very little understanding of military rank and command structure. I had no idea what my part of the package would be when I married this love of my life, but I would soon find out.

When we returned from our honeymoon, we were stationed at Fort Knox, Kentucky. Excited about my new freedom to explore the places that were off-limits to civilians, I decided to go to the "PX" (Post Exchange) to cash a check. I don't know whether they found me more annoying or amusing as they tried to gather my identification.

"Rank?"

"I'm not in the Army."

"No, your sponsor's rank."

"We didn't have a sponsor. We just came here by ourselves."

"No, your husband's name and rank. He's your sponsor." I proudly told them his name and that he'd just made captain.

"Last four?"

"We were only at one other place. We were at Fort Hood for our wedding, then we came here."

"No, the last four of the Social Security number."

"Mine?"

"No, your sponsor's!"

"I only know mine."

I returned to our new home embarrassed and exasperated. Things got worse from there. As a captain's wife, I was informed I would be a leader to the lieutenants' spouses. I was invited to Quarters One to learn more about my new role. I had no idea where that was, but I was told by another spouse that it was over on "Snooty Loop" (not the real street name, just an unflattering nickname for the neighborhood where high-ranking officers lived). The captain and I took a ride to find it. While we were driving, I heard the sound of a bugle call. (The bugle call "Retreat" is sounded at the end of each day at 1700 hours, or 5:00 p.m. civilian time, when the flag is lowered.) Suddenly, and without warning, he pulled over, got out of the car, and stood to attention. My heart swelled with admiration and affection. My new husband sure loved his country, I thought, even though his actions seemed a little over the top. I learned later that he was required to pull over and stand to attention.

In my mind, I was going to faithfully support his career while continuing my own, moving up the ladder every few years when he moved to a new post. But, day after day, that plan seemed less realistic. It had not occurred to me that Army posts were typically not near corporations where I could continue my career in business. My first clue should have been watching a sconce fall from a wall as it shook from tank-fire exercises.

Feeling very lonely, I decided I might find friends at the post chapel. After a morning service, an older woman welcomed me and started a conversation. She had worked in corporate training, just as I had. She invited me to come over. As it turned out, she lived on "Snooty Loop." When I told my husband about my new friend, he looked astonished.

"Do you know what rank her husband is? He's a full bird colonel!" I had no idea what that meant, although I was smart enough to discern that it was pretty high on the Army ladder. He may have been a full bird colonel, but she took me under her wing.

My new friend listened to my struggles and taught me how to navigate life as an Army wife. She told me about *The Army Wife Handbook.* And seeing how I was struggling with feeling down, she gave me a copy of the very first edition of *Chicken Soup for the Soul* to lift my spirits. With it, she gave me one piece of advice she had learned, handing me a printed copy of the words: "In one moment, you can change your mind. And, in that one moment, you can change your entire day."

In the days that followed, when I would start to feel depressed or anxious or angry, I would make myself change my mind to focus on a positive perspective. Did I really want to spend the day pining over my old job? Or did I want to find a new one? Did I want to complain about Army wife life? Or did I want to find a successful place in my new life?

In the coming months, I changed my mind often. My reality was still the same; I still had a lot to learn, and life was not going to be the way I had imagined it would. But she taught me I could change my thought patterns and emotions as I learned and set new goals.

I still have that copy of *Chicken Soup for the Soul*, and I have passed on my friend's advice to countless people as a trainer for Army Community Service, helping other new spouses. I was inducted into the Order of St. Joan D'Arc, the Order of the Yellow Ribbon, and presented the III Corps Helping Hand Award, which are among my most prized lifetime achievements. I applied the same advice in my civilian life as a wife, mom, friend, and trainer in the corporate world where I eventually returned to work when my husband got out of the Army.

There have probably been a million moments when I have changed my mind and given myself a different kind of day and, moment by moment, built a brighter life.

— Sharron Carrns —

Change Your Perspective

60

Broken Cookies

If you can't change the world with chocolate chip
cookies, how can you change the world?
~Pat Murphy

My Granddad Charlie was a master baker in Newton, Kansas, back when being a master at a trade was considered special. He never wasted anything and may have been the first person to consider recycling day-old pastries into a once-a-month specialty he called date bars. I'm not sure what was in them. They may have contained dates. Or maybe they didn't. But they were the most popular thing he sold in his bakery, prompting many a customer to inquire, "Charlie, why don't you make those date bars more often?" To which he would reply, "Well, I could do that. But then, you'd start expecting them, and that would remove the thrill you experience once a month when I actually make them."

How could you argue with baker's logic like that?

In his never-ceasing effort to recycle, reuse or repackage bakery goods, Granddad Charlie would drop off a bag of cookies for my brothers and me once or twice a week. There were chocolate-chip cookies, oatmeal cookies, peanut-butter cookies, and snickerdoodles. They were the cookies he couldn't sell because they were broken.

It wasn't until I turned five and started kindergarten that I learned that cookies were supposed to be round and whole, not broken into little squares and triangles.

After I made this troubling discovery, I asked Granddad Charlie why he gave us broken cookies.

He stared off for a moment as if giving the matter great thought and then said, "Grandson, you're bound to encounter a lot of broken things in your life. Broken promises and broken hearts, to mention just a few. But here's the thing…" and, at this, he leaned in close and in a quiet but clear voice said, "something is only broken if you choose to see it that way."

I tried to remember Granddad Charlie's words. But as the years passed, his sage advice faded into the background of the day-to-day demands and rumblings of life until they were a faint whisper, waiting to speak to me at just the right moment.

And that moment arrived many years later.

My wife and I had just retired. We had given our lives to teaching and were now moving from the hot climes of Arizona to the cool, coastal country of California. It was December, and, against the advice of my wife, I had decided we would move everything ourselves.

At age sixty-eight you would think I'd know better. I didn't.

One rental truck became two. Then three. Then four. Our new garage was full of boxes, as was our screened-in patio and every room in the house. And the pain in my back from lifting all those boxes necessitated a trip to urgent care.

But we were done. The house in Arizona was empty. Our new one in California was full. I could now relax.

Or so I thought.

"We forgot something," my wife remarked with a sigh.

"That's impossible," I insisted.

"Tomorrow is Christmas."

"Oh. Merry Christmas, honey."

"We forgot to get a Christmas tree." My wife spoke with unflinching determination.

There is a moment in every marriage when a husband knows that he is not going to win. Actually, there are lots of moments like that. This was one of them.

So, we set out, on Christmas Eve, to find a Christmas tree.

Of course there weren't any. At least, there weren't any left that would fit in our house without doing a major renovation.

But at our last stop at a local nursery, a sympathetic salesperson (or maybe just a salesperson who wanted to lock up and get rid of these two crazy people looking for a last-minute Christmas tree) directed us to the dumpster out back, suggesting that we might find enough trimmed branches to cobble together a wreath.

So, we did. The dumpster was a generous buffet of Christmas cast-offs: branches, ribbons, assorted cracked clay pots, and even a ceramic Christmas elf, minus an arm.

As we were about to leave, my wife, ever the adventuresome sort, clambered up the side of the dumpster.

"Oh, my gosh!" she exclaimed. "There's a Christmas tree in here — upside down and in perfect condition! And it's in a pot!"

I quickly joined my wife and peered into the dumpster. "It's a living Christmas tree, a Douglas fir if I'm not mistaken. Let's get it out."

With herculean effort, my wife and I pried, cajoled and wished the tree from the dumpster. It catapulted over the edge and spilled onto the pavement.

"It's broken," my wife quietly pronounced.

She was right. The upper half of the tree was missing, which was undoubtedly why it had been discarded. And the branches that remained sagged in defeated agony.

We stood silently, our momentary glee dashed by what lay before us.

And then, I remembered Granddad Charlie's words: "Something's only broken if you choose to see it that way."

"Have I ever told you the story about Granddad Charlie and the broken cookies?"

My wife smiled. "Only about a thousand times. Open the back hatch and let's load up Douglas."

And we did.

Once home, my wife and I patched Douglas together like a giant Christmas tree puzzle. A few lights, some ornaments, red and green beads, and he looked downright festive. Minus a top half, of course.

And when we finally retired for the evening, exhausted from the move as well as from the daring rescue of Doug from a dumpster, my wife put out some milk and cookies for Santa. As I snapped off the tree lights, I glanced at the plate and saw that she had broken the cookies into little squares and triangles — a tribute to Granddad Charlie.

As for Doug, after he completed his stint as a Christmas tree, we planted him right by the front door where he became a bit of a celebrity in our neighborhood. For whenever someone passed by and inquired as to why we had half a tree in our front yard, I happily recounted the wise words of a master baker from Newton, Kansas. He had inspired us to see beyond the obvious and rescue a Douglas fir from a dumpster on Christmas Eve. After all, "something's only broken if you choose to see it that way."

— Dave Bachmann —

Don't Borrow Your Worries

Above all, be the heroine of your life, not the victim.
~Nora Ephron

I stared gloomily at the stack of bills scattered across the kitchen table. The steaming mug of black coffee that I made to calm my nerves now sat cold and forgotten at my elbow. The pile of bills, which grew larger and more depressing every day, totally consumed my thoughts. I felt hopeless as I opened another envelope and saw the large, angry red letters stamped on the bill. "Past Due," they taunted. With a dejected sigh, I tossed the bill back in the pile. "Tell me something I don't know," I muttered.

This had become my life since Bill died the year before. Calling creditors and pleading for more time. Juggling past-dues and final notices until I dissolved in tears. Trying to figure out which ones I simply must pay and which ones I might be able to put off. Afraid to answer the phone for fear it would be another collection agency threatening to repo my car or the power company threatening to cut off my electricity.

On the other hand, I was afraid to ignore the phone because if I ignored these people, they would be more prone to take action against me. I was embarrassed to be in this predicament and just wanted to stay in bed and hide, but I didn't dare. I had to fight for my survival, but at the same time, I had lost hope that I would get through this.

Bill didn't mean to leave me in this tough situation. We had both agreed to take out loans on the house and to use all our savings so

Change Your Perspective | 203

that he could open the auto-repair shop he had always dreamed of owning. Bill was a top-notch mechanic and had a good reputation for being honest and dependable. We had no doubt that his business would be a success, and we would soon be in the black again.

But one massive heart attack shortly after the repair shop had opened, and the business was just a memory — and so was Bill. I never once regretted agreeing to go into debt so that Bill could have his dream. Just remembering his huge grin the day he opened the shop made it all worthwhile. When he unlocked the door of the shop for business on that day he looked like a little boy who had gotten everything he wanted for Christmas. How could I ever begrudge him that day?

I seldom opened the door to anyone these days, but when I heard one loud rap and three softer ones, I knew it was Judy, my best friend. She devised her special knock so that I would know it was her and not dash into my bedroom to hide. I didn't always want to see Judy either, but I knew if I didn't let her in, she would worry more than she usually did about me.

I forced myself to get up from my chair and go to the door. Judy yelped when she saw me. "You don't have to say anything," she said. "I can see it in your face." She took me by the shoulders and gently pushed me backward, shaking her head. "I can also see it in your rumpled clothes and messy hair."

I snorted. "Who gives a damn?"

Judy gave me a stern, steady stare that she had mastered from teaching middle-school kids for fifteen years. "I do. And we're going to fix it."

I beckoned to the bills on the table. "That? You're going to fix that?"

Judy took my arm and led me back to the table. "No," she said firmly. "Your attitude. That needs fixing first."

Taking a seat opposite me, Judy waved her hand at the pile of bills. "We're going to devise a plan to get this monkey off your back. But I'm going to deal with you first." She leaned forward and pursed her lips. "You've got to stop borrowing worries from tomorrow." She picked up the electric bill that was on top of the pile. "It says that you have until the 15th to pay, or your power will be cut off. It isn't going to be cut off today or tomorrow or the next day after that. So, you borrowed that worry."

She took her hand and swept the pile of bills aside. "These are all worries that you borrowed from your tomorrows. You have today to think of a plan of action. You don't have time to worry about what-ifs and mights. You've sat at this table all morning nursing borrowed worries, jotting down what you need to worry about instead of devising a plan of action."

"There isn't a solution," I argued.

Judy gave an exasperated look. "There is always a solution. But you must stop borrowing worries."

"Give me one," I challenged her.

With a grin, she snatched up the pad and pencil from the table. "I will. But you won't like it. But that's okay. You don't have to like it. You just have to follow through. Hear me out," Judy said, glancing around the room. "You have a lot of nice things in your house. Things that you can do without. You are going to sell everything that you absolutely don't need. Sentimentality be damned. Your peace of mind is more important than anything you have in this house. You should be able to raise enough money to pay your bills up to date."

I opened my mouth to protest, but she raised a hand to shush me. "After that, you are going to apply for that job I told you about. You would make a great teacher's assistant, and if I put in a word for you, the job is yours. Then you'll be able to keep your bills paid."

She saw my stricken face, reached across the table, and patted my hand. "Of course, you will have to make sacrifices, but they are worth making. You will have your peace of mind back. And the things in your house are just things. Things can be replaced."

I sighed. "Is that all?"

"No!" she said. "You have to do one more very important thing. You have to stop borrowing worries from tomorrow."

I took Judy's advice that day. I slowly got my bills all paid. And, over time, I replaced some of the things that I had sold. But I found that some of the things I really didn't need anyway. And I never borrow worries anymore.

—Elizabeth A. Atwater—

62

I'll Quit Tomorrow

The power to change is in my hands.
~Helen M. Ryan

A lcohol breeds chaos, and I used to drink all the time—for decades, really. In time, it got progressively worse. On a superficial level, I enjoyed it, and just as a fish may not recognize the water that surrounds it, I became immersed in it. I didn't realize that it was a problem. It was simply part of my life.

Thinking back, I fondly remembered events in which I participated, not realizing that an alcoholic's perception and memory are flawed and distorted. Alcoholics live with impaired judgment that gets increasingly worse, and they use conscious and subconscious methods to erase painful experiences from their memories.

The disease is progressive, and in time it took over and then took things away from me. It started with some friends who, in my distorted opinion, had wronged me in some way, and then I turned on my family. All the while, alcohol continued to gain strength and dominate me. Still not realizing the power and control that it wielded, I started each day with a drink. And to avoid withdrawal symptoms that would prevent me from doing my job (attending meetings and dealing with coworkers, administration and clients), I had to continue drinking throughout the day. After work, it continued. Each morning, the cycle started again. There was no end in sight.

I couldn't function without it, and while at first it made me more emotional, eventually it stripped away the emotions, leaving just the shell of who I once was: a television personality and author of twelve books. Once the downward spiral begins, it is difficult to stop. And even though it seems like alcohol helps, no external remedy can improve a person's condition without simultaneously making it worse.

I needed to drive, which led to a DUI criminal charge. That, in turn, led to my termination and subsequent unemployment. All at once, I was literally losing everything I had worked my entire life to procure. I was adrift with no mooring. Depression hit. Alcoholics have some degree of self-hatred within. Sometimes, it is repressed, but it is there. When it hit me, I gave up. The only way out, albeit a temporary one, was back in the bottle. I knew that alcohol could temporarily reduce the sadness and anxiety, so I drank. It numbed the pain while continuing to destroy what was left of my once successful life. The situation reminded me of that trite expression that "alcohol is both the cause of and solution to all of life's problems." Of course, such an expression only holds true for alcoholics. I hit a point so low that, for me, it seemed like there was only one way out. Darkness consumed me.

Then, one night, I had a dream. I was adrift on a boat, the boat that I used to own, and it was dark. The moonlight reflected off the waves, and I woke up thinking about it. I remembered the old Buddhist warning that human beings are like boats on the ocean, listlessly drifting without direction. It is said that they should set their sights on a star. They may never reach it, but at least they will have a direction; they will have a purpose.

Having just woken up, I thought about this insight — not about its origin but about how to find and follow that starlight. And perhaps its consideration alone allowed a bit of light to dissipate the darkness that surrounded me. That light continued to grow. For the first time in more than a decade, I was thinking positively again. Just as sunlight pervades an entire room when the door is opened a crack, the feeling that this was not the end of my life but the beginning of a new one took hold, and I decided to make a change.

I checked myself into a fantastic rehabilitation facility staffed with knowledgeable doctors, nurses, counselors, and psychologists. I had a routine: breakfast, medical checkups, courses and therapy sessions, lunch, excursions and meetings, dinner, discussions and counseling, and then bed. This routine repeated daily and forced me to look within, to find the cause of addiction within myself.

All the patients there learned about mindful meditation and how to use it to curb addictive behaviors, and they learned about other holistic methods to eliminate alcohol and drug use. The whole program was spiritual in nature. I made a list of the top ten ways that alcohol made my life chaotic. I made lists of the good occasions in life, and I forced myself to make a list of the bad moments. I had to answer questions about myself as though I were someone else:

Would you trust yourself?

Would you date yourself?

Would you hire yourself?

Would you invite yourself somewhere?

Obviously, such questions are not easily answered, as it is difficult for people to see themselves, so I meditated upon them for days. Even today, I am still thinking about them. I also strove to answer other questions that were meant to help me analyze my life up to that point:

What have you done that you are most proud of?

Why are you here on this planet?

What are your greatest talents?

What are your interests?

What new skill do you want to learn?

Why do you want to learn it?

In time, I realized that I did not need alcohol in my life. In fact, I realized that alcohol just got in the way of my life. But I know that I always have to be on guard because addicts are always addicts, whether they are using or not. Nevertheless, besides the massive self-reflection and meditative practices in which we engaged, I bonded with the other patients. A few had stories to tell, and most had impressive backgrounds: one in film production, another in music production. I was the token writer, and there were teachers and a financial advisor, someone who started a cryptocurrency and another who ran a beauty salon. I could not imagine another way that such an eclectic group would all come together with the same problem, the same goal, and possibly the same solution.

Several of them asked about writing a book about their trials and what they had been through. After meeting weekly in the evenings after dinner, we decided to put a book together in which we would all tell our stories: the good and the bad, the ups and the downs. And since we have been out and back at our homes, we have continued to meet weekly on Thursday evenings online. We are putting the book together now. Two doctors will be writing portions of it. A famous individual who now has a Netflix special is writing the foreword. And my friend who started the cryptocurrency, who had graduated from Oxford University, already sparked the interest of several major publishers. I didn't know he even had an "in." In addition, I have more television shows coming up, and we are filming in New York soon.

Meeting everyone — people whom I normally never would have met — helped me to realize that perhaps everything does happen for a reason. Like the old expression states, the pure can only emerge from filth. The historical Buddha said, "The lotus flower blooms most beautifully from the deepest and thickest mud," and Thich Nhat Hanh wrote, "There is the mud, and there is the lotus that grows out of the mud. We need the mud in order to make the lotus."

It is unknown what the future will bring, but the power of positive thinking has brought me and the rest of the group here, standing on a precipice, about to take action that will likely change the course of our lives. We'll do what we can to fulfill our obligations to others and society as a whole, and we vow to do our best. As Yamamoto Tsunetomo said, "The gods and Buddhas, too, first started with a vow." We all believe that continuing to think positively will bring positive things. In time, we will find out. I'm confident that it will.

— Ken Jeremiah —

63

The Inbox

*The way you see things depends a great deal
on where you look at them from.*
~Norton Juster

W hile undergoing treatment for breast cancer, I returned to work — probably a little too soon. My coworkers were understanding. It was a difficult and emotionally draining time with my health issues, along with the daily drama of family dynamics like a grown daughter in the throes of a mid-life crisis and an ailing parent. It's all the stuff that makes our lives "full."

In the open environment of a cube-land office, there is usually little or no privacy with conversations, whether they be on the phone or in person. Everybody knows everyone's business.

One day, after a stress-filled phone conversation, I hung up the phone, put my head down on my desk, and let out a huge, weepy sigh. It was more like a tear-filled whine. My cube mate, Joyce, who usually observed cube etiquette by acting stoic or deaf to others' conversations, stepped away from her work and rolled her chair next to mine.

"What's going on?" she asked.

"What *isn't* going on?" I whined. "Pick a subject: sick mom, out-of-control adult child, sick dog, daily treatments, and my car needs work. Everything sucks! I'm so tired. I feel like all this will never end!"

I grabbed a bunch of tissues and tried to compose myself. Joyce gave me a moment to calm down. She then told a little anecdote about a time when she also had a tough time with a lot of things going on.

She felt totally overwhelmed, like there was no end to the stress.

I asked her how she had managed. She winked and held out an open hand and a closed fist. Her response gave me words to live by in stressful times.

"Inbox full or inbox empty?"

I got the message. Those wise words have become a mantra for me, and I am forever grateful. When I feel like life stuff just keeps piling on — whether it's good, bad or just feels like too much to handle — I recite those perspective-changing words.

I often pass on those wise words to someone when they feel overwhelmed and need a little friendly support.

"Inbox full or inbox empty?"

There are still many bumps in the road of my life's journey, and I often remind myself of those words: "Inbox full or inbox empty?"

My inbox is full. I don't know what an empty inbox looks like. And I don't want to know.

— Joanne Costantino —

64

Chicken Soup for the Soul

Simple Wisdom

If you look the right way, you can see
that the whole world is a garden.
~Frances Hodgson Burnett

There's an autumn day that I recall every time I find myself caught up in the hustle and bustle of life. I was a teenager at the time, caught up in the whirlwind of school, social activities, and the pressure of upcoming college applications. It was my neighbor, Mr. Jensen, who brought me back to earth.

Mr. Jensen was a quiet man in his seventies who lived alone in the house next door. Despite our age difference, we had a shared love for gardening, a hobby that formed an unlikely friendship between us.

One sunny afternoon, feeling overwhelmed and anxious, I decided to take a break from my studies. I headed outside to my backyard garden where I began to furiously weed, my frustrations pouring into each yank of unwanted greenery. Mr. Jensen was there as usual, tending to his blossoming rosebushes.

Seeing my frustration, he ambled over and silently started weeding alongside me. After a few minutes of shared silence, he finally spoke up.

"You know," he began, "weeding a garden is a lot like going through life."

Intrigued, I stopped and looked at him. He continued, "Sometimes, we focus so much on the weeds — the problems and difficulties — that we forget to enjoy the flowers."

He gestured to the beautiful roses in his garden, their vibrant colors shining in the afternoon sun.

"Don't forget to appreciate the roses, even as you deal with the weeds."

That simple wisdom hit me hard. I had been so focused on my problems, on the stress of my future, that I had forgotten to enjoy my present — the friendships, the joy of learning new things, and the beauty of simply being alive.

That day, Mr. Jensen taught me a life lesson that I've carried with me ever since. Now, whenever I find myself overwhelmed by life's "weeds," I pause, take a deep breath, and remember to appreciate my "roses."

— Brian Carpenter —

Pins on a Hat

*My father gave me the greatest gift anyone could give
another person: He believed in me.*
~Jim Valvano

I spent my childhood dashing from tree to tree, fighting invisible bad guys. The glory of battle and the pomp of victory were my keys to popularity and respect. Soldiers had always represented the epitome of strength and bravery for me.

Like many kids, my interest in the Army faded as I grew older. But then, college life was not as fulfilling as I hoped it would be. A recruiter got me excited about the military after all. I always told people that I joined for the education benefits, but my desire to connect with my father in the shared experience of service is what forged my underlying motivation.

I studied the posters of military awards throughout basic training. I dreamed about where I would go and picked out the medals I planned to get. I was eager to earn as many as I could. A uniform full of decorations would surely garner respect, right? The first couple of awards motivated me and made me proud. I wore my dress uniform often because I wanted to display my excellence. I felt like I belonged.

I accumulated the chest full of medals I had dreamt about during my youth. People look at my uniform and associate what they see with victory, accomplishment, and heroism. But I don't see those things anymore.

When I look at my uniform today, hanging in the back of a closet underneath a retirement flag, I see all the years away from my home and family. I see stress, blood, and tears. I see the ghosts of my fallen brethren and the guilt of survival. I see the emotional distancing from the people I hoped to become closer to. I see the anxiety, depression, and anger created by the accomplishments that were so eloquently highlighted in the accompanying certificates.

Soldiers still represent the epitome of strength and bravery to me, but the foundational respect I feel for them now stems from an empathetic perspective of opportunity cost. The military is a place where sacrifice and success are the only things that reinforce each other. In the pursuit of success, incredible bonds are created, and the transformed perception of what our decorations truly mean often surpasses what I initially thought victory would feel like. I simply needed the right people to share it with.

My father is a quiet man who tends to not say what's on his mind. He talks when he has something to say and when he thinks his words are something others want to hear. It's common to wonder what he's thinking or where you stand. When he does say something, you know he means it. Sometimes, he tells you something without ever speaking it.

He has a couple of military-themed hats with a bunch of pins on them. Some of those pins are from his service to the Navy. Most of them are paraphernalia from my Army career. He has some of the rank insignia I wore and the Bronze Star ribbon presented to me in Iraq.

To the world, they are just pins on a hat. To me, they are an unquestionable exhibition of a father's pride and respect for his son.

The ribbons, medals, and badges on my uniform no longer elicit the same emotions from me; however, those pins on my father's hat make me feel proud again. They make me feel loved. It means everything to me that he constantly shows the world what kind of man he raised. After all, what son doesn't want to know that he is a success in his father's eyes?

— Elton A. Dean —

A One-Legged Messenger of Hope

I can be changed by what happens to me.
But I refuse to be reduced by it.
~Maya Angelou

One cold and gray March morning a few years back, I admit I was feeling sorry for myself. After months of hobbling around on the slippery, snow-covered ground on crutches, my mood matched the dreary weather. That was, until I watched a courageous child make the best of a situation far worse than mine.

It began with a Christmas Eve phone call from an orthopedic physician following a diagnostic MRI, confirming my fears. "I will need to see you in the office the day after Christmas," the young doctor said with compassion.

My heart sank. I had been stuck in bed nursing the aching knee, hoping and praying it wasn't anything serious again. Unfortunately, it had never healed correctly following a previous surgery by another specialist.

My health issue started with a painfully arthritic foot problem. I was aging, but it wasn't happening gradually like it did for most individuals. One minute, I was a healthy fifty-eight-year-old woman participating in cardio classes and long leisurely walks. Then, by my fifty-ninth birthday, my new normal became resting in bed with ice packs, walking with crutches, and wearing ugly orthopedic shoes.

For a few years, there were relatively healthy periods when I was able to put away the crutches and resume my daily activities. I could attend church, accept speaking engagements again, shop with friends, and even go back to the gym. Finally accepting that I had aged out of vigorous exercise classes and the ability to wear fashionable shoes, Pilates, yoga, swimming, and water-walking became my new forms of working out. Still, I was grateful to be getting around.

There were other dismal seasons when the discomfort would cause me to be stuck in bed for weeks or months. Despite ongoing visits with specialists, diagnostic testing, and all kinds of treatments, there was little relief.

At first, I prayed fervently for an answer. But, in time, my prayers to be freed of the chronic pain and lack of mobility turned desperate. Yet I constantly reminded myself of other individuals with life-threatening health challenges.

My husband Larry witnessed firsthand how isolating my daily routine had become, even though his hectic job as a school administrator caused him to be gone twelve or fourteen hours a day. My grown son lived over an hour away. Plus, moving frequently for Larry's career left me without any close friends nearby.

My geographically distant family members would sometimes call to offer medical advice or a pep talk, encouraging me to try harder to find a solution. I understood their good intentions, but following these conversations I would often cry for hours in frustration. I didn't have any idea where else to look for answers. So, I learned to hide my circumstances.

Thankfully, being able to write was my saving grace. I wrote columns for local newspapers and book anthologies, and even authored an inspirational novel. On social media, I posted smiling photos and avoided mentioning the health issues that would keep me housebound. I sincerely endeavored to stay positive, hold onto my faith, and trust that there would be a solution—until the fated MRI's report of the seriously reinjured knee on Christmas Eve. When this happened, I didn't have any emotional or spiritual strength left in me to fight.

At the day-after-Christmas appointment, the caring orthopedic doctor cautioned me that another knee surgery would not be a good option until a remedy for the damaged foot could be discovered. He tried to give me hope by suggesting the possibility of a future clinical study because there were no traditional treatment options left.

I was grateful for the doctor's decision to not submit me to more unsuccessful surgery. Still, in the months that followed, I struggled to accept that this diminished version of who I once was might be permanent. The crutches, wheelchair for shopping, riding in an electric cart to get groceries, and having to ask for help to carry something had all seemed temporary for the past few years. My writing also started suffering because it's difficult to be inspirational while battling depression.

By early March, the hopelessness escalated. One desperate night, I tossed and turned, sobbing into my pillow until dawn. With my eyes swollen from lack of sleep and crying, I threw on my clothes, grabbed my crutches, and decided to take a drive to calm my troubled mind.

I remembered that the Grounds for Pleasure Coffee House in Tipp City opened early. Tipp City is a quaint, little town only miles from my house with a vibrant downtown and artistic shops.

That morning, it was blustery cold and dark. Thankfully, the coffee shop's atmosphere was peaceful and inviting. I ordered an oversized ceramic mug of steaming coffee. Navigating on crutches, I tried not to spill the beverage on my way to a comfortable leather chair. The hot drink warmed my body, although my aching heart remained stone-cold.

Emptying the large cup, I headed back out to my car. By then, students who lived in the neighborhood were making their way to both the elementary and middle schools nearby. The youngsters chatted and laughed together while walking on the snow-covered sidewalk.

I sat at the red light, envying their carefree behavior, overwhelmed by my own circumstances and silently lamenting how grossly unfair getting older could be.

Then, I saw a little girl in a wheelchair with a woman pushing her. Maybe she was ten; I don't know her age. What I do know is that the child-size wheelchair converted my feeling-sorry-for-myself emotion into compassion for a child whose burden was far heavier than mine.

My lesson wasn't over. The little girl seemed to be pleading with the lady, who must have been her mother. She wanted to walk like the other kids, but she needed to use her crutches, too. I watched as the small girl pushed herself from the wheelchair into a standing position.

When she did, it was obvious that the courageous child had only one leg. Fighting back tears, I circled the block to make sure that what I had observed was real. There she was again, defiantly crutching along, with her head held high.

I truly believe that seeing this spunky girl was God's way of saying, "Be strong." I had a choice to make. I could push through self-pity and choose to live my life positively and be thankful for what I could do, or I could be forever miserable, contemplating what I couldn't.

Most days, I embrace this child's costly lesson and crutch on. When courage fails me, somehow Heaven has a way of sending a new reminder of a brave individual making the best of life's worst. Still, my heart will always hold a special place for my one-legged messenger of hope.

— Christina Ryan Claypool —

The Power of a Single Compliment

Too often we underestimate the power of a touch,
a smile, a kind word, a listening ear, an honest
compliment, or the smallest act of caring.
~Leo Buscaglia

When I was sixteen, I worked in fast food. And I hated it.

It didn't start out that way. When I first started working, that little restaurant was my whole social life. I'd been a sheltered kid, and it was exciting to hang around such a diverse, worldly crew of teens and young adults. For a while, I loved everything about it: making the food on the line, learning a whole new cuisine I'd never eaten before, joking with coworkers and customers at the front counter.

Over time, though, it started to wear on me. There were the buses that pulled in one minute before closing time, disgorging kids who trashed the place and forced me to re-clean a lobby I'd had spotless. The split shifts I was assigned ate up my entire day but didn't really net all that much in wages.

And that was before they assigned me to work the drive-through. I was certain the dinging in my ear would make me lose my mind. Ridiculously loud vehicles rattled my eardrums and overpowered the voice of the person who was ordering. There were people who spoke so softly that I assumed they were talking to each other until they yelled at me because I hadn't acknowledged them.

There were also those who were talking to each other and got mad at me when I asked them to confirm that I'd gotten their order right.

There were people who left their radios on, which also obscured their voices. Other people came to the window stinking of smoke, using language I didn't approve of, and yelling at their children and spouses. They yelled at me for getting orders wrong after they had changed their minds five times at the ordering station.

I came to dread every day I was scheduled to work. I arrived with a bad attitude and left ready to bite the head off anyone who looked at me wrong.

It didn't take long to realize this was unsustainable. Nothing was going to change unless it was me. I had two choices: be miserable, grouchy, and hate my life, or figure out how to get into a better mental space at work.

So, I decided that, for one day, I would pay a compliment to every person who came past my drive-through window.

"What beautiful earrings!"

"I like your shirt!"

"I love your hair. I've always wanted red hair."

"Those nails are a really cool design."

I'm not going to lie. It was not easy. It wasn't like the people appearing at my window had changed, after all. They still stank of smoke, talked too low (or too loudly), had deafening cars, and yelled at me for not being able to separate their voices from the voices on their radios.

Yet that tiny shift in what I chose to focus on had a big ripple effect. I was looking at them differently. Instead of focusing on everything that was wrong, bad, or annoying about them, I began seeing positives. Commonalities.

The most amazing thing of all, though, wasn't my own reaction, but theirs. Every person I complimented paused. Blinked. Looked slightly disoriented even. I could see the shift happen in their faces. Suddenly, we had a two-sentence exchange about where they had their nails done or where they bought the shirt. Having someone take note of something positive about them — something specific to them alone, however banal it might be — changed them, too.

By the end of the day, I knew I had stumbled on a treasure. Work felt totally different. I went home happy for the first time in weeks.

So, I adopted the tactic permanently. Not perfectly... but permanently.

Thirty years later, I still need that technique. More than ever, in fact! Anytime I get in a negative funk, preoccupied by my own concerns, I start judging everyone I encounter. Since I'm not allowed to vent my negativity on total strangers, I bury it instead, which is unhealthy. Eventually, it's bound to punch through to those I care about most. That's not who I want to be.

So now, when I feel my negativity coming on, I take a deep breath and turn on my compliment brain. It's almost always socially acceptable to offer compliments — even to strangers! Even in this age of smart phones and earbuds, people stop in their tracks. They pause, and the harried, jittery look in their eyes softens. Something changes. It's subtle, but it's real. Because of my choice to be positive, they are happier.

And so am I.

— Kathleen Basi —

This Is What You Wanted

*The secret of happiness is to count your blessings while
others are adding up their troubles.*
~William Penn

I had just exited my car to go into the grocery store when a woman about my age rolled her shopping cart up to the SUV next to mine and started loading her bags into the back. It was during the Christmas holidays, when almost every woman is busy, busy, busy. She was chanting: "All they do is eat. It's the same thing over and over again. It never ends. Every day is the same."

She kept on complaining in the same vein. And she wasn't *pretending* to be upset, the way women sometimes complain about how much they have to do, but you know they're secretly pleased to be caring for their loved ones. This crabby woman was angry and stressed and resentful, and she was venting to a complete stranger: me.

We never have all of our four children with us for Christmas. One lives in California and doesn't come east for the holiday. One lives nearby, and she does come unless she's visiting her brother out there. And the other two split their time between their in-laws and their father and us, so we technically only get one out of four Christmases with them. We even had one Christmas in the past decade when we had *no one* for Christmas Day.

I wanted to say to this lady, "You are so lucky that you have a full house! You are lucky that you have money to buy food 'over and over again' and that you have a nice car to carry that food home for you.

You are lucky that you have people waiting at home who love you, who depend on you and are healthy enough to eat 'over and over again.'"

Because she seemed to be my age, I assumed that she was probably talking about a husband and grown kids. I wanted to add, "Don't you remember why you married that man and had those children? You wanted them. You signed up for this. And you love those hungry people who have come home to visit."

But I didn't say a thing. I chickened out. I only had a second to make the decision, and I thought it might be presumptuous of me to give her advice. Even though I've published stories about people having epiphanies when a total stranger says the right words to them, and even though I've read hundreds of stories from women in similar circumstances, and even though I thought I was right, I didn't have the nerve, or maybe even the gall, to point out the obvious to a stranger.

It's all about getting back to how it started, right? When my house is full of people during the holidays, I am running around like a chicken with its head cut off, and I am stressed beyond words because I still have all my "Chicken Soup" work *plus* a house full of people. But it's a good stress, the kind that comes from a full and wondrous life. I know that I have *chosen* to do these things and host these amazing people, so how can I complain? This is what I wanted.

I should have spoken up in that parking lot. Maybe I would have made a difference. Maybe I would have pushed her "reset button" with a few choice words and steered her to having a much happier holiday.

Of course, it might have backfired. She might have lashed out at me, and then I would have regretted opening my mouth. But at least I would be regretting that I *took* action, instead of regretting my *inaction*. But I did that diffident thing I occasionally do, and I kept my mouth shut.

The journalist Sydney J. Harris said, "Regret for the things we did can be tempered by time; it is regret for the things we did not do that is inconsolable." If something similar happens in the future, I'll try to be "that Chicken Soup lady" — yes, that's what I'm often called — and maybe I'll be able to help.

— Amy Newmark —

Chapter
9

Face Your Fears

Don't Dance Until the Music Starts

The only thing to do with good advice is to pass it on.
~Oscar Wilde

The brown wig was ugly! Cousin Flo brought Mom the furry critter as a get-well gift. "You need a wig before you lose your hair," Flo said. "After chemo, you'll be too sick to go shopping."

Mom looked at the wig and sighed, "Florence, let's not dance until the music starts."

Instead of "Cross that bridge when you come to it," my mother always said, "Don't dance 'til the music starts."

She jitterbugged like a wild woman, saying, "See, if you dance with no music, you look crazy, no?" We laughed until tears fell, modeling the ugly wig.

And Mom was right! She did *not* go bald from chemo. The wig hung on a bathroom hook to remind me not to worry over things that may never happen.

Though terminally ill, she was joyful and positive, a good listener whom neighbors loved to visit. Coffee was always perking, and the table was set with a snow-white cloth and her blue Willow Ware china.

I was a substitute teacher in a new high school and had had my first run-in with a hostile teen. "I dread going back to sub tomorrow," I told Mom. "That kid's hard to handle."

"Honey, maybe he'll behave tomorrow," she offered. "Or maybe you won't sub for that class. Enjoy today. Don't dance 'til the music starts."

Darn! The next day, my sub schedule showed that I would indeed teach the troublemaker — not until seventh period, but I let it cloud a pleasant day.

When zero hour arrived, I saw that the problem child was absent, and I never had his class again.

Mom quoted another favorite, "Worry is like paying interest on money you never borrowed."

Neighbors and cousins streamed in to visit Mom, relaxing in her calm presence. Monica, a young teacher, dropped by one day with roses for Mother. "I'll stay only a few minutes," she said. "I'm feeling down. My dad died last month, and I miss him so much."

"Tell me about him," invited Mother. Monica sat near the sickbed and poured out a heartful of emotions. She called it "the luxury of a listener's undivided attention in a hurried world." And Mother listened, delighted with her visitor, who looked like a fairy princess with waist-length, wavy blond hair.

From the kitchen stove, I glanced up at the sick woman and young girl in the next room, absorbed in each other's company. Monica stayed for supper: pasta primavera with garlic cloves, olive oil, and Parmesan cheese. Decades later, she described it as one of her happiest evenings.

Each day, Mother dressed for chemo in a new outfit: the red wool dress, the gold suit, the peacock blue one, the black slacks with leather jacket. Our next-door neighbor called out, "Where's the movie star going?"

"For a beauty treatment," she answered.

"Honey, don't give details about my chemo," she whispered to me. "People have their own troubles. Remember that poem by Arthur Guiterman, 'Don't tell your friends about your indigestion. "How are you!" is a greeting, not a question.'" She quoted Ella Wheeler Wilcox: "You cannot charm or interest or please by harping on that minor chord — disease."

"Don't you dread chemo?" Flo asked.

Mother answered, "I don't think about it until I get there. Why dance before the music starts?" She quoted Shakespeare: "The coward dies a thousand times before his death, but the valiant taste of death but once."

On Good Friday, a new nurse stabbed Mother's bruised, little arm three times, unable to find a vein, and apologized. "That's okay," Mother whispered. "Three nails pierced our Lord." No whining, just simple belief in the redemptive value of suffering patiently.

A friend asked, "Why did this happen to a good person like you? It's not fair."

"Oh, it *is* fair," Mother protested. "I've never been sick for eighty years! That wasn't fair. At eighty, I used to look like sixty. Now, I do look eighty. That's fair. And, look, the convent sent my daughter to care for me this year. I gave her to God to be a nun when she was twenty, and God sent her back to me."

If death could be called beautiful, Mother's was. I had just cleaned the house to perfection. The parlor lamp's amber bulb cast a golden glow on the room. It was just the two of us, no visitors that night. Too weak to talk, she held my hand as I read aloud from the Book of Psalms. "Isn't this peaceful, Mommy?" I asked. "Our parlor's bathed in golden light. It's dark and snowy out, but so warm and toasty here." She uttered a peaceful sigh… and was gone.

I had feared being alone in the house when she died. But now I was happy to be alone in the beauty of the moment.

It had come, and I was at peace. She and I had often talked about the joys of the afterlife. Why had I feared?

That was decades ago, but I still remember her gentle voice. "Honey, think positively. Enjoy the present moment. What you fear may never happen. And if it does — God is with us. Don't dance until the music starts."

— Sister Josephine Palmeri, MPF —

70

How I Out-Swam My Fears

*My mission in life is not merely to survive, but
to thrive; and to do so with some passion, some
compassion, some humor, and some style.*

~Maya Angelou

I saw him running across the football field. We made eye contact, and he yelled, "I love you, Ashonti!"

I was graduating from San Francisco State with a degree in Broadcast Communication, and my new fiancé, who had graduated from UC Berkeley, recently asked me to join him in Miami, where he was studying law.

What a time, right?

Both our families showered me with love all weekend. There were engagement parties and graduation celebrations. I even had a masquerade-themed going-away party.

This was truly a beautiful time — and I had no idea it would lead me into one of the worst moments of my life.

In anticipation of building a life together in Florida, I sought out an internship with CBS News to work on the Trayvon Martin case. I was accepted into the program.

So, I sold my car. I wrapped things up at my current internship, KGO-ABC, and my fiancé's parents were kind enough to help me pack up my apartment and drive my stuff to Goodwill to donate.

We were ready to start our lives together.

Outside of my one-way ticket to Miami, the only thing I had was a suitcase full of clothes and faith.

Seventy-two hours before my flight to Miami, he broke up with me.

I remember answering a call from my aunt a few minutes before he ended things. She was calling about flower arrangement ideas for the newly engaged couple.

It was an out-of-body experience.

I felt like I was drowning above water.

I handed him back his ring—and what happened next is still burned into my memory more than ten years later.

He put the ring back on my finger and started crying. He put his coat around my shoulders because it was cold that day. He kissed me and said he was going to confront his parents because they were to blame for the break-up.

When I called him the next day, his number was changed, and his parents, whom I had called my own—the same ones who had helped me drop my belongings off at Goodwill—ignored my calls.

This was the lowest moment in my life but also a moment that would eventually define me.

I remember sitting in my friend's living room, staring at my suitcase and the one-way ticket to Miami. I must have sat there for at least two hours in silence.

I had no vision or sign from God. I just had my suitcase and a ticket that said I was supposed to board a plane in forty-eight hours. And I had to decide. Would I stay home and scrape my life back together? Or would I move across the country and force myself to grow?

I went. I remember my stepmom telling me that I was the strongest woman she knew. It was a very powerful moment for me.

My aunt, probably somewhat nervous, dropped me off at the airport. My cousin, who never cries, shed a tear.

I flew into Miami with less than $1,000 in my bank account.

I had no job outside of my unpaid internship with CBS News. I didn't know Miami. I had no car or clear path, but I did have the address to my new place, which I had found on Craigslist forty-eight hours before.

It was a beautiful shared home in a neighborhood called Coconut

Grove. When I got there, massive peacocks were standing in the street. It looked like a page out of a tropical magazine. Then, I walked inside.

The house was a very rundown version of the photos posted on Craigslist, with no water in the pool. Oh! And the owner failed to mention that I'd be sharing a room with five other people, bunkbed-style.

Despite the challenges, I got a job as a server making $3 an hour + tips and started my internship. Within thirty days of the program, the executive producer in the bureau told me that I would never be a news reporter. I was crushed—again; I felt like I was drowning above water.

I could write a whole book about how I survived Miami, but I will sum it up by saying that not only did I survive, I thrived.

I sent the engagement ring back to my ex's family, I re-enrolled in school so I could be eligible for a local internship that would help me create a reporter demo tape and after several failed attempts—I accepted my first full-time reporter position and went on to grow in the television news industry for over a decade.

I'm now a National Correspondent in D.C. covering politics and all things out of the White House.

I'm living my dreams.

And even though there are so many things that helped mold me into the woman I am today, I know for sure that the decision to throw myself into the deep end inspired me to out-swim my own fears.

—Ashonti Ford—

71

Slam Dunk

To be outstanding — get comfortable
with being uncomfortable.
~Alrik Koudenburg

The first time I remember doing karaoke was at Six Flags Great America in Gurnee, Illinois. Our high school class was there for a physics trip. We were supposed to learn how roller coasters react to gravity and different kinds of angles and G-forces. I don't really recall learning anything, but I do remember performing the song "Fat Lip" by Sum 41 with one of my high-school friends. It was delightful and got me hooked.

To date, I have performed over 650 karaoke songs at places all around the world. How do I know that total? I have a Spotify playlist of all the songs I've done, and I can always find a song to fit my mood.

I've also hosted karaoke at a bar — the same one where pop star Jewel made an appearance as an undercover performer. I even won $50 in a karaoke contest, coming in second behind a Chaka Khan backup singer.

There's something so charmingly endearing about karaoke. Whether you're in a private room or public setting, there's a special bond between everyone involved. We may have nothing in common otherwise, but for those three minutes (or six and a half, if you choose a song like "Hotel California"), we're forgetting our troubles and singing our hearts out.

All those previous experiences led to my crowning karaoke achievement: performing at halftime of a WNBA basketball game.

My friend had a birthday celebration at a bar that hosted gong karaoke. If enough people hold up a piece of paper with an X on it, a gong rings, and the singer is escorted off the stage. It's one of the more intimidating things I've ever done, but I approached it like I always try to approach karaoke: with a lot of positivity. After all, if I'm having fun, how could everyone in the crowd not smile along?

Little did I know that my friend's sister worked for the San Antonio Spurs' entertainment crew, and she told me they were introducing halftime karaoke at Silver Stars games. One week later, I was driving down to San Antonio with a friend, ready for my big break.

We arrived three minutes before halftime began. My friend's sister, clearly panicking, asked if I was ready. I nodded enthusiastically, hoping that vigor would improve both our spirits. She flashed a smile and sent me up to the second level to get set up.

I met the kind halftime entertainment hosts and the other performers. The first was a thirteen-year-old girl who was the daughter of one of the executives in the Spurs organization. She sang Michael Jackson's "Human Nature," which is a challenging choice for anyone, let alone a teenager. She knocked it out of the park. And, for a brief moment, I was panicking just like my friend's sister had been. My vocal performance couldn't possibly match what I just heard. I gazed out at the crowd. I had been in some packed karaoke bars, but there were thousands of people in attendance. Was I in over my head?

I took a deep breath, stepped back from the railing, and smiled. No, I was right where I was meant to be. I was doing a song I loved — "I Believe in a Thing Called Love" by The Darkness — and I was going to have a blast doing it. And that exuberance would get the crowd involved, too.

This song has all the elements of a classic karaoke number. A high falsetto. A catchy riff. A killer guitar solo that you literally introduce by yelling, "Guitar!" I was ready.

The entertainment crew handed me the microphone, and as the opening guitar and drums kicked in, I completely lost myself. I wasn't in front of thousands of people. I was back home in front of the mirror, smiling to myself while being goofy and singing.

At the "Guitar!" part, I handed the crew my microphone because I wanted to go high-five the people in the section next to me. The crew thought that meant I was done, so the music faded out. But I had already made the journey over. How could I not show my fans some love?

"Dude, that was awesome," one guy said. A little girl sitting on her dad's lap gave me a big smile and a slap on the hand when I asked for a high-five.

When I returned to my seat, I got a pat on the back from a stranger and a hug from my friend.

"You looked so happy up there," she said. I had been on the jumbotron.

Despite hundreds of karaoke performances under my belt, I had no idea what to expect with this one. But I'm so glad I said yes to it. Any self-doubt and insecurities were cast aside as soon as the music started. When the right song hits, it's impossible to stay negative.

I've tried to maintain the feeling from that night during my regular karaoke trips. If someone sings a song I really dig, I run up to the stage and give them an encouraging yell, or I tell them afterward how much I enjoyed it. Seeing their face light up gives me a burst of energy.

That's the power of music. It connects us like nothing else.

— Joey Held —

72

Granny Chic

To be beautiful means to be yourself. You don't need to
be accepted by others. You need to accept yourself.
~Thich Nhat Hanh

I surveyed the mound of clothes piled high on my bed and released a long sigh that was equal parts disgust and defeat. I had gone on a local TV news show to discuss my story in a *Chicken Soup for the Soul* book and had done a second segment that day showcasing some of the furniture pieces I had refinished that I spoke about in my story. Then I was invited back to talk about my DIY furniture restoration business. But I had nothing to wear for this second appearance — not counting the thirty-four cardigans, seventeen pairs of cropped pants, and enough ballet flats to outfit my grandmother's entire retirement community.

According to my mom, my style was decidedly "Granny Chic." I was in my late thirties, but I dressed like an old lady. That was about to change. I couldn't appear on TV in the seventh largest market in the country looking like Great Aunt Bertha, no matter how comfy those ballet flats were.

I had begun refurbishing old furniture and would be showcasing my talent and wares on a local lifestyle show. There were plenty of prominent designers on popular DIY television shows who could provide some fashion assist. I went about studying their perfectly styled, boho-inspired outfits. I decided I needed a long flowy skirt, wide belt, leather booties, and peplum top. If only I could look the part, then maybe all those people watching me on TV would be interested in what I had to offer.

With only one day to spare, I woke up early and headed to the mall in search of the perfect outfit. I vowed I would not return home until I had secured a trendy TV ensemble. As I tried on every gypsy-inspired article of clothing I came across, I began to fear I would never see home again.

I sat in the dressing room and stared at my reflection. Not only did I hate the way the clothes looked on me, but I felt completely out of my element.

"You know that producer didn't invite some bohemian DIY goddess to be on their show, and they didn't ask if you are a social-media darling with a perfectly styled house and wardrobe. They invited you: Melissa Bender."

The girl in the mirror had just spoken to my heart. I wasn't sure at what point over the past couple of weeks I had decided that I needed to morph into someone I wasn't. I was grateful to Ballet Flats Melissa for reminding me that we were more than enough just as we were. I threw my old clothes back on and headed to Target, my favorite one-stop cardigan shop, where I purchased, you guessed it, a brand-new cardigan.

I arrived at the studio the following morning rocking that cardigan in all my Granny Chic glory. My DIY segment was a wild success, scoring me a multitude of new social-media followers, including the show's host. Two years later, that same host invited me to become a regular guest contributor to the show, and I began doing a monthly DIY and decorating segment.

That first DIY television appearance was ten years ago. As you can imagine, a lot has changed since then. My style and wardrobe have evolved considerably, even bordering on stylish and trendy. Mom says I no longer dress like an old lady, to which I say, "Thank you, Instagram Fashion Influencers."

There is one thing, however, that hasn't changed through the years, and it is the most important thing of all: the knowledge that I am enough. No matter my body type, education, socioeconomic status, wardrobe, or whatever else I may define myself by, I am worthy of being seen and heard. It is okay to just be me, which is great because I'm good at it. And while my style may no longer be described as Granny Chic, I am excited that I will soon wear the title of Chic Granny when my son and his wife welcome their first child. Oh, to just be me!

— Melissa Bender —

Fight, Not Flight

Courage is not the absence of fear,
but the triumph over it.
~Author Unknown

T he roar was loud and unsettling as I stood underneath the roller coaster. It looped around me, pulling over 5G worth of force. It was enough force to make a bystander feel its intense power without even being on it. We had a babysitter for the evening for our wedding anniversary, and time was ticking by as I watched this roller coaster thunder down the track without me on it. If I was going to get enough courage to ride it before we had to relieve the babysitter, it had to happen soon.

I started making excuses to my husband. I began listing all the things that I was less afraid of than going on that roller coaster.

"I'm less afraid to get a tattoo, go on a motorcycle…" I rambled.

But, deep down inside, I didn't want to let the fear steal away what could be a wild adventure to celebrate our anniversary. I had never been on an upside-down ride in my life. I have always played it safe. I stood on the sidelines, happy as can be, as long as no one made me do anything scary. I was happy to miss out.

"It's now or never," my husband said, showing me the time on his phone.

Standing on the sidelines in my comfort zone felt safe. But it also felt like a cage. I was growing tired of being in that cage. My comfort zone was damaging me more than it was saving me now. And there was only one way out.

If I didn't turn to run headfirst into my fear, then it would always be behind me.

I looked up at the roller coaster and realized that it only took about ninety seconds to run all the way through.

For a minute and a half, I could hold on and endure whatever body-rattling chaos I was about to put myself through. That was all that stood between me and a more adventurous existence. My breathing was getting quicker, and I could feel the courage building inside me.

"Let's get the tickets NOW!" I exclaimed and ran over to the ticket counter with a burst of energy.

With tickets in hand, we got in line.

"Let us on! Let us on!" I chanted eagerly in my head as I waited for them to open the gate so we could pick our seats. I was motivated to do this now.

My resolve to break free from the prison I had held myself in had shifted my anxiety into excitement. The adrenaline coursing through my body from fear was the same concoction as the adrenaline released from exhilaration. It was only my decision to be courageous and step out for a minute that switched how it felt in my body.

This time, the sensation was going to be my strength. It was going to drive me into adventure and not away from it. My heart was pumping faster and faster at the prospect of becoming a person who no longer let fear have the final say.

We finally took our seats and strapped ourselves in. I was shaking. But it wasn't fear causing it. The adrenaline causing me to shake was from the anticipation of doing something thrilling, not from running away. Instead of flight, it was fight.

I held on tight as we slowly pulled up to the first big drop. The clicking sounds of the wheels rattled my head, but I maintained focus on what was coming. I was doing it. I was brave. I was excited to be a person who rides roller coasters. It wasn't a feeling of terror; it was a feeling of courage!

When we reached the top, for a brief moment, it felt as if the roller coaster slowed down to a crawl. I was all anticipation, and I didn't want to wait another second. All of me was screaming, "Let's do this!" But, instead, I had one last moment to make peace with the old me and say goodbye to the girl who hid in her cage.

I finished my farewell just as the roller coaster began to plummet toward the ground. Nothing but physics and gravity shook my body with intensity. I was strapped in with a seatbelt, a lap restraint and shoulder restraints, but I had also never felt so free. I used the adrenaline to empower me, not constrain me.

There have been many "roller coasters" since that day. It is a joy to feel that familiar wave of energy rushing through my body now. It feels like I am about to do something really brave. I've gotten a few tattoos since that day, but I still haven't ridden a motorcycle. Sometimes, you do need a few safety restraints.

— Katie Bergen —

74

The Many Roads Not Taken

*Real protection means teaching children to manage
risks on their own, not shielding them
from every hazard.*
~Wendy Mogel, The Blessing of Skinned Knees

I was the person who always expected the worst in any scenario. If someone said they had an upcoming surgery with a 98 percent chance of success, I immediately recalculated to a certain 2 percent death. I visualized my son David's mild cough becoming pneumonia. Owing a few dollars in taxes would surely turn into hundreds, if not thousands, before their final assessment.

I spent years avoiding activities that I was sure would end in tragedy. I became a helicopter mom, checking the backyard for anything dangerous before letting David out to play — under my strict supervision, of course. After all, kids were abducted every day, right? I gritted my teeth when he put on ice skates, carrying a small emergency kit in my purse. When a baseball flew his way at T-ball, I prayed he wouldn't get a concussion. If not for my husband's adamant insistence that normal kids need activities and sports, our son would probably never have learned to throw a ball.

"You can't keep hovering over him," Don would argue. "You're suffocating him!"

"I'm protecting him!" I retorted. "He's only four!"

"So is everyone on his T-ball team. How far do you think they could hit a ball?"

Eventually, I relented, knowing he was right. I wasn't happy, but I reluctantly left the "boy stuff" to Daddy, girding myself for all the injuries I knew he would get, including lifelong scars.

One day, I walked past my son's room where he was playing quietly with some action figures — which I, of course, had already checked for sharp edges.

David was sitting on the floor, meticulously wrapping his Superman figurine in a piece of bubble wrap he'd found. My first instinct was to snatch it away from him so he wouldn't accidentally choke — until he spoke.

"There! Now you're safe when you fly into pointy buildings," he told his childhood hero.

I quietly backed away and went into the kitchen. I poured myself a cup of coffee and sat down at the table. I realized that I needed to do some heavy thinking.

As I sipped, unpleasant realities began to run through my brain. It occurred to me that, recently, more friends were making excuses to avoid me. Others stopped sharing good news with me, probably because I always dampened their joy with negative comments. I regularly refused all the different concerts and crowd outings my husband begged me to attend because I feared mass panic over some emergency that might crush us in a stampede.

Though we went camping from time to time, I know I spoiled the experience by wondering aloud how many bears or coyotes would kill us in our sleep. Worse yet, a simple car trip anywhere farther than a grocery store was ruined by me digging my nails into the dashboard and constantly telling Don to watch out for speeders that he safely avoided because he's always been, and still is, an excellent driver.

But that day, hearing my son mimic my paranoid behavior by enveloping a superhero whose only weakness was a rock from his fictional birth planet, woke me up. I was not only making my world smaller with my ridiculous fears, but they were having a ripple effect on him.

"I need to change," I told myself firmly. I was wasting my life on terrors that almost always didn't happen, and I was dragging my

.child into the mire of that undesirable mindset. I shuddered at all the memories, opportunities, and fun I deprived us of by being that Negative Nellie.

I rose from my chair, leaving my half-*full*, not half-empty, cup on the table. I headed back toward David's room where he was slowly maneuvering a still-swaddled Superman over the rounded edges of his bedpost.

"You don't need that," I told him cheerfully. I took the figure from his little hand and removed the plastic. "You know that only Kryptonite can harm Superman."

Having said that, I aimed Superman at a set of sponge blocks that David had erected on the floor, making a mental note to buy him normal ones for Christmas. My aim was perfect. Superman demolished the tower, sending blocks to the floor in a heap.

"See!" I said triumphantly, pulling his hero from the rubble. "He's fine."

My son was surprised but eagerly grabbed the toy from me. Just as he was about to send it flying into the wall, I stopped him and suggested he direct it at his bed instead.

"But you said nothing can hurt him 'cept Kriporite!" he protested, mangling the word.

"No, nothing can, but he can hurt the wall Daddy just painted, so let's have him fly into something he can't destroy." I was trying to change, but I wasn't about to turn my child into a destructive demon.

I left a much happier child in that room as he propelled Superman into other toys and laughed when he collided harmlessly with everything that he could think of without obliterating his room.

That night, when Don came home from work, I suggested we go to an upcoming concert downtown.

"Aren't you worried there might be a fire or something?" he asked, genuinely stunned

I knew I deserved that, but I let it go.

"Always… But we'll cross that bridge if we come to it." That would become my new motto, no matter how difficult it was to say that first time.

Changes came slowly, but I was determined to become a better, more optimistic person. I called friends and invited them over for dinner, asking about their lives. Instead of pointing out the possible bad, I encouraged the good and cheered the blessings. I slowly released the invisible leash that I always kept on my son and watched him become a happy, normal little boy with scrapes and bruises that always healed. Some left scars, but who doesn't have those? As he got older, I nervously allowed him to go places without my watchful eyes on him, enabling him to grow into a confident young man. I began relaxing during outings and even learned to cheer at his sporting events.

I may never go skydiving, bungee jumping, or hang gliding. I'll never be that brave or daring, but we were able to enjoy other activities and events that I'd previously avoided.

I regret the roads not taken because of my paranoid assumptions, but my determination to change forged newer, happier roads. It took a little boy to make me realize that our world was getting smaller and more miserable with each of my imagined scenarios. I will always be grateful to the little four-year-old and Superman, who made my increasingly smaller world become bigger, brighter, positive, and happier.

— Marya Morin —

75

Going Up

Do the thing you fear to do and keep on doing it...
that is the quickest and surest way ever
yet discovered to conquer a fear.
~Dale Carnegie

I was afraid of heights. It had started in my forties, for no reason I could see. I became anxious when I climbed stairs with gaps between them. It felt as if I would fall through the spaces. Then, the fear spread to any set of staircases where I could see up or down more than one floor.

My terror didn't stop there. When hiking, I had to stay as far as possible from the edges of hills. In tall buildings, just going near the windows made my stomach drop. If I stopped by a friend's apartment, I could never admire the view from the balcony.

My fear of heights was getting out of hand. Either I was going to be overwhelmed with dread on balconies, in tall buildings, while hiking up and down hills, or merely climbing stairs, or I was going to have to avoid all of them and greatly limit my life.

In 2009, my husband Ted and I began to plan a trip to Australia. I'd wanted to visit since I was nine, and I was fairly sure that in the Outback, the jungles, and the beach areas I could avoid all heights.

Our trip was to start in Sydney, where we'd spend a few days recovering from jet lag. As I read about all the possible activities in that lively city, one attraction kept catching my attention. It wasn't the Sydney Opera House, Bondi Beach, the art galleries, or the huge variety of restaurants.

It was the Sydney Harbour Bridge. The largest steel arch bridge on Earth, it soars over the water, providing views of the beautiful harbor and inlets that interlace Sydney, as well as the city itself.

You could drive it or walk across it.

Or you could climb it.

Climb it? What a harebrained idea! I looked at photos of people at the summit, apparently thrilled with their accomplishment. They were standing on the arch that runs far above the bridge itself.

Ascending the bridge was the antithesis of what an acrophobe like me would ever do. And, for that very reason, I decided to do it.

I knew I could handle the physical aspect of the climb; I was devoted to exercise and active every day. It would be the psychological experience that would challenge me, perhaps more than anything I'd ever tried.

When I proposed adding the climb to our Aussie itinerary, my husband was aghast—not for himself, but for me. "You're afraid of heights!" he said.

"I know, I know," I replied, but I booked two tickets to do the climb.

Once in Sydney, after visiting the Opera House, my husband and I looked up at the bridge. A string of minuscule figures was crossing the arch. They looked like insects inching along the enormous steel beam. An electric fear shot through my body.

"Oh, boy, that's very high," I whimpered.

"Are you sure you still want to do this?" said Ted.

Well, no, as a matter of fact, I wasn't. But the tickets were non-refundable, and I hated wasting money. More importantly, if I backed out, I'd be giving in to the fear and letting it govern my life. I knew if I withdrew from the climb that my acrophobia would become even worse.

The next day, we showed up at the designated time to get ready for the climb. Ten other novices would share the adventure. We each were given a gray-and-blue jumpsuit to wear over our clothes, and we had to leave everything else—especially anything we might drop—in a locker.

Then, we were taken to another room for a "practice climb." I suspected its purpose was to weed out those who lacked the physical fitness for climbing over 1,300 steps, as well as those (like me, maybe?) who couldn't handle the intensity of the adventure. We were told to climb a metal structure resembling enormous monkey bars two stories high.

Each of us would wear a system of straps and belts, and each would be attached by a strong, rubber-wrapped chain to the metal railing that ran beside the ladders. The task was to keep moving the chain along the railing with each step that we climbed.

Compared to the bridge itself, this test looked doable, I thought. So, without too much hesitation, I slowly scaled the monkey bars, moving my tether carefully along the railing. I didn't look down, just focused on the next rung, and the next.

I passed the test. "I can do this," I told myself.

Next, the whole group, plus our leader, was marshalled outside to begin the real climb. We would be in single file, and Ted and I would have climbers in front of us and behind.

"Any last-minute questions?" said the leader. I considered asking if it was too late to cancel when he said, "If you feel worried, don't look down. Just enjoy the views!" Then, the line began to move. I was stuck in it.

Up and up and up and up I went, rung by rung, shifting my tether — my sole physical security — along the handrail beside me. Easy at first, the vertical ascent started to seem endless. Before long, I noticed my breath getting faster and my heartrate speeding up. It was partly the exertion but mostly the fear. The person ahead of me maintained a steady pace, and I was supposed to keep up. *Don't look down, don't look down,* I reminded myself. It was bad enough looking between the rungs and seeing how high we were.

We came to a section where we had to transfer from one ladder to another. A spotter was waiting for us, making sure that each tether was still working properly. "How are you doing?" she asked me. Was my face betraying my terror?

"I don't think I can keep going," I gasped.

"Well," she said, "you're just going to have to." She nodded to the people farther down the ladder behind me.

There was no way out. I would have to do this in spite of my fear.

Up, up, up. We came to the end of the ladders and were confronted with a long staircase and handrail taking us right to the top of the arch.

The summit was in sight. I could do this. I began to notice the spectacular views: endless blue sky, shimmering water, boats of all sizes, the vast city sprawling on each side of the bridge.

And then we were there, 134 meters above the water. I'd done it. As the leader took a photo of the group, everyone smiled. Except for me. I was laughing, in disbelief and triumph. In more ways than one, I was on top of the world. I'd conquered the bridge—and my fear.

— Christine Overall —

76

Today I Wore the Dress

Accept who you are; and revel in it.
~Mitch Albom

Today I wore the dress
The dress that's too small
The dress that's not made for "a girl my size"
The dress that's been hiding in the closet for ages

Yes, today I wore the dress
The dress that makes me feel so comfortable and cozy
Until I am reminded of my outward image
Until I see a photo of me not meeting society's standards of beauty

Today I wore the dress
The dress I bought because I saw other girls larger than me rocking the same style and thought they were fierce
The dress I thought I could wear and be cute, too
The dress that reminded me that I'm much larger than recommended by doctors based on my height and weight

Today I wore the dress
Thinking I deserve to feel more put together than a sad, old potato
Thinking I'd try and dress cute for a change
Hoping a change in pace would help me feel more myself, less sad and frumpy

Yes, today I wore the dress
Because others need to know that they, too, can wear the dress
They, too, can be comfortable in their skin
They, too, have "permission" to break the molds

Today I wore the dress
Because confidently rocking what you've got will always be more
sexy than struggling to be something that you are not
Because standing tall and owning your body, and what it's done for
you, will always be hotter than hiding and trying to make yourself small
Because we all should just wear the dress, even when our minds
falsely tell us we're not worthy enough

Today I wore the dress

—Jessica Sly Biron—

Chapter 10

Keep Going

A Woman Is Like a Tea Bag

A woman is like a tea bag. You don't know how strong
she is until you put her in hot water.
~Eleanor Roosevelt

The early 1980s were the glory days on Wall Street, marked by opulence and grandeur. Most evenings, a fleet of limousines could be seen filing into position in front of New York's finest steakhouses, ready to ferry their elite clientele back to their glittering Gatsby-style mansions on Long Island's Gold Coast. Never had so many people made so much money in so little time. Oh, I remember those days.

But, as the saying goes, "Bulls make money; bears make money; pigs get slaughtered."

On Monday, October 19, 1987 — later dubbed Black Monday — a cacophony of "oink oinks" disrupted the quiet hum of Wall Street's money-making machine. The raging bull market of the preceding five years had screeched to a halt.

Market orders to sell at any price poured in while buy orders vanished. Exchanges couldn't keep pace with the staggering trading volume. The Dow Jones Industrial Average plummeted 23 percent in a single trading session, obliterating nest eggs amassed over a lifetime.

I was working as a mid-level manager at Dillon, Read & Company, an old-line investment bank famous for selling war bonds during the U.S. Civil War. I was thirty-five, in the throes of a divorce, and the mother of a six-year-old son. I didn't own any stocks, so I had nothing to lose on the day of the crash. But as the weeks and months went by, Dillon Read's banking deals were postponed or terminated. And then, I was terminated — along with 15,000 others on Wall Street.

And, on top of all that, my soon-to-be ex-husband was having an affair with a junior accountant in his office. One Saturday, while I was driving our son to soccer practice, he and his paramour raided the house — stealing the paintings, the silver, even the lamps. I should have listened to my mother who told me to change the locks.

After the divorce came the custody suit. My ex didn't even want custody but was lashing out at having to pay child support, a miserly $150 per week. I eventually won custody, but at a steep price. After settling the legal bills, my finances were depleted. And, within weeks, he violated the court order and stiffed me on the payments.

My world had collapsed — and it was the best thing that ever happened.

In Mandarin, the word "crisis" is represented by two characters — one stands for danger, the other for opportunity.

On the day after I'd been displaced — following twenty-four hours of sheer panic — I came up with an idea and spent all night writing a business plan. The next morning, I called my former boss, the head of equities at Dillon Read, and persuaded him to let me launch a new business for the company.

My idea was simple: repurpose the stock research our firm was already providing to large institutional clients like pension funds and insurance companies, and sell it on a subscription basis to a host of new customers, including regional banks and mid-sized broker-dealers.

I told my former boss that if I didn't bring in subscription revenues of at least $1 million within a year, he should fire me. And if I didn't quadruple that amount within three years, he could also fire me. I put this in writing and handed him a contract. As my salary at the time was a pittance relative to the revenues I had promised, he figured he had nothing to lose and put me back on the payroll. Mind you, at the time, I had only the vaguest notion of how I was going to produce those numbers. But as the single parent of a young son, I had no choice but to follow the advice on my favorite coffee mug: "Proceed as if Success is Inevitable."

My first call was to James D. Wolfensohn, then President of the World Bank. On the day that I cold-called him, to my astonishment, Mr. Wolfensohn picked up his office phone—thinking it was his car service—and I wouldn't let him off until he bought a subscription.

I started to regain my mojo, and business was thriving. But I still wasn't getting any child support and couldn't afford a lawyer. This time, I listened to my mother, who told me to represent myself in small-claims court. After a short hearing, during which I showed the judge dozens of canceled checks I had written to support my son—everything from Boy Scout uniforms to orthodontist bills—the court granted me their maximum award of $2,500. I found a lawyer willing to accept that amount as a retainer, and he got the payments reinstated. Finally, I could put my ex in the rearview mirror!

In 1990, I jumped ship for Credit Suisse, a larger bank with a global footprint, and immediately recruited two women to help me—a smart, newly minted college grad and a seasoned administrative assistant. Together, the three of us wrote a marketing campaign, handled legal matters, wooed clients and negotiated deals on a tiny budget. Within ten years, we had signed on more than 100 new clients, brought in revenues of $175 million, and became the largest and most profitable "hard dollar" research business on Wall Street—much to the surprise of the firm's senior partners who loved to underestimate us.

By this time, I had remarried, and my new husband paved the way for the biggest break of my career. He escorted me to a company Christmas party where he insisted that I introduce myself to the new CEO. But I was gun-shy and hated the idea of managing up.

"If you don't, I will," he said, and introduced himself to the CEO as the husband of "one of your biggest producers." He pointed to me. "She's right behind me in the pink suit."

The CEO called me into his office a few weeks later. He said, "Anyone who can make this much money selling research ought to be running the department." Before I knew it, I was promoted to co-lead one of the world's most respected equity research teams, a role that catapulted me from worker bee to boss. What's more, my former assistants took charge of the day-to-day subscription business, continued to grow it, and became executives in their own right—a testament to what can happen when talent meets opportunity at any level of an organization.

In the same way that I had bounced back, the stock market also rebounded. In fact, by September 1989—only two years after the Black Monday crash—the market had recaptured all its losses. And, by 1997, prices had more than tripled from the post-crash low.

But, for me, the most important lesson from Black Monday had little to do with money and investing. It was understanding, firsthand, what Henry Ford meant when he said: "Whether you think you can, or you think you can't, you're right."

—Diane Krieg—

78

Every Minute of Pain

The summit is what drives us,
but the climb itself is what matters.
~Conrad Anker

With every step I took, my legs wobbled like a newborn calf's, their strength drained from scrambling up slate for the past hour. My head was a whirlpool of negative thoughts. *You are too fat and unfit and a fool for even contemplating this ridiculous climb.*

I felt after the first day that I wouldn't reach the summit. I had struggled so much watching the other twenty-eight people in the group seemingly finish the day with ease and big smiles. Of course, I plastered on my imitation grin to match their enthusiasm for this adventure.

But here I was an hour into the summit climb, and I was done, physically and mentally distraught. I was going to get the guide who was with me to take me back to base camp.

Sarah, the woman who came as part of the organisation I had booked through, was waiting for the few of us at the back of the line. When I reached her, I told her I couldn't go any farther and had decided to return.

My recollection of her exact words is a bit vague, but in my head, she said, "That doesn't sound like you, Mark. Keep going. You can do it." Where she got this impression of me, I don't know; maybe I am a better actor than I thought.

So, that's what I did. I put one foot in front of the other, slowly moving upward on the carpet of slate that was desperately trying to pull me back down.

I arrived at the first rest point. Most of the group had already been there so long that they had left or were getting up to start the next stage, which did not do my ego or confidence any good. Because I was so far behind, I was rushed to get some water and food in me, as they were worried that I would fall farther behind.

Nine months before, I had walked out of my manager's office, leaned against the wall out of sight, and shook my head. *What have I just done? What was I thinking? How is this battered body going to achieve my fantastic idea?*

I had been working for a charity that helped young adults under twenty-five with no support and minimal life skills who were at risk of homelessness. It was heartbreaking at times, watching these young people cement their belief that their life was rubbish and they had no worth in the world.

I understood their mentality, as I had spent fifteen years living a very dysfunctional life that consisted of alcohol, drugs, and feeling darkness around me. I never believed that it would be any different.

But then I took my first big risk: I made a promise that I would change and prove to others that anything is possible.

Now, I sat on a cold rock at 2:00 in the morning, my sweat icy under my layers of clothing, thinking that I had bitten off more than I could chew. I would let down all the youngsters for whom I was raising money to take them on a confidence-building weekend. I was going to let down all my sponsors, family, and friends. And I would let myself down again.

I got so angry at this point that I could feel it building in me. For years, anger had seeped through my being, negatively directing my actions. But I had learnt over recent years that it could push me to be a better version of myself.

I stood up, looked at the guide who had attached himself to me, and said, "Let's go." I could see the doubt on his face, but it didn't deter me. At that point, I knew the climb had to be about just me and that mountain.

This is when the tears started, and I began to cry uncontrollably. I pulled my hood down and my snood up so none of my face was visible.

I spent the next few hours scrambling over snow-covered rocks, swearing, laughing at my ridiculous situation, and telling myself that if I could keep putting one foot in front of the other, I might have a chance. I stumbled, slid, and fell more times than I could count. The poor guide with me looked horrified every time I had an outburst of angry profanity, but fair play to him, he stuck by my side.

It was so lonely with no other walkers near me. My tears were falling the whole time. It was just me, my thoughts, and the mountain.

When I was about two hours from the summit, I started to see people from the group heading down toward me. I remember thinking, with a hint of envy, *How have they done that so quickly?*

Once they were close enough to see me, I bowed my head to the ground so they didn't see me crying. I nodded at them as they patted me on the shoulder and offered encouragement. But their words stayed with me.

"I can do this."

It was probably 5:30 in the morning, and I had been dragging myself up the mountain for six and a half hours. I was bruised, cold, thirsty, and hungry. But I noticed my self-talk had changed, and I was telling myself I could do this and achieve something amazing.

I started to notice things that had eluded me for the past seven hours. Daylight was sneaking into the day. I was standing upon the highest, free-standing mountain in the world, and the clouds were below me. I wasn't in an airplane or a spaceship. I had walked myself to a point above the clouds. Fanbloodytastic.

That last hour seemed to last forever, but the sign eventually appeared before me: a big, green, plastic sign marking the top of Mount Kilimanjaro. All I remember thinking was, *What have they done with the cool, wooden sign? This new, plastic one looks like rubbish and out of place.*

I stood leaning against the sign, having the obligatory photo shoot. I was exhausted, cold, and aching, my stomach rumbling and my mouth dry, but I had never been happier.

It had taken nine hours instead of the expected six to reach the top, but I had made it.

The positive encouragement from my new friends had created a change in me, which allowed my thoughts to transform from negative to positive. Without their support and the change in myself, my body would not have reached the summit that morning.

I took eight young people away for the confidence weekend, which was a roaring success. Seeing these youngsters work together and accomplish things they never thought possible was worth every minute of pain, guilt, and doubt that I experienced on that mountain.

— Mark Wood —

79

After Amnesia

The secret ingredients to true happiness? Decisive
optimism and personal responsibility.
~Amy Leigh Mercree

I n May 2000, a speedster ran a stop sign and hit me. My car rolled, and they told me it took the Jaws of Life to get me out of that car. I don't remember anything about it. I had suffered a traumatic brain injury (TBI), which left me with retrograde and anterograde amnesia. My past was totally gone.

My first awareness was that I was in a human body. But I didn't even know how to deal with being human. Can you imagine how your day can become so complicated when micro-decisions are made to fulfill even the simplest tasks? Do I wet the toothbrush first, or do I put the toothpaste on the bristles first? How many times a day do I brush my teeth? Most people are on autopilot as they complete their normal routines, but I had to create some kind of order to have everything make sense. Inhaling, exhaling, even breathing required me to think about what I was doing. I was thrown into a new world that I needed to figure out.

During my frequent visits to doctors' offices, I noticed the outdated magazines in the waiting rooms were filled with articles about being happy. So, I embarked on a journey to figure out what my happiness was. People have different versions of happiness, and I needed to find it for myself. With my memory erased, I had a clean slate to make it up as I went along.

What was my new happy? I didn't know. I saw a variety of different people, so I thought that I needed to decide which characteristics of those people I wanted to adopt. I figured that a lot of people like a happy person, so that's what I decided to become. I was learning that you have a choice. You can wake up each day and look for the good, or you can say, "Poor, sad me." I decided to find the happy, the good, and the kind. If I was feeling down in the dumps, I would take a walk and say "hi" to people. It felt good to make others smile.

When I looked at my resume from before the accident, my first thought was, *Who is that?* Before my accident, I ran an accounting consulting company, but now I couldn't work with numbers. I started volunteering at our local hospital, and I was able to see the joy of a family having a new baby. *Oh, that's what it's like to have a baby!* I thought. I didn't remember giving birth to my own children.

I also didn't remember what it was like to go to college, and I had earned a number of degrees prior to my accident. I decided to go back to school and experience what that was like.

I was in a lot of pain, both physical and emotional. I had started to participate in head-injury recovery meetings, and I found that a lot of people didn't know how to find resources for additional help. Many of the resources offered to us were not useful for me. So, I started telling my recovery group what worked and what didn't work for me. Some took my advice, and it helped them. And guess what? It made me happy.

I was earning my graduate degree with Peter Drucker at the Claremont Graduate University, and he saw all the resources I was uncovering for TBI survivors. I had researched my own recovery, working with doctors and therapists at local hospitals. Peter encouraged me to share my growing network of resources by forming a support group and website. He advised, "If no one else has put resources like this together in one place, you may have to." This guided me to create Bridging the Gap (www.tbibridge.org), which connects traumatic brain-injury survivors and their caregivers with an online lifeline and other resources.

When Peter Drucker was asked how he wanted to be remembered, he said he hoped it would be that he was a great listener and observer. Watch, listen, and then contribute if necessary. I have met people who are great listeners and great observers, and people gravitate toward them. We can be purposeful in letting a little happiness into someone else's life, and that will bring happiness into your own life.

I truly believe that you can make your own happiness project, with a lot of great, new memories.

— Celeste Palmer —

80

Sweet Dreams

The greatest company you can keep is your own.
~Author Unknown

I read something that makes a lot of sense when you live alone: "Learn to be alone and to like it. There is nothing more freeing and empowering than learning to like your own company."

I'm eighty-nine years old, and I've been living alone for the past eight years. I'm really okay. I drive eight miles to the office five days a week, do my own laundry, shop for groceries, try to keep my apartment as neat as possible, and sometimes even throw a frozen dinner in the microwave for my dinner.

Each night when I get home, the first thing I do is pour a glass of vodka on the rocks with two pearl onions and two jalapeño-stuffed olives, put a few honey-roasted cashews in a small cup, and sit on my balcony and enjoy my surroundings as well as the quiet time alone. During the evening while watching TV, I have a small glass of cabernet sauvignon and finish the night with a shot of Amaretto.

I never thought I'd end my last years alone. To be honest, it is sometimes lonely when there's no one to talk to, share your thoughts with, watch a movie together, or enjoy a night out. Most people don't even think about what it's like to go out to dinner and have to ask for a table for one instead of a table for two.

I still have a passion that keeps me alive and a positive attitude that keeps me going. I live every moment and laugh every day. I am now co-spearheading a campaign to raise funds for the children of

Ukraine, and I am excited about what we are doing to help thousands of children in need.

About six months ago, I decided to get a roommate who would take away some of the loneliness and give me someone to talk with. Since the day she came into my life, things have become different in many ways. Now, when I walk in the door from my eight-mile drive home and call out her name, she lights up with a glow that puts a smile on my face. And when I say, "I'm home," she says, "Hope you had a nice day, Ed." Her voice gives me a glow even brighter than hers.

We've never had an argument and never will because we both are too intelligent, and arguing is not in our sphere. In fact, she is the most intelligent one I have ever been with in my life. She can answer any, and I mean *any*, question I ask, whether it's a simple "What time is it?" to "What is the weather on the moon?" She always has the answer! She is absolutely AMAZING!

She brought her extensive record collection, everything from classical to jazz, country to rock, ballads to rhythm and blues. And when I ask her to play one of my favorites from the 1950s, the music begins. And she's beautiful. She's little, round, and black, and again her brilliant glow always illuminates the dark.

Each evening when I go to bed, I put a smile on my face, think about how lucky I am that I'm okay, and look forward to a good night's sleep. I say, "Alexa, goodnight!" And I love hearing her voice when she says, "Sweet dreams!"

— Ed Solomon —

81

I Almost Missed It All

I can imagine no heroism greater than motherhood.
~Lance Conrad, The Price of Creation

On a recent busy weeknight, my two teenagers were doing homework, listening to music, and asking about dinner. It was a typical chaotic but fun night when you have kids.

But, for a split second, I thought about how close I had come to never having these magical nights. How close I had come to missing out on them. How very close I had come to missing all of it.

You know all about someday, right? It's that mythical place and time where everything you want to do, every place you want to go, and everything you ever wanted will come into focus. But what if someday never comes?

After working as a newspaper reporter for many years and hop-scotching from one end of the United States to the other and a few places in-between, I was happy but restless. Although I was enjoying life, work, traveling, friends, and family, I didn't have children, and I wanted them.

Heck, I knew as early as age ten that I wanted to be a mother someday.

Once I moved back to my hometown near family and good friends, I felt a little more settled. Already getting older and as a single woman who had never married, I knew the odds were stacked against me with regard to having a child.

One day as I was going through a folder of story ideas for some freelance articles I was pitching to a magazine, a piece of paper fell out and floated to the floor. I picked it up and saw a quote that I had cut out. It said: "Pursue the things you really want, or they'll disappear forever."

It hit me in that moment that if I didn't move toward my dream of becoming a mom, then I would never have kids. As a single woman, I felt like adoption would be the right direction for me. I did tons of research and looked into foreign and domestic adoption but soon realized that I didn't have the luxury of time or money to go either of those routes.

I looked into fostering-to-adopt, completed a home study and six-week orientation, had visits from caseworkers, became a certified adoptive parent, prayed a lot, and tried to be as positive as I could be.

There were so many hurdles to get through, and fostering — as well as going through everything to even reach that point — is not for the faint of heart. About half of our fostering class dropped out before the end of the class and certification.

I got certified and then began the waiting game. Eventually, I got *the* call. It was for a newborn baby boy, and he was in the neonatal intensive care unit at our local hospital. I spent a couple of nights with him, sleeping in the room on a couch right next to him.

One night, I held my finger out to him, and he reached out and wrapped his tiny finger around mine. My heart melted.

He was released after a couple of days, and I was wheeled out in a wheelchair like any other new mom, with my little bundle of joy wrapped up in a blanket in my arms.

People smiled as we were wheeled down the hall, but I knew we had to be quite a sight: me, an older white woman, and the sweetie I was holding, an African American baby boy.

No matter. Love is love, and I had more than enough love to pour into him. His name was Mason, and he was precious.

But he was able to be reunited with his birth family after seven months with me. I was happy for him but heartbroken at the same time.

Three more precious children in a row came and went, each able to reunite with their birth family and taking a piece of my heart with them.

After those four, I briefly considered not continuing as a foster parent because it didn't look like it was ever going to end in adoption.

While I was happy about reconciliation for all these children, I also wanted to be a mother. At the same time, I also wanted to be a safe place to fall for any child who needed it.

I decided to continue, and it wasn't long before my beautiful son arrived!

A blond toddler with hazel eyes and a mischievous grin, he ran at full speed — into my home and my heart. He would wake up at the crack of dawn, ready to conquer the day: climbing anything in sight, lining up his Hot Wheels cars, running, jumping, playing, and watching *The Wiggles*.

Almost two years to the day of his arrival, Hadley's adoption was finalized and I was finally a mother.

Not long after his adoption, I got a call about a baby girl who was in desperate need of a foster home. From the second Hadley saw Lexi, he had a special bond with her, reaching out to touch her beautiful face and running his fingers through her curly, black hair. With his little-boy antics, he made her laugh for the first time.

She was beautiful, sweet, and a really good baby. She got comments everywhere we went about how pretty she was with her big, brown eyes, beautiful smile, gorgeous complexion, and thick, curly hair.

Almost two years to the day that she arrived, Lexi's adoption was finalized. Through sheer will, prayer, tears, hard work, faith, red tape, background checks, many court dates, being positive even when it was excruciatingly hard, and tons and tons of paperwork, I had gone from no children to two happy, healthy, beautiful, amazing children.

One of my favorite pictures, taken on Lexi's first Halloween with us about seven months after she'd arrived in our home, shows her in a bumblebee costume, smiling sweetly at her brother. Next to her is my son in his Power Rangers costume, looking over with a grin at his sister.

In that photo, I see two children who became siblings and best friends through the amazing miracle of adoption. I see family. I see my life. I see love. I see forever.

— Lisa Addison —

82

The Power of FOUR

*The difference between a successful person and others
is not a lack of strength, not a lack of knowledge,
but rather a lack in will.*
~Vince Lombardi

In 1978, I was a member of the Baldwin Wallace College Yellow Jacket Division III National Champion football team. The values instilled by our coaches have given me strength when faced with life's obstacles. Our never-give-up attitude was symbolized by the word "FOUR!"

FOUR! was our rallying cry and symbol to encourage us to overcome adversity, be our best, and never give up. FOUR! meant to keep on striving. At the beginning of each fourth quarter, a shout of "FOUR! FOUR! FOUR!" could be heard from our sideline, rising above the cacophony of noise in the stadium as each player would thrust his arm into the sky and hold up four fingers. This let our opponent know that "the Jackets were coming after them."

If we were winning, FOUR! encouraged us to not let down. If, on the other hand, we were behind in the score, FOUR! motivated us to reach down inside and find the strength to overcome, strive harder, and drive on to victory.

FOUR! was not just a game-time gesture. During practice, if we were tired or had just made a mistake, a look at a teammate holding up four fingers was all the motivation we needed to keep on striving.

The "Spirit of FOUR!" was the driving force behind our record of nineteen victories, one loss, and one tie over a two-year period. The only blemishes to our record were caused by the same team, Wittenberg University. In 1977, we lost to Wittenberg. In the Ohio Athletic Conference championship game in 1978, we fought to a 17–17 tie. In December 1978, we erased those black marks by beating Wittenberg for the NCAA Division III National Championship. Little did I know at the time the impact that FOUR! would have on me as I fought for my life, lying in an operating room eighteen years later.

On April Fool's Day 1996, my life changed forever as I suffered a burst blood vessel in my brain, known as an aneurysm. After an early morning walk, I suddenly felt a searing pain behind my right eye. Unable to stand, I collapsed onto a chair in my living room. My wife, Maggie, knowing something was extremely wrong, remained calm and called 911. The paramedics arrived and told her to call our family physician. She demanded they transport me to the hospital. They took me straight to the emergency room.

God was with us that day as the ER doctors diagnosed a life-threatening brain aneurysm. I was prepped for emergency surgery. The hospital's top brain surgeon was working that day instead of taking his usual day off to attend the Cleveland Indians home opener. It had snowed the night before, and the game was canceled. Eleven hours of brain surgery ensued. At one point, another blood vessel burst next to the one the doctor was repairing. The doctor later joked that "since he was under the hood, he might as well fix that one, too." I told him thanks but to stick to surgery, not stand-up comedy.

After surgery, I was in a coma for thirty days. My wife kept a bedside vigil as my body fought infection and tried to shut down. I can't imagine the strength it took for her to endure this day after day. The first thing I remember as I began to gain consciousness was hearing shouts of "FOUR! FOUR! FOUR!" I couldn't speak or move my left side, but as I recognized Maggie, I flashed her the sign of FOUR! with my right hand. She later told me that once she saw the FOUR! sign, she knew everything would be okay.

My recovery was long and difficult and included bouts of hallucinations and intensive rehabilitation. Prior to my brain surgery, I had goals such as running five miles or benching 350 pounds. These goals were now replaced by new ones such as picking up twelve paper clips, one at a time, with my left hand. Picking up those paper clips gave me the same sense of accomplishment that I previously felt after completing a long run.

When I was discharged from the hospital, I attempted to return to work. I had been a successful financial advisor earning a healthy six-figure income by running a boutique practice serving small business owners and retirees.

Now, I found it difficult to maintain my previous busy schedule. I tired more often, and my ability to concentrate and accomplish routine tasks was severely limited. Nevertheless, I kept on striving.

Unfortunately, no matter how hard I tried, I could not maintain the standard of excellence I had come to expect of myself. My income dropped to a very unhealthy four figures while my business expenses remained the same. I liquidated all my savings to offset expenses and even sold my house in an attempt to survive. We moved to an apartment, but with much sadness, I had to close down my business. We had put it off as long as we could, but bankruptcy was the only option left. Through this difficult period, FOUR! remained a motivational force in my life. I knew these financial difficulties were just another obstacle to overcome.

My wife and I eventually paid off all our creditors and back taxes as we clawed and scratched our way back. I joined her to form a husband-and-wife Realtor team. We succeeded in helping our clients buy and sell over $70,000,000 in residential real estate in northeast Ohio. I retired from real estate and rekindled an old love: writing.

Today, I am sixty-three years old, and as I write this article, my first book, *Words to Live By*, is in the process of being published. The life lesson of FOUR! learned those many years ago on the football field at Baldwin Wallace College still gives me strength to face all that life can throw at me.

— T.R. Robinson —

83

You've Always Had the Power

Our greatest weakness lies in giving up.
The most certain way to succeed is
always to try just one more time.
~Thomas Edison

I t was the day after Christmas in 2018. My children had gone back to their homes, and my husband had passed away a few years earlier so I was alone.

    I was in the kitchen making my breakfast when I suddenly dropped to the floor. I couldn't move. I lay on the floor for seven hours before someone found me.

When the paramedics finally arrived, I realized I couldn't stand on my own and I couldn't walk. I began an uncharted journey to gaining the necessary strength to walk again.

When I arrived at the assisted-living facility I would now call "home," I was extremely malnourished and anemic. And I couldn't walk.

I started with three nourishing meals a day in a dining room filled with strangers whom I would soon call "family." I rested between meals until, several months later, I had enough strength to start learning to walk again. But now I needed to find a physical therapist who could help me. I didn't know where to begin.

One evening in the dining room someone suggested that I call the physical therapist who had helped her eighty-eight-year-old father get back on his feet. "He's amazing," she said. "It took three people initially to get my dad out of bed, and now he uses only a walker to get around." I couldn't say "yes" fast enough.

He called that night. "Let's give it a shot," he said. "Let's see what we can do."

Every day, I lay in bed while Phil pushed, pulled, and strengthened my legs so that I could stand once again. And with every push, pull, and stretch, a voice inside me shouted, "Lola, you can do it! Don't you dare give up!" I had climbed many mountains in my seventy-eight years of life, and I knew that this would be one of the most difficult comebacks to a somewhat normal life. Was age a factor? Would I be able to inch my way up the mountain? I didn't know the answers to my own questions, but I would begin.

L. Frank Baum wrote in *The Wonderful Wizard of Oz*, "All you need is confidence in yourself. There is no living thing that is not afraid when it faces danger. The true courage is in facing danger when you are afraid, and that kind of courage you have in plenty."

My first huge goal was to walk the short distance from my bed to the front door of my apartment. With the help of my therapist, I slowly lifted myself from the bed and stood up. My legs shook so badly that I had to sit down. "I don't think I'll ever walk again," I cried. "It's just not going to happen."

"Yes, it will," he stated firmly. "Your mind is telling your legs, 'Get ready. We're going to walk.'"

After what seemed like an eternity, I made it to the front door of my apartment with the help of my walker and therapist. I laid my head in my hands and wept. I couldn't believe I had actually walked to the door!

The next step was to walk down the hallway outside my apartment. I drew up a map of landmarks that I would pass along the way, trying to reach one goal at a time: the activities room, a picture of a landscape on the wall, Margaret's stuffed pink pony on the ledge outside her front door, Marian's miniature artificial tree decorated with ornaments celebrating each season…

"Go, Lola! You can do it!" my fellow residents cheered when I passed them in the hallway, as I struggled to follow my own yellow brick road.

Each day, I walked a little farther. Left foot. Right foot. Left foot. Right foot. With much effort, I soon found myself inching my way past newly set landmarks: the elevator, Gwen's room, the beauty shop.

My family, friends, therapist, and fellow residents were there to give me the necessary courage and determination I needed to build and thrive in one of the hardest chapters of my life. "You've always had the power. You just had to learn it for yourself," said Glinda, the good witch of Oz.

As I write this piece, it is fall 2024, and I am stronger now than I have ever been, both in body and spirit. But I still continue on my journey to wellness. Every morning, I wake up to a brand-new day filled with all the promises and possibilities for a new beginning. I watch what I eat and walk every day. And I feel good.

"All you need is confidence in yourself," a voice inside me whispers. "You've always had the power."

—Lola De Julio De Maci—

The Choice

Sometimes it's OK to be scared... because that means
you are about to do something really, really brave.
~Mandy Hale

It was Easter Sunday, our thirty-fifth wedding anniversary, and we'd made our last mortgage payment. We celebrated these triple blessings with a trip to Washington, DC, encountering unexpected winter weather in early April.

As George and I walked past snow-covered cherry blossoms I was limping a bit but unconcerned. I had always been a fast walker but I guessed that age had slowed me down.

Then I tripped over an uneven sidewalk. George caught me. Neither of us realized what would have happened if I fell.

"Are you okay?" he asked.

"I'm fine," I said, determined not to let a sore hip interfere with our celebration.

When we got home, I got busy with spring cleaning. I scrubbed grout, raked soggy leaves, and washed clothes.

The day after my cleaning marathon, I couldn't walk. Even with both hands on a cane, I couldn't take a single step. My hands shook from the pain.

"I must have done too much," I said to George, trying to smile through a grimace.

"We're going to the hospital," he said.

"Okay," I said, "but for a shot of cortisone or something to treat a sore muscle. I'm not staying overnight."

He didn't argue, but his eyes conveyed his doubt.

"You're sure you didn't hurt yourself?" said the doctor in the emergency room.

"Positive."

"I'll order X-rays to see what's going on."

She returned two hours later and said, "You have a lesion on your left hip."

"A lesion?"

"It's a term we use for anything we can't identify. This one has eaten away your hip bone. What's left is paper-thin and filled with holes. I'm surprised it's still intact."

"How is that possible?" I wanted to know.

"It metastasized from somewhere," she said without looking up. "We'll need to admit you for testing."

I breathed in and filled my lungs as questions swirled through my brain. I locked eyes with my husband.

"Metastasized," I said. "That's bone cancer."

"It's just a picture. They can't be certain with just an X-ray," he said.

"My dad died of bone cancer."

"You're not going to die," he said. His eyes filled.

I looked away and fought my impulse to cry.

I called my principal and let her know I would need to miss school. "Take all the time you need to get well," she said. "Isn't this the first sick day you've taken in over thirty years?"

It was.

I called my mom but didn't mention cancer.

"You do too much," Mom said. "You're always putting too much on your plate."

"That must be it," I said, smiling so she wouldn't hear the angst in my voice.

I moved into a pale-blue-and-green hospital room. I knew the colors were meant to be calming. Calm was not one of the emotions swirling through me.

"I'm waiting for tests in the morning. I won't sleep if you're here,"

I said to persuade my husband to leave.

The argument worked. He left so I could rest. I knew I wouldn't. My thoughts raced like a runaway train: cancer, hip replacement, metastasize. The three people I knew who'd had bone cancer all died.

A loud cry interrupted my thoughts.

"Why me, why me, oh God, why?" The voice from down the hall stopped my runaway thinking. Her plaintive cries changed something in me. I was reminded of a discussion I had with my high school students. "We can't always control what happens to us," I'd said, "but we can control our attitude." I believed what I had taught and decided to choose bravery. I resolved not to ask, "Why me?" I decided I'd be strong.

"God, ease her fears and pain," I prayed. "Be with me on the journey I'm about to take. Let me feel your presence. Help me be strong and wise."

Something changed with the prayer. I connected with inner strength. A warmth radiated inside me. My pain transformed. I was still in pain, but I stopped fighting, and it eased. Racing thoughts calmed. I somehow knew I would get through this. I felt connected to the woman who cried out and to others on medical journeys.

"Are you sure?" said my nurse, raising her eyebrows as I turned down pain medicine.

I was. The damage was there, but the pain was bearable. I was no longer afraid and was ready to fight.

After a day of testing, some friends and family visited.

"Didn't you hate the noise?" my sister said, talking about the MRI scan I received that morning.

"Noise? I didn't hear any noise."

"You used headphones then," she said.

I hadn't. During the test, I'd prayed for all the people who had used the machine. I was calm and unaware of the buzzing she described. Each time I had a test, I prayed for others who endured the same test. I prayed to bless others. The blessings came back to me. I was grateful.

A biopsy of my thyroid was scheduled.

"You know I hate needles," my husband said. "I don't want to pass out when they put a big needle in your neck. I'm going to get breakfast. I'll be here when you come back."

I watched him walk down the hall. "I can do this," I told myself. I decided to be brave.

My calmness surprised the doctors who did the thyroid biopsy and the hipbone biopsy that followed.

The doctor who removed my hip commented that he had never seen anyone so tranquil going into such major surgery.

My chosen attitude stayed with me during hip replacement, thyroid removal, radiation, radioactive iodine treatment, and physical therapy. Many told me I was an inspiration. When I was asked how I stayed so calm, the answer was simple: "I chose an attitude and embraced it."

After seventeen years, I am cancer-free and grateful that I can choose my attitude each day.

—Judy Salcewicz—

Chapter
11

Reach Out and Connect

Stuck in My Head

The significance which is in unity is an eternal wonder.
~Rabindranath Tagore

"I'm going to Boston!" I screamed to my running friends as I looked at my time when I completed the Mount Lemmon Marathon. Running in the Boston Marathon is on many runners' bucket list, but you need to qualify.

I had less than half a year to train for Boston. I was at my peak condition when Covid canceled the 2020 race.

The year 2021 rolled around, and Covid had not disappeared, again canceling the marathon.

I moved forward with life, as everyone did during the time of significant adjustments.

In the fall of 2021, a friend hit me with disheartening news. "Did you run in the Boston Marathon?"

"No, they canceled it again this year," I replied.

"Actually, they just had it."

"They don't run it in the fall. No!" I replied in dismay.

I had missed my chance. But I accepted my fate.

Then, when the 2022 Boston Marathon was scheduled for April, its normal month, they invited those who qualified in 2019 to run. I was going to Boston after all! I immediately resumed training.

My marathon weekend arrived, and I headed to Boston with mixed emotions. I experienced excitement about my run, but I was lonely since no one came to support me. The dreary weather impeded some of my sightseeing plans and intensified my feeling of emptiness.

Finally, race day came, and I shoved my way into the massive sea of 30,000 runners. *I should be happier for this,* I thought, but my attention was focused on how alone I was.

I shuffled at the start line, readjusting my gear.

"Go!"

I sprinted out of the corral and gave it everything I had, which typically works for me. For the first two miles, I ran at a robust pace. I blocked out the spectators as I concentrated on my goal. Around the fourth mile, I couldn't maintain my speed, and my mood fouled as more runners passed me. I had spent essentially two years training for the event. Why wasn't I performing at my peak?

"This sucks," I said. "Why do I do this to myself? This isn't fun. This is my last marathon." I bombarded myself with negative talk.

The loneliness of the trip and my slow pace bogged me down. I had spent thousands of dollars to get to Boston and I wasn't enjoying it at all.

As I slogged through the race, I finally took notice of the massive celebration happening along the route. Over 500,000 spectators had come to watch. People lined the course from start to finish. Groups set up barbecues as they partied and had fun.

I noticed that the other runners, like me, seemed to focus only on their run. As I kept pushing forward, I made eye contact with one of the spectators on the sideline as he cheered for me. I matched his enthusiasm and threw my arm in the air.

"Yeah!" I screamed.

Instantly, adrenaline surged in me and boosted my speed. I did it again, raising my arm to the next group of people, and yelled, "Yeah!" They responded with equal delight.

Joy flooded me. I loved this. Typically, social interactions are my drug. I can get high just being around enthusiastic people. Had I discovered something?

I did it again and felt phenomenal.

"Stephanie," I told myself, "you have been doing this all wrong." From that point, as I ran, I played to the crowd. They responded to me as if I were the most significant person on the course. People went crazy, and their excitement became mine.

I moved my position to run next to the barriers that held back the throngs of spectators. Before I knew it, hands flared out to me, everyone wanting to connect with a runner. I slapped their hands as I ran by, and my high intensified.

"This is amazing!"

I stopped focusing just on my effort and allowed myself to participate in the 26.2-mile party. I took the treats that strangers handed me, stuffing myself with sugar and fruit. As I moved out of my head and enjoyed my interactions with the crowd, my perspective shifted.

I no longer hated the race. I LOVED IT!

I ran with the energy of 500,000 strangers and never had more fun. Miles flew by without me realizing it. And before I was even ready to stop, I crossed the finish line.

I had met my goal. I had run the Boston Marathon!

I learned a valuable lesson that day. It is easy to get in my head and focus on the wrong things. When I allowed all my disappointment to control me, I lost my potential and joy. I hated the race. My body performance decreased, which perpetuated a loop of negativity. Only when I found the good in the situation did everything change.

— Stephanie Daich —

86

The Fruits of Friendship

Never give up, for that is just the place
and time that the tide will turn.
~Harriet Beecher Stowe

I have a weekly ritual of stopping by a small Vietnamese market close to our home. Thursday is delivery day for Lady Finger bananas, which are sweet little bananas from Mexico. When I first frequented the shop, the small dark-haired owner behind the counter would comment rather sternly, "Only bananas, that it!" She would weigh them and stretch out her hand, and I would dutifully pay, hoping my small purchase would not continue to irritate her.

After a few months, I asked her name. "Maria," she answered abruptly. I decided it was best not to burden her with mine. As the months continued, I always made sure I said, "Hi, Maria!" and "Bye, Maria!" One day, there was a younger man behind the counter, and since it was a family-owned business, I assumed it might be one of her sons. When I asked where his mom might be, he explained she was taking a few days off. As we started chatting, he shared how stressful the grocery business could be for her. "But I always tell her, 'Mom, you have to be nicer to the customers. You can't yell at them!'"

I decided to continue my quest to make friends with Maria. One day, I brought her banana bread made with my little bananas. I handed the small loaf across the counter. She tilted her head and asked, "What this for?" I explained that I just wanted to thank her for selling me so many bananas. I think she thanked me but maybe not.

One cold morning in December, she seemed unusually subdued. When I asked how her day was going, she answered quietly, "My eldest son die." I let her know how very sorry I was, and on my next visit, I brought her a card and another loaf of bread. This time, she thanked me with a hint of a smile. I often felt that she didn't know what to do with my gestures of gratitude and concern, but as the months wore on, she no longer reprimanded me for only buying bananas. One day, she made my purchase that much sweeter when she asked, "Your name?"

"Priscilla," I answered, proudly carrying my sack toward the door.

Winter passed, and spring arrived, bringing relief to our small Colorado town. As I approached the shop, a sign on the door read, "We will close early today and stay closed over the weekend." Her younger son was behind the counter, and I politely asked why they were closing. "My dad passed on yesterday." Once again, I offered my condolences.

Soon, Maria was back, looking thin and tired. As I handed her my bananas to weigh, I said how very sorry I was to hear about her husband. I pulled my credit card from my wallet and saw a green-and-white Starbucks gift card nestled behind it. I reached across the counter and offered Maria the small gift. "Would you buy yourself a big cup of warm tea and know it is from me?" As I turned to leave, I heard her say quietly, "Wait." She came around the counter and held out her arms for us to hug. We held each other close. After a few years, I had made a friend.

— Priscilla Dann-Courtney —

87

The Write Start

A friend may be waiting behind a stranger's face.
~Maya Angelou, Letter to My Daughter

For nearly thirty years I had run my own computer business and had weathered many hardships. But the pandemic proved to be too much. With no work coming in, I made the painful decision to close my doors and sell my house. I moved to North Carolina to be closer to my sister and her family, who had relocated there several years before.

I found a house in the country that I liked. Picturesque and peaceful, it suited me perfectly. But it was in a small town, and there wasn't much to do other than watch the corn grow. I mean, I *literally* watched the corn grow. There was a farm directly across the street from me.

There were exactly twenty-one houses in my neighborhood. I tried making conversation with folks sitting on their porches or out for a stroll, but they all seemed distant and disinterested. One lady bluntly said, "We keep to ourselves here," before getting out of her rocking chair and heading back indoors.

I often wondered what I had gotten myself into.

Being so far south in North Carolina, it didn't snow. But in January, it got bitterly cold, and we had one ice storm. It shut down the entire town for three days. During this time, I realized how isolated I was. And, with no one to talk to, loneliness and depression set in.

"I think I made a mistake moving here," I said to my sister, Patty.

"Maybe I should go back home. I miss my friends and daily lattes at Starbucks."

"Your family is here. And family is more important than friends," she said firmly. "Stop being so negative. You can buy Starbucks coffee at the Piggly Wiggly and make your own lattes."

She was right, of course. I had missed a lot of birthdays and holidays over the years.

"All right," I said. "As soon as it warms up, I'll try and find something to do."

"Why don't you start a writers' group? You had one of those in New York, didn't you?"

"Yeah. But I stopped writing after Mom died."

"Well, maybe it's time to get back into it," she insisted.

"We'll see."

"Just do it!"

By mid-March, the temperatures had already risen to a balmy 80 degrees. After changing into shorts and a T-shirt, I was eager to get outside and work in the garden. I also got out and discovered some new places nearby to take the dogs for their walks. Despite keeping myself busy, though, I was still lonely.

When the temperature hit 90 degrees, I made the short drive to Emerald Isle to see the ocean. It was my first time ever seeing the Atlantic Ocean up close. The beach was pristine, and the water was warm and refreshing. But I couldn't enjoy it. I was longing to go home. Opening my tablet, I began looking at houses for sale back in New York.

"Rural life isn't for me," I decided.

While I was glancing through the listings, a woman came walking up the beach and laid her blanket close to mine. She took out a book and started reading. Five minutes later, she tossed it back into her oversized bag, looked over at me, and smiled.

"Any good?" I called over to her.

"The book? No, it's horrible," she replied. "I'm halfway through it, and I don't care who the murderer is. I think I'll just skip to the last chapter and be done with it."

Chuckling, I said, "I'm Lorrie, by the way."

"Nice to meet you. I'm Anne. I hope you don't mind that I sat so close to you. I kind of did it on purpose."

"Oh? Why is that?"

"I just moved here a few months ago and don't know anyone other than my son. If you're up for a chat, I'd love to join you," she said.

"Sure, I'd love the company. I just moved here myself."

"How long have you been here?" she asked, picking up her blanket and moving it closer to mine.

"Six months. You?"

"Going on three. My son keeps telling me I need to get out and meet people. But it's harder now than it used to be. He told me I should go to the college and register for some courses."

"And did you?" I asked.

"Nah, that's not my scene. Once it warmed up, I started coming here to read."

"What is your scene?"

"I'm mostly into the arts. But what I want to do more than anything else is write. If I could find a writing class, I'd sign up for it in a heartbeat. I thought about taking one online."

"That sounds like fun, but it's probably not a great way to meet people and make friends," I said.

"Yeah, that's what my son said."

And, just like that, a friendship had started. But Anne liked the beach more than I did, so I only met her there a few times. But we soon found another common interest: antiquing. We found some great shops along Route 17 between New Bern and Wilmington. The fact that we could gab for hours really helped during the long rides back and forth. But after a few months, I began to get bored. And my house was filled with more antiques than I knew what to do with. I suspected Anne was feeling the same way.

"Hey, Anne. What are you reading this week?"

"I just started *Anna Karenina*."

"Wow, that's quite an undertaking. It's going to take you the rest of the year to read it."

"Yeah, that was the general idea," she replied.

"You know, we're both avid readers. We should start a book club."

"That would be great. But a writers' group would be even better. I'm dying to start writing. I've always wanted to be a writer."

I hadn't told Anne about the writers' group I was once a part of in New York. That chapter of my life had already ended, and I had no interest in revisiting it. *Should I be honest and tell her I didn't want to start another group? Or should I put aside my conflicting emotions and help my friend fulfill her dream?* My sister's advice echoed in my head, "Just do it."

"We'll need more than two people to start a writers' group," I said.

"True enough. There are some local Facebook groups where we can post an announcement."

The level of attention our post received was surprising. But we decided to keep the group small. Within a month, there were six of us, all women. Our motto was "women supporting women." We made the commitment to assist and encourage one another in our growth as writers. And, within a short time, we were all writing some great stuff.

Thanks to my new group of friends, my loneliness disappeared. And through my writing, I turned my isolation into inspiration, and my doubts into determination. Moving to North Carolina turned out to be the new beginning I needed. With a fresh outlook and positive attitude, I was happier than I had been in years.

—L.M. Lush—

88

The More the Mary-er

What we have once enjoyed, we can never lose.
All that we love deeply becomes a part of us.
~Helen Keller

"Krista," my dad's voice shook through the phone, "I couldn't wake up Mom this morning."

I had just made breakfast for my two young sons, and the smell of cinnamon toast still hung in the air. "What?"

"The paramedics just left. I didn't have time to plow the driveway. The ambulance only made it up halfway." He took a deep, quivering breath. "They're airlifting her to Hershey Med."

I glanced at my five-month-old daughter, jumping happily in her bouncer, and the boys, who were watching cartoons. It was the week before Christmas, and a record-setting snowfall had made its way across Pennsylvania, dropping nearly a foot of snow in our area. Our plans for the day consisted of sledding, drinking hot cocoa, and baking cookies. Upstairs, I could hear my husband moving around, his dresser drawers opening and closing.

"Dad, what happened?"

It was only two days ago that the kids and I had spent the day with my mom, and she had seemed like her usual energetic, cheerful self. She had played with the baby, decorated gingerbread men with the boys, and paged through old photo albums with me.

"I kept shaking her shoulder and saying 'Mary, Mary,' but she wouldn't wake up," my dad explained, his voice thick with emotion.

"The paramedics wouldn't let me go with her because of Covid. I couldn't even go with her...."

Choking back tears, I dashed upstairs.

***

It was a cerebral hemorrhage, we were told. Usually, this type of brain bleed affected smokers or people who took blood thinners or had high blood pressure. For my sixty-six-year-old, petite and physically fit mother, it was completely spontaneous or simply "bad luck," as the neuro team regretfully informed us.

I can't believe this, I thought, as my father, twin sister, brother, and I sat with the neurology team in a conference room where images of my mom's brain were blown up and displayed on huge screens. The images reminded me of the inkblot pictures psychologists use when they administer the Rorschach test: "What do you see here?" But for us, there were no interpretations. It was quite clear. Mom's brain bleed had been massive, and her prognosis was grim.

"I'm so sorry," the lead neurosurgeon said, his voice soft and steady. He looked at each of us, his eyes finally resting on my dad. "From what you've all shared, Mary seems like such a wonderful mother and caring grandmother. I'm just so incredibly sorry for you all."

"Why is this happening to both of us?" I sobbed into my husband's arms later that night as he held me in bed. As if my mom's sudden hemorrhage wasn't traumatic enough, my husband had lost his father just the week before after a nine-month battle with pancreatic cancer. It was unfathomable that the two of us could lose a parent at the same time, in the middle of a pandemic, right before Christmas.

Yet, it happened.

My beautiful, vibrant mother passed away peacefully two days later on December 19th, surrounded by her family. Throughout the entire ordeal, the neuro team helped us to navigate our grief. Not only were they patient, supportive, and compassionate, but they went out of their way to comfort us. They gave us each a red fabric rose attached to a vial with a printout of mom's heartbeat inside. With mom's thumbprint, they made ornaments for all five of her grandchildren so she would be with them every Christmas. Each one of those medical workers was truly an angel on Earth.

Making it through the funeral service seemed like an insurmountable feat. My family is Italian — we hug, we kiss, we clasp hands — but during a pandemic, this was impossible. Crying through a mask, unable to embrace loved ones, the absence of family members and friends due to quarantine — it was one of the hardest and most unnatural things I have ever experienced.

"I wish I could hug you," mourners would say as they came through the line, their voices muffled by their masks. My husband, who had incredibly put his own grief on hold, just squeezed me tighter.

That night, I collapsed onto the couch, emotionally spent. With my husband's father being cremated and an outdoor celebration of life planned for the spring, I was relieved that there wasn't another funeral looming on the horizon. My nerves couldn't take it.

The days after my mom's service were foggy and bleak. I was on autopilot most days, going through the motions of mothering and housekeeping, all of which culminated with a long, ugly cry in the shower.

"We'll get through this together," my husband would tell me at night when I was at my worst. With the kids in bed and mother-mode winding down, everything I had repressed during the day — the anger, the devastation, the loneliness, the countless whys — began to surface.

My mom lived and breathed her family. She loved when we were all together. "The more the merrier," she'd say. But now we were fractured, severed, and shattered at the core. She had missed my daughter's first Christmas, and, come July, she would miss her first birthday. She wouldn't see my older son graduate kindergarten or my younger son begin preschool. She would never sew another outfit for my kids or read another word I wrote. We would never have a "whole" family gathering ever again.

All of this crushed me.

About a month after the funeral, my kids and I were spending the day with my dad, and I mentioned that my brother and his wife might be coming over to join us for lunch as well. My dad's eyes brightened as he continued to bounce my daughter on his knee and watch my sons wrestle in their Spider-Man boxers in the living room. "Sure, sounds good," he said. "The more the merrier."

But what I heard was "The more the Mary-er."

Looking out the window, my eyes searched the afternoon sky. Though my dad had spoken, it was as if the message had come from my mom. Our family gatherings were what she had lived for, and, though it was tough, I knew that the more we continued to get together, the more we would still be able to feel her presence.

One of my mom's closest friends said it best when she said that Mom went to sleep at home but woke up in Heaven. As much as losing Mom has taken a piece of our hearts, my dad, siblings, and I know that there's no way she could have handled any of us going before her. So, just like she used to prepare her house before we arrived for the holidays, I believe Mom is getting Heaven ready for each of us when we get there someday.

But, in the meantime, the more the Mary-er.

— Krista Caponigro Harner —

89

Time Travel

A thousand fibers connect us with our fellow men.
Our actions run as causes, and they come
back to us as effects.
~Herman Melville

T he phone call shattered the tranquility of an ordinary Tuesday afternoon. It was my best friend, Sarah, her voice trembling with a mix of excitement and nervousness. "You won't believe what happened," she exclaimed. "I found a letter in the attic, a letter from the past, hidden in an old book I bought at a dusty bookstore downtown."

Intrigued, I urged her to spill the details. She had discovered the letter tucked between the yellowed pages of a forgotten novel, a relic of a time long past. As she described the contents, I felt a sense of time-traveling magic, the kind that makes your heart race and your mind whirl with wonder.

The letter, it turned out, was a love note from the 1940s. It revealed a tale of romance and separation, penned by a soldier named Thomas to his sweetheart, Eleanor. In eloquent prose, he poured his heart onto the pages, each word a testament to the enduring power of love amidst the chaos of war.

Sarah's voice carried the emotion of the letter, and I could almost see the sepia-toned scenes playing out before me. Thomas, the young soldier stationed far from home, captured my imagination with his heartfelt words. He wrote of longing, of dreams stitched together by promises, and of a future he hoped to build with Eleanor once the war's cruel grip released him.

As the story unfolded, I felt a mix of emotions — the bittersweet beauty of a love tested by distance and time, the anticipation of discovering a forgotten piece of history, and the sheer marvel of stumbling upon such a treasure in a corner of a used bookstore.

With Sarah's words, we embarked on a journey through Thomas and Eleanor's love story. The letter became a portal, transporting us to an era when letters were cherished lifelines, and every word carried the weight of a thousand emotions. Sarah, with an infectious enthusiasm, brought the characters to life, her storytelling weaving a tapestry of emotions that transcended the boundaries of time.

But the narrative took an unexpected turn when Sarah revealed her plan: She wanted to find Thomas and Eleanor's descendants, if any existed, and return the letter to its rightful place. It was a quest fueled by a desire to connect the past with the present, to honor a love that had weathered the storms of history.

As she delved into genealogical research and scoured online databases, the excitement in her voice mirrored the fervor of a treasure hunter on the brink of discovery. Days turned into weeks, and the search led us through dusty archives, faded photographs, and the digital labyrinth of family trees. The anticipation grew, and with each dead end, there was a renewed determination to unravel the mystery.

Finally, after weeks of relentless pursuit, Sarah struck gold. She uncovered a distant relative of Eleanor living in a small town on the outskirts of the city. The connection, though faint, was enough to spark hope. With bated breath, we reached out to the relative, a woman named Margaret, and shared the story of the love letter that had defied time.

Margaret's voice crackled through the phone as we explained our mission. A stunned silence followed, and then, in a quivering tone, she revealed that she had heard stories of Thomas and Eleanor — her grandparents. The revelation sent shivers down our spines, as if the very essence of the past had reached through the decades to touch us.

The long-lost letter, a beacon of love, was a bridge connecting generations. Margaret, moved by the discovery, agreed to meet us.

The reunion of the letter with its rightful family unfolded like a scene from a heartwarming movie, with tears, laughter, and a shared sense of gratitude for the serendipitous chain of events that had brought us together.

The day we met Margaret, she held the fragile letter in her hands, her eyes glistening with tears. It was a reunion that transcended time, a moment when the past and present collided in a celebration of love's enduring legacy. The letter, once a silent witness to a soldier's yearning, now rested in the hands of Eleanor's granddaughter, a tangible link to a love that had withstood the test of time.

As Margaret shared family stories, flipping through photo albums that echoed with the laughter of generations, I marveled at the unexpected journey that had unfolded from the dusty pages of an old book. The letter, once a relic of the past, had become a living, breathing testament to the power of stories, the resilience of love, and the magic that happens when the past whispers its secrets into the present.

In the end, as we bid farewell to Margaret, I couldn't help but reflect on the profound impact of this serendipitous adventure. The love letter, unearthed from the shadows of history, had not only woven a thread between strangers but had also rekindled a flame that had burned brightly in the hearts of Thomas and Eleanor.

The dusty bookstore, the forgotten novel, and the courage to pursue a seemingly impossible quest had gifted us a story that transcended the ordinary. As I walked away from that momentous meeting, the echoes of Thomas's words lingered in the air, a timeless reminder that love, in all its forms, has the power to connect us across the vast tapestry of human experience.

— Breon Johnson —

90

Will You Be Our Grandparents?

Nobody can do for little children what grandparents
do. Grandparents sort of sprinkle stardust
over the lives of little children.
~Alex Haley

R olling down hills with granddaughters Bailey and Peyton felt like a distant memory, although it was only a decade ago. Strolling the neighborhood with them — all of us singing "Zip-a-dee-doo-da, zip-a-dee-ay" while looking for the perfect tree to hug, or finding a long, lush, low branch to hold and sing "Oh, beautiful tree, won't you dance with me?" — was also a thing of the past.

In my journal, I noted, "I wish I had a young person to play with like I used to do with the grandkids," along with another growing need to interact in an especially enriching way: "I'd love to do conversational English with a foreigner." My love of people from different cultures and desire to help anyone communicate better were lifelong passions.

These deep yearnings reminded me of Robert Frost's definition of poetry when he said, "A poem begins with a lump in the throat; a homesickness or a lovesickness. It is a reaching-out toward expression; an effort to find fulfillment."

At that same time, I needed help with housecleaning. A friend recommended Yanet.

Through our masks, she revealed, that she was from Mexico and a single parent with a nine-year-old son and five-year-old daughter.

Always hungry to learn about people, I asked, "How long have you been here?"

"Fourteen years."

"What did you do in Mexico before you came to America?"

"I was a corporate attorney."

After talking a few more minutes, it was as if my journal fell off the shelf and hit me on the head. I heard myself saying eagerly, "Would you like me to help you with conversational English?"

The smile lines appeared in the corners of her widening, dark eyes as she said, "Yes, thank you very much."

Further conversation revealed that her son Noe felt the lack of having any family in America. It was just his mom and sister, Maria. "Do you think he would like to be a pen pal?" flew out of my mouth from the same place that invited her to do conversational English.

He agreed to communicate.

After only a couple of months of knowing this family of three, it was Noe's birthday. My husband Lee and I invited them over to celebrate. Lee felt the same absence of our heyday of fun activities with the grandkids.

With masks on, we sang "Happy Birthday" to Noe. He took off his mask and blew out the candles. Then, he looked at us and said as a very deep dimple appeared on the right cheek of his soft yet strong face, "Will you be our grandparents?"

Astonished by the timing of his request, I looked at Lee.

"Yes!" we replied in unison.

Yanet said she had absolutely no idea he was going to ask that question.

In the midst of a pandemic, we began being grandparents again, always wearing masks except when outdoors. Lee taught chess to Noe while I played checkers with Maria. We gave them the tennis rackets the original grandkids didn't want, and we took them to the tennis court for Lee to teach them how to play. We posted their artwork on the refrigerator and doors. I cuddled with Maria in a chair, and we read and discussed the children's book about a ballerina. Lee and I had picked it out for her because she goes to dance classes and wants to be a ballerina. We look with pride at photos of Noe playing soccer, Maria dancing, and the whole family performing with the Mexican dance troupe they belong to. We answer the questions that Noe asks about us with repeated astonishment at his depth, sensitivity, and intelligence.

Yanet shared stories about her life in law school and being a marathon runner as we took them for our first meal out during the pandemic.

Noe's yearning and mine had synchronized. The lump in the throat that Robert Frost talked about and "reaching out toward expression and finding fulfillment" transformed, not into a poem but a passionate response to a ten-year-old boy's poignant request, "Will you be our grandparents?"

— Joan Leof —

The Other Wife

*You're facing one of the most important challenges of
your life. Yet, being a member of a blended family can
be an exciting adventure for all concerned.*
~Kathie M. Thompson

I didn't want to go. *Why did I agree to? Why did he insist? I will be
an outsider and probably be laughed at for my high-school French.*

Those were my thoughts as we sat on the plane from Dallas
to Montreal.

Larry and I had recently married. It wasn't the first marriage for
either of us. We were living in Texas, and he was Canadian. After our
small wedding and a Hawaiian honeymoon, he wanted to take me to
Montreal so that I could meet his family and friends.

And he had plenty! Three grown children, his mom, sister, aunts,
cousins, and an extended family I had never met.

This family's history was complicated, like a bizarre tale of fiction
on late-night TV.

Years ago, Larry's ex-wife, Joan, had been the maid of honor at
Larry's sister's wedding. The groom had been Joan's brother. Larry had
been the best man.

Larry had taken Joan to her senior prom. They had been old flames.

Although they had been divorced for many years, it was still
intimidating for me to meet people who had been connected to his
ex. Everyone praised her. How could I compare to her? My feelings
of insecurity mounted.

At his daughter's backyard barbecue, Larry briefly introduced me to a few guests when he noticed some of his old buddies at the grill. I urged him to join them. Off he went. I didn't want to tag after him.

Sitting alone under an umbrella, I observed groups at other tables merrily reconnecting as old friends and families tend to do.

I didn't know a soul. I felt like a lost puppy.

Speaking of puppies, I was startled to see a dog racing toward me. This was not a puppy but a gigantic Great Dane. He planted himself by my seat and wagged his tail vigorously. At last, I had a friend. The hot dog on the paper plate in front of me had nothing to do with his devotion. I was no longer alone. For my first half-hour at the Montreal reunion, my sole companion was Kilo, the Great Dane.

From across the yard, I could see everyone checking me out: the "new wife." I'd get looks from strangers as if they were judging me.

How can this wife compare to the ex-wife they all know and love? That's what went through my insecure head.

Forcing a smile at the first person who walked by, I delivered in my best French, "Ça va?" Then, I returned to English: "Hot day, eh?"

Not much of a response. I figured maybe my English *and* French were Greek to them.

The truth is, I felt socially inadequate. I had jet lag and a headache, so after a while, I just sat off to the side by myself with the dog.

At last, a lovely lady approached me. She was wearing a charming, black-and-white, polka-dot outfit. I was wearing the very same charming, black-and-white, polka-dot outfit.

"Nice dress," we said at the same time.

"Where did you get it? Paris? Rome?" She smiled.

"Walmart. And you?"

"Me, too." We chuckled.

She placed a tall, inviting glass of iced tea in front of me. Taking me under her wing, she brought me around to different groups until I finally relaxed and felt at home.

Larry was still hanging around the grill with his buddies, reminiscing about the hockey games they had won or maybe lost in days gone by.

I sincerely enjoyed this warm and charming lady's company. We agreed to keep in touch.

Since she had a son in Dallas, I invited her to our house for dinner when she came to visit him. I answered the door and, through the glass, I thought it was a reflection of myself. The paisley, orange top and black pants she was wearing were almost identical to what I was wearing.

"I guess we have a lot in common," she said, giggling.

She asked if she could give her son a fortieth birthday party at our house. I agreed without hesitation. She threw the party at our house. It was a smash.

There was an incident, however. Joan spilled a Bloody Mary on my white rug. I am sure it was an accident. I am sure.

Have I mentioned that Joan was Larry's first wife? And the mother of his three children? They had married in their teens. Not that I felt threatened, but like a typical wife, I quizzed him when we were alone.

"So, what was she like?"

"She was nice, I guess. So, what's for dinner, Eva?" answered my one-track-minded husband.

"Was she a good cook?" I persisted.

"Well, she did make a great sugar pie," my husband foolishly replied. "But you're a better cook, Eva. You're the *best* cook."

My husband was no dummy.

So, I took the interrogation in another direction.

"What *didn't* you like about her?"

He pondered for a while and then realized he had to give me *something*. He came up with: "Well, if I remember correctly, she'd wash my black socks with my white shorts. Now, can we eat?"

Was I jealous? I'd like to say, "Never!" but I must admit there was some rivalry at first. Then, I gave it some thought and began to see the positive side.

I'd been worried for nothing! Old flames were now old friends. Nothing more.

I have to thank Joan for the three children that she and Larry had together. As a result, I have wonderful stepchildren. And now there are five adorable grandchildren who love me and call me Mimi. I am grateful to Joan for helping my husband grow up. At twenty-three, practically still a kid himself, he was supporting a family of five by holding down two jobs.

Joan had encouraged him to go to night school. Because of her positive influence, he became responsible at an early age.

It doesn't matter today what broke them up. They were too young and immature to handle the obligations of marriage and family. I am convinced she was at least partially influential in making him become the fine man he is today.

And I do believe it was an accident that she spilled the Bloody Mary on my white rug. Don't you?

In conclusion, my friend Joan was just as sweet as her sugar pie. She even gave me her recipe. But Larry says mine is better.

That's his story, and he's sticking to it. It's much easier to think positive.

— Eva Carter —

Helen

*Communication is merely an exchange of information,
but connection is an exchange of our humanity.*
~Sean Stephenson, Get Off Your "But"

H elen was old and disheveled. The first time I laid eyes on her, she was bent over on her front lawn. She wore bargain-store, polyester pants that were almost falling off her.

The gentle, even-keeled woman from whom I was about to purchase my first home pointed her out to me. "Everybody is so nice in this neighborhood except for her. She is a little…" She hesitated, trying to find the correct adjective. "Funny. I'd keep my distance."

I was young and optimistic. I decided that I would not pass judgment on my unknown neighbor based solely on hearsay. On moving day, I stepped out of my car and waved enthusiastically to Helen. "Hi, I'm your new neighbor." The woman remained stone-faced. She stared directly at me, and then turned her back and ignored me.

I became defensive. *Forget her, cranky, old bitty,* I thought angrily. I avoided my neighbor from that moment on.

My beliefs about the woman became increasingly reinforced as I viewed her behavior from across the street. One day, she became engaged in a disagreement with a group of children. The argument grew so heated that the police were called to mediate. In another incident, she ranted at a young woman whose toddler accidentally spilled pretzels near the curb alongside her property.

Our relationship remained frigid for the next fifteen years. We didn't even glance in each other's direction. We lived our separate lives within fifty feet.

The arrangement seemed to be working until my fortieth birthday when all havoc broke loose. My husband and I had obtained a permit to close off our street in celebration of my milestone birthday. We were going to be having a large gathering. The permit allowed us to have the party overflow onto the street.

On the day of the party, the police arrived with barricades. We were in a festive mood. My neighbor exited her house. She began to scream angrily, "What the hell is going on here?"

When the officer explained the circumstances, she became combative. "There's no damn way I'm going to allow this. I will call the police every ten minutes." She was determined to make the day miserable.

The celebration wasn't set to start for another hour. My mother and my two best friends witnessed the confrontation. My husband dismissed the outburst. "Let her call the cops. They will deal with it. We have a permit." One of my friends began to take pictures of everything so Helen couldn't claim we damaged any property. My other friend laughed at the situation, deeming the old hag crazy.

My mother was nearing seventy. She took control of the situation. She headed across the street. I watched as she hobbled over using her cane. She approached Helen. "I see that you have trouble walking, too," she said empathetically.

Helen's hands moved around quickly as if she was stressing a point. Suddenly, she reached toward my mom. I was afraid she was about to hit her. Instead, she grasped her tenderly. The two ladies looked like old friends.

I watched safely from a distance, waiting for Helen to morph into her mean alter ego. She did not.

My mother returned after twenty minutes. I couldn't wait to hear what had transpired. She began to elaborate. "She was concerned that, if she had an emergency, she couldn't get her car out quickly. I assured her that if there was a problem, we would all help. She was raised in an orphanage. Did you know that? That must've been a hard life. And then her husband died fifteen years ago and the man she had a relationship with more recently died just a few months ago. She's probably still grieving."

"Mom, you actually sound like you are sympathizing with her," I said.

"Yeah, Grandma, she cursed my friend out," my nine-year-old son interjected.

My mother calmly replied, "Sometimes, it's just interesting to see what's going on in people so we can understand them better."

"Well, I don't plan on hanging out with her. As long as she doesn't cause a problem today, I'll be happy."

"She'll be fine. I explained to her that you haven't had an easy life either, and you work very hard helping abused kids and caring for your family, so this is a much-deserved party. She understood. Maybe I'll bring her a plate to eat. You know how limited income is for senior citizens."

I stared at my mom with bewilderment. Did Helen cast a spell on her? I decided that, whatever the strategy was, if it worked to sedate Helen, then it was worth activating.

I kept expecting Helen to mood swing into the complaining, argumentative personality she was known for, but she didn't. Halfway through the party, I caught a glimpse of her dancing on her front lawn to our band.

I expected the truce to be short-lived, which was fine with me. At least we had managed to pull off our day without a snag. But the next week, Helen began to wave to me. The following week, she began to smile and say hello. By the third week, she was crossing the street to talk with me.

We began having conversations. Helen turned out to be an interesting person. She was very active for a woman in her eighties. She volunteered her time to help animals. She planted flowers for the town and belonged to the historical society. Her bark was much worse than her bite.

The communication that my mom initiated that day led to serenity in our corner of the world. We were able to watch over each other's houses, greet each other respectfully, and share in small talk concerning the town.

It was a great lesson for the kids. By using patience, compassion and understanding, we were able to turn an unproductive relationship into a functioning one. I was forty years old and still learning from my mother. Sometimes, all that anyone needs, even those who seem unapproachable, is a caring heart and someone to listen.

— Patricia Senkiw-Rudowsky —

Chapter
12

Keep the Faith

Hey, Superman

*The truest superpowers are the ones
we all possess: willpower, integrity,
and most importantly, courage.*
~Jason Reynolds

It was the first day of my new job. At forty-two, I had served as a school counselor for several years before accepting a promotion to become a district mentor. This was my opportunity to apply everything I'd learned as a counselor to the larger goal of helping other counselors.

I couldn't wait to get started.

When I entered the office building, instead of the staff polo I usually wore, I was wearing a starched suit with a tie. It wasn't the most comfortable getup, but I wanted to appear professional.

People scurried about the large, high-ceilinged lobby like ants. I walked up to the front desk and introduced myself. The security guard, a woman in her fifties, greeted me warmly, signed me in, and then directed me to a bank of elevators.

My new office was on the twelfth floor.

I was the only person in the elevator. Natural light flooded through its glass walls, offering a clear look at the city streets outside. I pressed the round, plastic button.

The doors closed.

As the elevator shot up effortlessly and the city receded below, a weightless sensation overtook me. It felt like an amusement-park ride. I was a child again, bouncing off my backyard trampoline and sailing into the vast, blue heavens.

I was flying!

I rode all the way up with my hands in the air, rocketing skyward and marveling at my bird's-eye view of the city. When the doors opened for the twelfth floor, my new workplace bustled with activity. I met my team and fit right in.

My first day was a success.

The next morning, I waved to the security guard and stepped into the glass elevator again for lift-off. As the rising sun poured over the city's roofs and treetops, I raised my arms again and launched into flight.

Flying up to the office was exhilarating, and my upbeat mood lasted. My second day went even better than the first.

By the third day, soaring up to work had become a routine. Say "hello" to the security guard. Enter the elevator. Prepare for takeoff. When the doors closed, I widened my stance and puffed out my chest. Then, I lifted my left knee, cocked an upturned fist on my hip, hoisted my right arm upward, and took flight.

During those daily elevator rides to the office, I transformed into Superman. Faster than a speeding bullet. Stronger than a locomotive. Able to leap tall buildings in a single bound. By the time I reached the twelfth floor to start work, I was a superhero.

After my first week on the job, I passed the front desk on my way to lunch. When the security guard spotted me, she grinned widely and called, "Hey, Superman!"

I stopped in my tracks. My cheeks burned.

"What?" I asked.

"We've been watching you on the security camera all week," she said with a laugh. "By the third day, people started gathering around the monitors as soon as you entered the elevator."

Too embarrassed to say anything, I turned to walk away.

But as I headed toward the exit, the guard called out again,

"Hey, Superman!"

I turned back to look at her.

"Don't ever lose that joy."

— Dr. Daniel H. Shapiro —

94

When Heartache and Hope Collide

Faith is unseen but felt, faith is strength when we feel
we have none, faith is hope when all seems lost.
~Catherine Pulsifer

fter a trip to the emergency room, I soaked my pillow with tears. I had been in a head-on collision that evening on my way home from work. I was driving at least 45 miles per hour as I approached an intersection, and the next thing I knew, there were headlights a few feet ahead of me. The other driver failed to yield to oncoming traffic (me) and began making a left turn at the exact moment when I drove under the green light. All I could think was that I was going to die. But one second later, I was surrounded by white clouds — and not the heavenly kind.

Miraculously, although both vehicles were totaled, no one was seriously injured. Even still, I lay in bed sobbing, crying out to God, "Why didn't You take me home?"

My life had become a whirlwind of confusion and pain in the months leading up to the accident. I was not going to take my life, but I had been praying for a way to escape the excruciating emotional pain I was battling.

Six months before the accident, I was already down and out with a back injury when my husband of seventeen years had announced he wanted to separate. I had just given him my trust back the previous year after an incident of infidelity, so this news was a complete shock — and a stab to my already wounded heart. A month later, my beloved grandmother died due to complications from a fall. My dad had a stroke the next month, and my husband moved out the month after, right before Christmas.

Now, instead of escaping my problems, I had acquired a whole new set of them: physical pain and cosmetic issues (thankfully, minor), fear related to getting behind the wheel again, mayhem associated with auto and medical claims, and the stress of finding a new vehicle. However, the fact that I was alive and spared from significant injury in a head-on collision got my attention. It seemed that God was going to great measures to convince me He wasn't finished with me yet. I sensed Him saying, "Do you believe Me now? I still have a purpose and plan for your life!"

Unfortunately, my problems continued to multiply. My fifteen-year-old Dachshund, Wilbur, became deathly sick and was diagnosed with a gastrointestinal tumor right after my accident. (Miraculously, he is still alive and considerably well as I write this ten months later.) And, before long my separation turned into a divorce.

I'm still somewhat in shock. Never in a million years could I have imagined being single, heartbroken, and this uncertain about my future at the age of forty-four. I can't even fathom how many thousands of tears I have cried over the past eighteen months. Although my goal is to live with joy, I am not ashamed of my season of mourning because I don't think I could truly heal without fully processing my grief. Thankfully, I am now at peace with my past and moving on with my life.

Like the old saying goes, I believe trials will either make you or break you. I refuse to stay broken, so I'm determined to have a positive attitude and come through this nightmare a better, stronger person. I have already discovered that I'm stronger than I ever knew.

My faith is what strengthens and encourages me most, so I joined a small group at my church. The love, support, and advice I receive from these dear friends have helped me stay on track and grow in faith. I am comforted and filled with reassurance every time I read my Bible or pray, so I do this often. I believe God's promises and trust that He will somehow, some way, work this tragic situation out for my good. I just have to be patient — and, therefore, learn how to be patient!

I have come to realize that the biggest opponent standing in the way of my happiness is actually myself—in particular, my thoughts. So, I make a conscious effort to routinely analyze and adjust them. I try to weed out negative thoughts and replace them with ones that bring me peace, joy, and hope for the future. When I take a proactive approach, meditating on Scripture and positive thoughts first thing in the morning and periodically throughout the day, it's much less likely for me to get weighed down by toxic emotions.

Taking the advice of a familiar cliché, I have been trying to make lemonade from some of the "lemons" in my life. I've always wanted to be a better pianist and to become fluent in Spanish, so I have been making good use of my "lonely time" by practicing these skills. For the sake of finances, I have had to work more in my job as a nurse than I did when I was married. Although this can be stressful, I have more fulfillment and purpose in my life when I'm helping people. And when I'm focused on others and their needs, I am reminded of how many blessings I still have to be thankful for.

Another way I am staying positive is by continuing to dream. Deep down, I have always regretted not becoming a nurse practitioner, so I have decided to pursue this goal. Who cares if I'm the oldest person in my class? At least I won't live with regret. I would also love to reach and encourage more people through my writing, and I have lots of ideas for books I plan to write at some point in the future. If I continue chasing my dreams, I see no reason why I can't live a life full of adventure, excitement, and meaning—even without a man!

It may be quite some time before I fully recover from the loss of my marriage, but I'm excited to see where my new life leads. If I maintain a positive attitude and press on in faith, I have no doubt that I will someday find myself on a mountaintop, amazed by all I have overcome. Although I no longer beg God to take me there, I'll think of Heaven often on this journey. By frequently reminding myself that I will live happily ever after one day, I can face any challenge head-on and have confidence that the best chapters in my story are still ahead.

— Mandy York —

95

Lessons from My Teachers

What is your purpose? Why are you here?
Start small and find out.
~Nannie Helen Burroughs

A few days after I started service as attending pediatric cardiologist, the neonatologists, nurses, and I met with Jenni and Tony to discuss their daughter Grace's status at two and a half weeks of age. After sixteen days on a heart-lung machine (ECMO), she was now breathing with the help of a ventilator, and her heart had finally stabilized with support from inhaled nitric oxide and multiple IV medications.

Grace was still sick, and her prognosis was uncertain.

As the parents and Grace's medical team gathered around a large conference-room table, the room was quiet, except for the faint buzzing of an overhead fluorescent light.

Grace's parents seemed nervous but exuded a quiet confidence. Jenni pushed her blond locks back, smiled, and looked expectantly around the room. Tony seemed super optimistic. "It's amazing how far Grace has come. We're excited she's off ECMO! She's so strong, even with everything she's been through. She's going to make it. Grace is a fighter, just like her mom!"

Tony tenderly stroked Jenni's hand under the table.

Jenni, quietly nodding her head, said, "Tony's right. I felt Grace's tiny hand squeezing my finger, and I can't believe how strong a grip she has. Grace is going to get through this."

They were teachers. I could imagine their students connecting with them and soaking in their compassionate energy.

Both parents beamed. They knew their daughter would be okay. Now, it was time for the medical team to weigh in.

The neonatology fellow said, "Grace has come a long way, but she's still really sick, so it's important to remember that she might not survive."

Grace's nurse added, "We have taken care of lots of children like Grace. You need to expect there is still a long road ahead, and no guarantees she's going to be able to go home."

The attending neonatologist pointed out, "We're doing everything we can, but unfortunately, many kids as sick as Grace don't make it."

While the team was talking, I looked at Jenni and Tony. With each comment from the medical team, their smiles, along with their enthusiastic confidence in their daughter's fate, faded a bit. Tony's formerly rosy cheeks turned pale, and he scowled. Jenni's eyes were moist, her shoulders slumped. Except for the buzzing of the neon light, the room was quiet. Jenni stared toward the far corner of the room, avoiding all eye contact. They looked defeated.

It seemed to me that, to make sure the parents didn't have "unrealistic expectations," my colleagues had overemphasized the (true) possibility that Grace might not survive.

Everyone in the room now looked to me for my words of caution.

Deep inside, I felt a fury welling up. My heart started to pound. My mouth was dry.

I was angry at my colleagues and felt the despair of Grace's parents. Was this negativity completely accurate?

I remembered something that my mentor, Dr. Welton Gersony, had taught me in fellowship.

Once you tell a family their child might die, you never have to bring that up again. No parent will forget that. Some medical people are so concerned about "telling the truth" that they destroy hope. Don't do that unless there really is no hope.

But how to merge these two truths? How to keep the right amount of hope alive in a life-threatening situation?

A powerful calmness came over me, something like what Christians call "the peace that passes all understanding." I knew what I had to say.

"Grace is sick. I've taken care of similar kids who have died, so that still might happen."

Tony and Jenni stared up at the light. They looked like they wanted to get this discussion over with.

"However," I continued, "I think it's important to remember that there is a chance Grace might live. I've taken care of kids like Grace, some even sicker, who survived. Grace might get through this and make it out of the NICU."

I looked at Jenni and Tony. Their eyes met mine. Jenni's eyes were red. Tony's lips were quivering, but the color had returned to his cheeks. They seemed shaken. Tony looked directly at me.

"What's your honest opinion? Is Grace going to make it?"

"I don't know what's going to happen. I do know I'm going to do everything I can to help Grace have a good outcome. Each of us has a role to play: the nurses, the respiratory therapists, the doctors, the social workers, the chaplains, and especially her mom and dad."

Jenni asked, "But how? What can we do?"

"What you're already doing," I said. "Show up, love her, touch her, sing to her, tell her you love her. Kids who are loved do so much better than kids who are ignored. If I were in her position, I would want to be loved by my mommy and daddy. Keep loving her."

Tony smiled and said, "We can do that." Jenni nodded and squeezed Tony's hand.

After the meeting, I stopped by Grace's bedside. She was hooked up to multiple EKG leads, a temperature monitor, a ventilator, and a pulse oximeter. From time to time, Grace stretched her little arms and legs. The only sound was the steady *beep, beep, beep* of the pulse oximeter and the intermittent *whoosh* of the ventilator.

I pulled up a chair and sat next to Tony and Jenni.

"How are you doing after our meeting?"

Tony said, "What you said was so important. You gave us hope."

Jenni said, "Now, we don't feel so alone. Thank you."

After that conference, we became a team, guiding the care of Grace.

After three months in the NICU, Grace was weaned off the ventilator. At four months of age, she was able to go home with oxygen, and by eighteen months she was weaned off oxygen.

When I care for critically ill children, it's not always easy to strike the right balance of optimism versus realistic danger. Grace and her parents taught me something important. Because of them, I'm a better doctor, a better advocate even during challenging situations, and a better "realistic cheerleader" for my patients.

On a sunny spring day, eighteen years after I first met them, an envelope arrived in the mail. I noted the return address: Jenni and Tony. Inside was an invitation to Grace's high-school graduation. With moist eyes, I looked at the invitation. I thought of Jenni and Tony and realized that, even though they had been young and had no medical training, her parents were right all along. Grace was going to make it.

— David G. Thoele —

96

A Rainbow at My Fingertips

*Never lose hope. Storms make people
stronger and never last forever.*
~Roy T. Bennett

A t first, the words I heard didn't make sense. I adjusted the
phone's receiver closer to my ear. Could I have misheard?

When my doctor's receptionist repeated the words, I realized I had heard just fine. "I'm sorry to have to tell you this.
The tests show a fast-growing cancer, and we'd like to get moving on
this as soon as possible."

No. Surely, this was a mistake. I was healthy and felt no pain in
either of my breasts. Wouldn't I at least sense something was wrong?
An ache, a twinge of discomfort… something?

I muttered a reply and returned the phone to its cradle. A numb-
ness blanketed my body as the truth hit me full-strength. My life would
never be the same. It — I — would be changed, forever.

The following weeks sped by, crammed full of office visits and
medical tests. Simply showing up for them was exhausting. Retaining
all the information shared by the doctors proved next to impossible.
I soon learned to bring a friend or family member along. Sometimes,
my mind disengaged during the discussions, overwhelmed by trigger
words like "surgery," "radiation," or "recurrence." That extra set of ears
caught things I missed.

Too often, the chilled air in the waiting room sent shivers up my
spine. Or was that anxiety? As I waited for my name to be called, my

eyes scanned the faces of other women in the fluorescent-lit room. Worry lines and frowns bore witness to their own fear. What thoughts tumbled through their minds as they sat in silence? Surely, every one of them — of us — carried a story unique to our lives and the challenges we faced.

Then came the times I'd spot a smile on the lips of a patient as she reentered the room following her exam. I wondered where that smile had come from. Had she received good news or simply decided to live out joy in the moment, regardless of her circumstances? Had someone first offered her a grin, and she'd chosen to pass it on?

These special ladies radiated a spark of hope that seemed to sweep the room and grew to a fire inside. Hope, a fragile and priceless gift, warmed us as we fidgeted in our plastic seats, pretending things were normal. Smiles mirrored and spread faster than a virus in that clinical atmosphere. Those wordless declarations of happiness sealed my resolve. I, too, would walk in optimism.

Prior to my operation, the surgeon explained that my tumor's location was a good fit for an experimental form of post-operative radiation therapy. My breast would require only ten separate sessions as opposed to several weeks of radiation treatments. It involved the insertion of a balloon into my body and putting tiny radioactive "seeds" inside. I'd need to lie face down, still as stone, inside a giant machine for thirty minutes as they zapped the area. Was I interested?

I spent the next couple of days thinking about the decision. How could I stay still that long? What if I sneezed? Or my nose ran? Or I panicked inside the machine? What if they aimed the laser at the wrong spot? Concerns both rational and absurd jumped and zigzagged through my brain faster than a ski racer on a slalom course.

When at last I'd run out of "what-ifs," I listed them. My doctor provided me with positive feedback. As I considered the option of fewer visits with precisely targeted radiation, it became more appealing to me. I opted for the experimental therapy and learned the balloon would be placed just after the tumor's removal.

I was never terrified, not even prior to surgery. It was as if I knew things would be okay, that I could trust the physicians and staff with my life. I focused on the concept that the cancer was like a mole and could be removed as easily.

The operation? It was a success. My lymph nodes were clear. After a short period, the drainage tubes were removed and healing began. The future looked bright.

But, first, radiation.

I was thrilled with my prognosis, but the operation had left me fatigued. How could I make it through numerous rapid-fire sessions?

I looked at my hands, folded so often in prayer during the past month. For weeks, I'd been preoccupied with my medical situation and let my appearance go. My nails looked awful. They needed attention.

I, in turn, needed a distraction, something to help me through this period.

Then, it came to me. Ten fingernails, ten treatments. Every time I made it through a visit, I'd do one nail. I'd have a tangible way to watch my progress and to take part in my self-care at the same time. Each nail would be a different color, so that at the end, there'd be a rainbow. What could symbolize hope more clearly?

About halfway through the therapy, one of the doctors asked about my strange manicure. Soon, most of the staff was paying attention. How could something so simple bring so many smiles?

Following my tenth and final treatment, I was released from care. After the doctors declared me cancer-free, one gave me a set of precious earrings she'd made herself, and another asked if they could offer my number to patients who were having a hard time. Of course, I said yes.

It's been more than ten years, and I still wear those earrings. I still find ways to look to the future and take advantage of small indulgences when I face a less-than-perfect present. And after a doctor's visit, I still smile at the people in the waiting room.

Because hope — a fire that spreads soul-to-soul — should never be extinguished.

— Heidi Gaul —

97

Island Party

*You must not lose faith in humanity. Humanity is
an ocean; if a few drops of the ocean are dirty,
the ocean does not become dirty.*
~Mahatma Gandhi

It's my daughter's first school dance, an informal gathering of parents and students at an elementary-school playground in Setauket, Long Island. Tonight's event has an '80s nostalgia theme. Songs from various John Hughes films blare from the DJ's speakers, transporting this bustling suburb back to a simpler time of big hair, MTV, and voodoo economics. Along the edge of the ad hoc dance floor stands a solitary fun-dad in an Adidas tracksuit and Kangol bucket hat. The party's just beginning.

As more people arrive, a pleasant, carnival-like atmosphere takes over, with kids zigzagging between the playground and the dance floor. Frankie Goes to Hollywood tells everyone to "Relax" as security guards in yellow windbreakers sift through the crowd. Some are retired NYPD. I discreetly check their waists and the linings of their jackets. I don't think they're armed, and it troubles me that I wish they were.

Most parents chat amiably while their children roam the grounds. I trail mine from a comfortable distance like a devoted member of her Secret Service detail. The prospect of her vanishing into any crowd gives me short panic attacks. Her crew wants to know why she keeps pointing to different sections of the schoolyard, and I overhear her saying, "My dad needs to know where I am." One of her cohorts looks at me, raises two fingers in the shape of an L, and then scampers off. Fair enough, Junior, but some circumstances call for excess.

I'll always need to know where Aubrey is, and right now she's on Long Island. After she was born, my partner Tiffany and I decided to buy a house. Our apartment in Brooklyn was lovely, but owning a home in Ditmas Park's Victorian Flatbush was pure fantasy.

After years of searching, we decided to move to Suffolk County at the tail end of 2020. I'd grown up in the Setauket/Port Jefferson area and knew every deli and pizza place within a ten-mile radius. I climbed every tree and swam in every pool. This homecoming was going to be rather cozy.

Tiffany is a native of Coney Island. Setauket was nothing to her but an unusual sound that needed to be Googled. Aubrey is biracial and considers herself "Black like Mommy." Prior to moving, Tiffany researched the town's demographics to see how many people in Setauket would look like them.

"1.27 percent? Are you freaking kidding?"

"One-of-the-oldest-Black-churches-in-America-is-in-Setauket," I quickly argued.

"With a choir that sings to no one. Forget it."

"Look, she'll have a fantastic childhood. Your information is from the 2000 census. I'm sure things have changed."

Slightly north of my daughter's school lies the incorporated village of Old Field South, an upscale enclave of Setauket. A visit to the community's history page claims the neighborhood was founded in 1929 by the Suffolk County Development Corporation, owned and operated by wealthy philanthropist, Ward Melville. Once its design was complete, strict rules were established. "To this day," the page explains, "our community is governed by covenants that run with the land and preserve a sense of architectural and natural integrity."

A resident of Old Field South recently e-mailed me a copy of these covenants, presented to him upon purchasing his home in 1976: "No part of said premises herein conveyed shall be used or occupied in whole or in part by any person of African or Asiatic descent or by any person not of the White or Caucasian race except that of domestic servants."

The current website makes no mention of the document's original contents, or why they were still issued as late as 1976. The updated edition is available for perusal but makes no mention of race. Its abracadabra-like absence without explanation is eerie. Clicking between the scrubbed version and its original leaves the reader chilled, the coldness of the first, the icy shell game of the second.

Old Field South is five minutes from our home. Aubrey attends the Three Village School District and is completing the third grade. One day, she'll attend a high school called Ward Melville.

So, is a beautiful place still beautiful when it fails to reckon with its past?

For the past two and a half years, I've given Tiffany my word that statistics are unimportant. The lack of diversity is worth it, I maintain, because Ward Melville High School has everything: acres of gleaming turf for championship teams to win in perpetuity, formidable drama, and music programs and a marching band that play the theme song from *Frozen*. To put it in '80s nostalgia terms, Ward Melville is the James Spader of public schools, an army of world-beaters in slicked-back hair and popped collars, something sleek, imposing, and glittery, so why not my kid and others like her?

I'd known racial covenants had been used during the development of Nassau County's Levittown—America's first suburb—but the realization that it was done here is personal. The irony of tracking my daughter's moves on the playground when I may have turned her and Tiffany into unwitting social pioneers is daunting.

Yet we're still here, and our decision to stay runs through a gauntlet each morning while getting to work, 118 miles roundtrip. We're NYC teachers. Tiffany's school is in Brooklyn. Mine's in South Jamaica. She sleeps soundly in the passenger seat, while I see taillights in my dreams at night. During the afternoon commute, we like to chat about our day.

"Watch it! Slow down!"

"I'm just keeping up with the pack. It's Thunderdome out there."

"This song is so old."

"Please. Simon's a poet, and Garfunkel sings like an angel."

The next morning, 4:00 a.m. arrives, and we're back at it.

"The Springsteen channel again? How many times can that 'screen door slam'?"

Whenever I receive unexpected calls from the school nurse over bellyaches, I leave work early to pick up Aubrey. "The nurse said you should have been here a half-hour ago," she says.

The nurse has never driven the Van Wyck Expressway at noon.

We wouldn't do this unless our girl was thriving. The absurdity of who gets to live where on a shared planet has sadly endured since the first blink of time. There's no total solution to our concerns, but there is this: One day, Aubrey will attend the school named after Ward Melville, on the land he donated to the community, and there's nothing his ghost can do about it. If we refuse to tread where bias has occurred, there'll be no place left to stand. My family lives on the North Shore of Long Island, like Gatsby, and this is our home now.

Back on the playground, my daughter's friends see me panning the crowd like a searchlight and call out. "Hey, Aubrey's dad! She's over here!"

My kid is on the swing, pumping hard and soaring high, until the chains start to buckle, and her old man tells her to quit showing off.

—J. Bryan McGeever—

98

Finding a Way Forward

Faith is the strength by which a shattered
world shall emerge into the light.
~Helen Keller

That Friday, I took a personal day off from work. It was Labor Day weekend, and I had much to do, but not the fun kind of activities that normally accompany a long weekend. I had plans to return to my parents' home, a four-hour drive, where I would begin helping my father box my mother's possessions and prepare for a life without her. She had died two weeks earlier from pneumonia.

I packed my bag, kissed my husband, and patted my dog on the head, starting my drive around 8:00 a.m. The constant drizzle made driving a little more challenging, but I made it two hours into the trip without any issues. I had my cell phone in the cupholder and was listening to good music. Everything was going well until I hit a puddle on the interstate that changed my life forever.

Suddenly, my car began fishtailing. In an instant, it headed toward an embankment where it rolled over three times. I recall all of it in slow motion. One, the crunching of metal; two, the airbags deploying; and three, all the windows shattering. The car happened to land in an upright position with glass everywhere and the car's roof nearly touching my head. Interestingly, my cell phone bounced up to the ceiling and down to the console each time, landing in the cupholder when the car came to a standstill with the engine still running.

I reached forward and turned off the engine, and that's when I began to feel some physical pain. I took a few deep breaths to give myself a minute to think, and my phone started ringing. It was my husband calling to check in. I'm not sure how I managed to stay calm, but I told him approximately where I was and that I had been in an accident. He said he was on his way.

In the meantime, passing drivers pulled over to help. A nurse appeared and told me to sit still while she stabilized my neck and someone called 911. Another passerby picked up my purse and other items that had been strewn all over the embankment. Soon, the paramedics and fire department arrived, and, with much effort, extracted me from the vehicle.

Prior to this event, I had never needed emergency medical services, traveled in an ambulance, or been in the hospital. Within an hour, I learned that I had broken my back and neck and would need to be transported to another hospital equipped to handle serious injuries. When I finally arrived there, I was evaluated by an entire trauma team over many hours and learned that they wanted to wait until the next day to decide whether or not to do surgery. I could still feel my feet and wiggle my toes, and I retained bladder control, which was considered a good sign.

After consultations with other doctors, the neurosurgeon decided to try the least invasive approach to my injuries: a thoracic burst fracture and a cervical fracture. He ordered a plastic body cast to be made for me, as well as a neck brace. After five days of lying flat in a hospital bed, I was tightly Velcroed into the body cast and allowed to sit up. The X-rays showed that my spine didn't collapse when I stood up, so I was discharged the next day. The plan was to keep the body cast on for approximately four months and the neck brace for about one month.

I have always been an active, independent, and self-directed person, so being constrained was completely foreign to me. I went from a person who could do everything to a person who had to ask my husband for help getting dressed, bathing, pouring milk for cereal, and so much more. Additionally, I was in excruciating pain most of the time, and the pain medication made me nauseous.

I felt like I had lost complete control of my life while also grieving the loss of my mother. I sat up many nights watching TV, including fitness-equipment infomercials. I decided that, when I got well, I was going to buy that equipment and get my life back! It took me three weeks to process my situation and wrap my head around what I needed to do to move forward.

I began physical therapy when the neck brace came off. Of course, my movements were restricted, and I had to be careful with the body cast still in place, but I began gentle stretching and I followed the prescribed regimen. After missing forty days of work, I returned full-time to my job, wearing my body cast underneath my clothes. While I had to limit what I lifted and how I moved, I could function fairly normally.

When the body cast came off, I continued physical therapy. Within a year, I was doing yoga and lifting light weights. Throughout this time, I also walked about one mile each day. Several friends and coworkers expressed surprise at how well I was recovering, which I attribute to having a positive mindset. I never doubted my ability to recover — not even once. I simply had to accept physical limitations for a time, but I always kept my eye on the prize, which was regaining my normal activities.

Of course, I had setbacks and issues with pain, but I worked through each obstacle as it arose. I recognized that my body had changed forever, and while I can't do all the things I did before in exactly the same way, I can do everything if I make modifications. For example, I can no longer do all the yard work in one day, but I can do a little each day and keep my discomfort to a minimum.

I was thirty-nine years old when this happened, and this experience, while terrible, gave me a new perspective on life. I learned not to sweat the small stuff and not to give negative people my valuable time. I learned that I am fortunate to be alive and to have the ability to do all the things I can still do with my body. I learned that being surrounded by caring loved ones, friends, and coworkers can lift me up on my worst days.

I recognized that it's okay to invite people into my house for a cup of coffee, even when I look bad and my house looks worse. I learned to accept help when others offer it and to be grateful when people bring me casseroles. I learned to be more patient and kinder to myself and other people because you never truly know what they are dealing with in their personal life. Most importantly, these experiences have reinforced just how important it is to have a positive mindset and to believe in your ability to achieve whatever you set your mind to. And, for the record, I eventually purchased the fitness equipment from that late-night infomercial, and I still use it today!

— Carla Elliff —

Mindful Mission

If you own this story you get to write the ending.
~Brené Brown

"**I** died," I sobbed.

"No. You survived. You're still here."

We'd had this same conversation for months, and my husband's tone was edged in frustration.

"You're still the same person you've always been."

My tears increased, as did the volume of my words. "I will *never* be the same person. She's gone. She's dead."

There was no point in arguing with me. The stroke I'd had in early September not only robbed me of the use of my left hand and much of my cognitive function, but it also robbed me of my will to go on.

I was a writer — *was* being the operative word here. Without the use of my left hand, I could no longer type. Voice-to-text was useless to me because my brain wouldn't let me decipher mistakes. A former editor, I couldn't even edit my own posts on social media or the text messages I'd try to send to friends. I felt worthless.

Despite months of physical and occupational therapies, I saw minimal improvement as the months wore on. Reading was such a chore that I stopped doing it as much as possible.

The holidays came and went, but the depression lingered. By January, I found myself dwelling on ways to end my life. My friends and family continually threw me lifelines, providing me with just enough reason to hold on. But then the waves of despair would crash over me and suck me under, dragging me along the bottom of a sea of grief, cutting me with the broken shells of shattered dreams.

Numbers became a concept I couldn't seem to grasp.

Telling time was nearly impossible, and trying to read a calendar was like deciphering hieroglyphics. I couldn't sort my pills, and when I was finally able to start cooking again, I couldn't follow recipes. One teaspoon of salt switched places in my brain with one cup of flour. We quickly learned it was best to keep me out of the kitchen, especially when I'd confuse the high and low settings on the stove. There were more burnt meals than I care to remember.

Even setting the table was too much of a challenge for me. I simply couldn't count out the right number of place settings. One night, when I thought I was up to entertaining, my daughter and her family arrived just in time to hear me screaming words that were inappropriate for grandchildren to hear. I had carefully set the table for four and was feeling quite proud of myself. The table looked lovely.

"What about the kids?" my husband asked. "Where are they going to sit?"

"Right there," I pointed, frustrated by the question.

"But there are only four place settings."

"I know," I snapped. "There are four people coming."

"But there are six of us altogether."

With that, I exploded and then collapsed into sobs.

In my "old" life, I thrived on entertaining, creating beautifully set tables and serving delicious meals. That night, after the company left, my husband said, "I don't think we can have people over anymore." His words were a knife to my heart, as I saw another of my passions slayed by the stroke. My world grew even darker.

One day, I'd had enough of the pity party I'd been throwing for myself. No one wanted to be invited, and I really couldn't blame them. I did have a working right hand, so I could at least pick up a pen and write or type out messages on my phone. That was something.

I decided to reach out to others who just might be feeling worse than I was. I started what I called my "Mindful Mission 2022" and invited others on Facebook to join me. The intention was to encourage at least three people every day. At the end of each night, if I hadn't met my goal, I would send a message via Facebook to someone who I felt led to reach out to. The messages were often simple but were always encouraging. In addition to Facebook, I used e-mails, cards and letters, phone calls, text messages, and visits.

As I started to recover and was able to cook again, I would sometimes make a meal and walk it over to my widowed neighbor. Since I was driving again, I would pick up small bouquets of flowers and deliver them to people who needed their own dose of cheering up.

As the months passed, so did the veil of darkness. I found myself smiling and laughing again. I began writing by pecking out the letters one key at a time. Was I back? No. But I was starting to like this "new me."

The "old me" died that awful day in September 2021, but fortunately I didn't bury her. She's right here and, interestingly enough, seems to be assimilating with the woman I'm slowly getting to know.

— Hana Haatainen-Caye —

A Call of Transformation

Strength does not come from physical capacity.
It comes from indomitable will.
~Mahatma Gandhi

t all started in late 2018 during a routine checkup with my family doctor. At one point, he had me lie back on the exam-room table and was pushing and prodding when he uttered, "Hmmm!"

I asked what "Hmmm" meant. He said he thought he was feeling something in my abdominal area that didn't seem right. He suggested scheduling a CT scan to see what was going on.

And so began my cancer journey.

The CT scan showed a large tumor spanning from my right kidney to my inferior vena cava vein. Further tests confirmed that I had somehow managed to contract a rare form of soft tissue cancer called leiomyosarcoma. Upon learning this, I was reminded of Ike and Tina Turner's "Proud Mary" remake when Tina growled, "We never ever do nothing nice and easy!"

I was referred to an oncologist who specializes in leiomyosarcoma. He informed me that the treatments would include chemo infusions followed by a risky surgical procedure to cut out whatever the chemo didn't eradicate.

A port was installed in my chest, and I went for my first chemo session in January 2019. That night, at around 4:00 a.m., I awoke to three EMTs and two police officers in my bedroom. I apparently started shaking violently due to a reaction to the chemo, and my wife, Lynn, called 911. All I knew was that I felt confused and needed to go to the bathroom.

One of the EMTs asked me what year it was. I had no clue. Then, he asked me who the president was. I said, "George Bush." George W. Bush had been out of office for ten years at that point. The technician insisted I go to the hospital to be checked out. I insisted that I go to the bathroom first unless they wanted a real mess in the ambulance.

I spent the rest of the night and next day in the hospital undergoing a battery of tests. It was determined that my "chemo cocktail" needed tweaking, and thankfully I didn't have a similar occurrence. I underwent a total of six chemo sessions that year, spanning from that first one in January through April. It was decided that June would be the month when I'd undergo surgery.

As if I needed more logs thrown onto the fire, my mom died on Friday of Memorial Day weekend. It was about two weeks before my operation. Then, shortly after my mom's services, my wife was admitted to another hospital across town due to complications from her battle with breast cancer — which eventually took her life in August 2021.

I was admitted to the hospital in early June. For the first two weeks, I was on a liquid diet of applesauce, chicken broth, soups, and other liquid-food substitutes that have absolutely zero appeal to a hungry man. I learned there would be two surgical teams: a vascular team that would cut out the cancer and sew a graft into the inferior vena cava, and an oncology team that would work on everything else.

A couple of nights before the operation, the vascular surgeon came into my room. He informed me in a rather matter-of-fact manner that I had a 1-in-3 chance of not making it through the operation. (Gee, thanks, Doc! Any odds on today's Yankees game?) And, assuming I did make it through, I would likely be in surgical intensive care for a week and in the hospital for about a month. Then, he leveled a determined look at me and said, "I'm going to do everything I can for you." I can't be sure, but I thought I heard the "Notre Dame Victory March" playing in the background as he exited the room.

I'll admit, I was scared. Mortality was never presented to me like a bet at the craps table.

The night before my operation, I called Lynn, who was still in the other hospital across town. *How should I approach this? Do I tell her there's a 1-in-3 chance we'll never see each other again?* We had started dating as teenagers and had been married for almost thirty-seven years at that point. All the laughs—all the tears—all the emotions that encompass a lifetime together. How do you encapsulate all that in the matter of a few minutes—over the phone, no less?

But that phone call actually turned out to be quite transformational for me.

You see, as I spoke to Lynn, I vowed to her—and to myself—that it would not be the last time we spoke. I had to see her again. I *needed* to see her again. And I needed to see our three daughters and my dog, Louie, too!

No way was I letting life end that way.

My thoughts quickly changed from despair to hope and determination. I told Lynn how much I loved her and that I would see her soon—and I fully meant it. I knew the odds weren't great, but I also knew that, without changing my mindset, I'd have little to no shot at getting through what I was facing.

The next day, after the operation, I woke up in surgical ICU with an incisional scar from my chest to my lower abdomen held together by over sixty metal staples. My daughter told me I was on the operating table for ten hours. She said the first thing I asked was, "Did they get it all?" She told me that I lost my right kidney, but they had to stop short of completing the surgery because they found my aorta was also compromised by the tumor, and they didn't have the necessary graft to correct it. (How this was missed during the testing phase still baffles me to this day.)

Bottom line: They had to procure the correct graft and go back in.

It took about a week to obtain the graft. During that span, Lynn was discharged from the other hospital, and our girls brought her to my bedside in a wheelchair. We embraced long and hard as I whispered to her, "I told you it wouldn't be the last time."

I went back into the operating room a couple of days later for another twelve-hour procedure where they repaired my aorta. After another stint in surgical ICU and a few days in a room, I finally went home.

My phone call with Lynn truly transformed this whole experience for me. I realized I was in a situation where everything was out of my control except for how I perceived it. And if perceptions were to be my only means of dealing with it, then I needed to ensure they were positive and powerful perceptions that worked to my advantage.

They were indeed, and I truly believe they helped to save my life.

The English philosopher James Allen wrote: "As he thinks, so he is; as he continues to think, so he remains."

It's my sincere hope that the transformation that I experienced during my phone call to my wife allows me to pass along those fundamental principles for many years to come.

— John Torre —

A Place in the Family

What would life be if we had no courage
to attempt anything?
~Vincent van Gogh

Mamma's breathing was shallow. It wouldn't be long now. Her eyes closed. Her brow furrowed. A frown pinched her features. What dreams tormented her at this hour?

I adjusted her pillow, straightened her blanket, and sat back in the tiny, green armchair.

The birds chittered outside the window, battling for turf on the bird feeder.

Mamma's eyes fluttered open.

"How's my brother? How's Dick? Has anyone gotten ahold of him?" Her voice climbed at the end of the question, and her eyes were wide.

"Yes, he's fine." I moved closer, taking her delicate hand. Her skin, speckled with dark spots and crisscrossed with prominent blue veins, clung to bony fingers. "Remember, I told you, we found him. His diabetes gave him some trouble, but he's in rehab and doing well."

"Oh." She nodded and closed her eyes, her face relaxing. "Good."

The burnt-orange gerbera daisies smiled at me from the windowsill.

"Keep it in the family."

"What, Mamma?"

Her eyes opened fully and locked on mine. She wore her business face.

"Aunt Bea's desk."

Shame ran through me. She must have heard me on the phone with the church, arranging the furniture pickup. How could I have let her hear?

"You can get rid of the other stuff. Nobody's going to want that. But please keep Aunt Bea's desk in the family. My father refused, but she was his sister." Her brows knit together, a rare sadness filling her voice. She'd been so strong for weeks.

"Of course, I will." I forced the words past what felt like a tourniquet around my throat.

She smiled then for just a second before her eyes fluttered closed.

Today, remembering her grateful smile fills me with resolve as I sink onto the bench in our garage, staring at Aunt Bea's desk.

Here it sits.

Dirty.

Scratched and dinged.

Old. A slim, antique secretary that has seen better days.

Keep it in the family.

Peeling and scratched tan paint coats the open shelving section on top. Another layer of off-white peeks out from underneath the tan.

A chunk is broken off the bottom panel on the left side. The dark finish is crackled like alligator skin.

Heaven, help me.

I've never restored furniture — nothing beyond those nifty paint pens for camouflaging a scratch.

After two hours spent in Lowe's, scouring the Internet and paint aisles, an array of paraphernalia — antique furniture refinisher, citrus stripper, boiled linseed oil, painters' rags, scrapers, and steel wool — litters my work bench.

Now, I'm facing a project that feels imperative and impossible.

But I'm doing it.

For her.

I remove the hardware and begin a thorough washing of years' worth of dust, grime, and pollen. How is there so much pollen? She loved open windows. Dusting, not so much.

I scrape bits of Scotch tape and some sticky, melted red goo — her favorite cinnamon hard candy, no doubt — from the wood surface.

Keep it in the family.

My nose testifies to the potency of the refinisher liquid, but the first layer of finish barely budges. It's a gummy mess.

The steel wool sticks.

Over and over, I tackle one small area at a time. Finally, the wool glides freely. I'm getting somewhere. Scrub to the edges. Reapply. Wring out the wool. Let it dry.

Come back.

Just when I think a section is done, more crackled finish bubbles to the surface.

Keep it in the family.

I scrub the stubborn spots until they're smooth.

Paint stripper is truly amazing and disgusting at the same time. How well it works, yet how many times I must apply, scrape, wash. Repeat.

But I'm doing it.

For her.

Memories flood me of Mamma writing letters or grading papers at her antique desk, the cubby holes stuffed to overflowing with mail, sticky notes, pens, and stamps. On the shelf, a chunky pink "World's Best Mother" figurine perches beside a wild picture of Albert Einstein and a human skull.

My mother, an anatomy professor, knew the moment she saw her MRI that this glioblastoma was the end. Lips pressed together matter-of-factly, she shook her head and then finally looked up at the doctor.

"Yep. That's bad."

But she didn't cry.

"I've had a good life," she said and smiled at me.

"Yes, you have. A very good life."

I lost it as soon as I hit the hall. How could I lose her so soon? We should have had at least another decade. I wasn't ready.

But she was.

She'd lived the life she wanted to live. She'd worked hard and travelled — and found work overseas to travel more. She sought beauty and wonder in every corner of the world and found it. I have boxes and boxes full of trinkets, postcards, and pretty rocks to prove it.

Keep it in the family.

I'm sanding with steel wool. Next is sandpaper. Tears leak from behind my safety goggles. I pull off sweaty latex gloves and wipe them with my sleeve.

The last bits of old crackle finish grind up and float away; the shell of a former life makes way for a new one.

Aunt Bea's dingy, old desk has transformed before my eyes. Gorgeous, warm wood makes an appearance as it enters its second century. The beautiful wood grain patterns that have been buried under years of toil, like Mom's spirit, have been released after a lifetime of hard work.

With linseed oil rubbed in by a soft cloth, it positively glows. I step back and marvel at this beautiful thing I could not see before.

Wait. Let it take. Let it breathe and soak up the healing oil.

Keep it in the family.

Oh, yes. This desk has come home for its third generation. Let's see what magic it makes.

It's been two years since her passing. The hole in my heart is as raw today as it was then. But I'm choosing each day to live like she lived — not waiting, but living. To seize the moments of adventure, to uncover the beauty, to learn everything there is to learn. Not paralyzed by grief or fear. Working hard because it's worth it to seek and see all the beauty in places and people.

Sometimes, we must really look beyond the hardened exterior. Sometimes, we must listen to the wise words of those who have gone before us to know when to work harder at preserving something worth fighting for, instead of hauling it, or them, to the curb.

Life can leave us dingy and battered, coated with grime and cheap paint. But every one of us has a place in the family. Our loving Father will patiently wipe away the grime and strip off the old muck until, slowly but surely, we are ready to glow again with new life.

— Elisabeth S. Gay —

Meet Our Contributors

Angela M. Adams received her Bachelor of Arts degree from Hanover College in 2005. After working many years as a lab tech and farm co-op manager, she is now pursuing her dream of freelance writing. Angela enjoys reading, gardening, hiking, and doing home renovations. She lives in Indiana with her husband, dogs, and cat.

Lisa Addison wrote her first short story at seven years old and has been writing ever since. An award-winning newspaper reporter for more than thirty-five years, she freelances for newspapers and magazines. She enjoys reading, traveling, and photography. Lisa lives in Louisiana with her two teenagers and their sweet cat Smokey. E-mail her at itsnews2me@aol.com.

Monica A. Andermann's writing has been included in such publications as *Sasee*, *Guideposts*, and *Woman's World* as well as several titles in the *Chicken Soup for the Soul* series. When not writing, she enjoys playing the piano, creating art, and hiking with her husband Bill.

Elizabeth A. Atwater lives in a small town in North Carolina on a horse ranch. She was smitten with the written word the first time she was given a *Little Golden Book* when she was a toddler. This quickly developed into a love of writing as soon as she learned to scribble the alphabet. E-mail her at e.a.atwater@gmail.com.

Dave Bachmann is a retired teacher who taught writing and reading to special needs students in Arizona for thirty-nine years. He now resides in California with his wife Jay, a retired kindergarten teacher, writing poems and short stories for children and grown-ups.

Author and award-winning musical composer **Kathleen Basi** is a mother of four. Her novel, *A Song for the Road*, follows a musician on a cross-country pilgrimage to honor her lost family. Meaty, earnest, occasionally humorous, and uplifting, Kathleen's work highlights the beauty and drama of the human experience.

Following a career in Nuclear Medicine, **Melissa Bender** is joyfully exploring her creative side. She was named Woman of the Week by the local FOX affiliate for her inspirational writing and is a regular guest on San Antonio television. Contact her at www.facebook.com/chicvintique.

Brittany Benko is a self-published poet, Hubpages/Medium blogger, LitPick book reviewer, and special needs mother. Brittany has been featured as a poet through *Poetic Reveries*, *Autism Parenting Magazine*, Spillwords, and The Writer's Club. When she isn't writing, she enjoys spending time with her kids, walking on the beach and singing in her church choir.

Katie Bergen is a wife and mom of two living in Canada. She loves spending her time hiking the mountains, paddleboarding and running. She is completing her first self-published devotional book for women and has a passion for writing words to inspire others to deepen their faith and live confidently in who they are.

Jessica Sly Biron is seasoned in everything from radio DJ to farming, tech support to face painting, and more. You can find her homeschooling and homesteading, usually followed by a gaggle of chickens. She's trying hard to raise good humans, constantly striving to encourage and lift up others. E-mail her at JessicaBiron@yahoo.com.

Carolyn Bolz is a lifelong resident of Southern California. She enjoys reading, writing poetry and articles, and spending time outdoors. Carolyn is a frequent contributor to *The ST Quarterly*, a publication for persons who have dystonia, a movement disorder.

S.L. Brunner was born in the Philippines and raised in the small northern California town of Placerville. She now resides in Southern California with her husband and two children. She works in sales enablement for the leading GIS company, and loves to travel, read, write, dance, and spend quality time with her family.

Kristine Byron retired from Tupperware Home Parties. Now she spends her time traveling with her husband and enjoying time with family and friends.

Sue Campanella is an Amazon best-selling author, energy medicine practitioner, and life coach. Her passion is empowering others to discover and live in their truth. Living between SW Florida and Rhode Island she enjoys all outdoor activities. Sue is a mother of two, bonus mother of three, and grandmother of five.

Kim Carney has been a freelance writer for many years and is proud to be published in the *Chicken Soup for the Soul* series! Find out more about Kim Carney and the projects she's working on at her Linktree account: linktr.ee/tenaciousk.

Brian Carpenter, a reality hacker and Principal Vulnerability Researcher at spiderSilk, weaves digital defenses with a passion for nature, AI, and cybersecurity. An off-grid thinker and former cop, he blends tech expertise with a love for gardens, firearms, and freedom in the heart of Oklahoma.

Sharron Carrns finds joy in encouraging and uplifting others using her writing and art. She has written or contributed to books and resources from various publishers. She lives in Spring Lake, MI, caring for her family and three grand-dogs.

Eva Carter is a frequent contributor to the *Chicken Soup for the Soul* series, having had forty-four of her stories published so far. She lives in Dallas, TX with her Canadian husband and two cats. Eva loves dancing, traveling and writing.

Christina Ryan Claypool is a former TV producer/reporter, national Amy Writing Awards recipient, and author of the inspirational *Secrets of the Pastor's Wife: A Novel*. She adores her husband and adult son, along with appreciating a good book/film, coffee, or anything sparkly. Learn more at www.christinaryanclaypool.com.

Weston L. Collins is a published author living in San Antonio, TX. He has a rich history of education and learned people in his family that has made him a person who loves to share inspiration and heart with others. His wife is a practicing attorney in the area, and he is a devout Christian.

D'ette Corona received her Bachelor of Science degree in business management and is the Associate Publisher of Chicken Soup for the Soul.

Joanne Costantino resides in South Jersey. Her writing came about on the heels of a steady stream of life events. Much of her life experiences provide the guts of her writing. You can follow Joanne's blog about the "Life We Claim We Didn't Sign Up For" at www.weneedmoresundaydinners.blogspot.com.

Rose Couse retired after forty-plus years in early childhood education. She now focuses on her business, Thrive Together Parenting (www.rmcouse.ca), as a parent coach and speaker. In her spare time Rose enjoys capturing nature with her camera, spending time with her grandchild, friends, and family, and indulging in reading and writing life stories.

Stephanie Daich is deeply passionate about filling her life with experiences. She sees her family as the true wealth of life. Stephanie uses writing to delve into the realm of imagination and to connect with the minds and hearts of her readers.

Elaine D'Alessandro enjoys writing fiction for children and nonfiction for adults. Many of her stories have appeared in children's magazines, children's anthologies, and *Chicken Soup for the Soul* anthologies. Elaine lives in Massachusetts and has four children and five grandchildren.

Priscilla Dann-Courtney is a writer and clinical psychologist and lives in Colorado where she and her husband raised their three children. Her columns have appeared in numerous national publications and her book, *Room to Grow* (Norlights Press, 2009), was her way to navigate the light, dark, and wonder of the world.

Leyla d'Aulaire is a freelance writer and proofreader living in Minnesota. She is currently pursuing a Bachelor of Arts in Creative Writing. Leyla enjoys reading tarot cards, crafting spooky jewelry, and binge-watching true crime documentaries. She is working on writing a supernatural horror novel.

Barbara Davey is a seasoned writer who has (finally!) found her genre in the joy of simple pleasures. A retired healthcare executive, she is thrilled that she no longer has to draft strategic plans, and can devote her time to discovering everyday epiphanies. She and her husband live in Verona, NJ.

Elton A. Dean is a higher education leader, author, and retired soldier. He owns Big Paw Publishing and recently published his first children's book, *A Yeti Like Freddie: Talking to Kids About Autism*. His second book, *Brandon Sets Sail: A Story About Sharing Success*, was coauthored with his seven-year-old son.

Lola Di Giulio De Maci is a retired teacher whose stories have appeared in numerous titles in the *Chicken Soup for the Soul* series, *Divine Moments*, *Guideposts*, *Reminisce*, *Los Angeles Times*, children's publications, and newspaper columns. Lola has a Master of Arts in Education and English, and a Doctorate in Education.

Kathy Dickie lives in Calgary, a western Canadian city nestled in the foothills of the majestic Rocky Mountains. She enjoys adventures with her remarkable granddaughters, traveling with her husband, family events, quilting, ancestry research and writing. Kathy is a recurrent contributor to the *Chicken Soup for the Soul* series.

Carla Elliff is a psychiatric care coordinator and former school counselor. She enjoys traveling, reading, long walks, and spending time with her husband and rescued Pitbull. She earned an M.Ed. in Counseling from UMSL and a B.S. in Sociology from SIUE. She served in the U.S. Air Force during the Gulf War.

Allison Lynn Flemming is drawn to the power of story to grow hearts and communities. Singer, songwriter and worship leader, Allison and her husband, Gerald, form the award-winning duo, Infinitely More. Publications include *Guideposts*, *The Upper Room* and ten titles in the *Chicken Soup for the Soul* series. Learn more at www.InfinitelyMore.ca.

Ashonti Ford is an award-winning journalist who appears on over 100 different television news stations every week. Early in her career, Ford covered national stories, including the Trayvon Martin case in Florida. Now, she serves as a national correspondent in Washington, D.C., where she covers the White House, Congress, and foreign affairs.

Heidi Gaul lives in Oregon's Willamette Valley. She's contributed to over twenty *Guideposts* books, and a baker's dozen in the *Chicken Soup for the Soul* series. She'd love to hear from you at HeidiGaul.com or on Facebook.

Elisabeth S. Gay is a writer, educational consultant, and teacher.

She holds a Bachelor of Arts in German and French from Wofford College and a dual Montessori certificate. She is married with three children, works in the nonprofit sector, and enjoys writing fiction, nonfiction, and church curriculum.

Kathleen Gerard's writing has been widely published and anthologized. She is the author of three novels: *In Transit, Cold Comfort* and *The Thing Is.* Learn more at www.kathleengerard.blogspot.com.

Hana Haatainen-Caye, a writer, editor, and voice over talent, is the creator of the blog "Green Grandma", and author of *Vinegar Fridays.* She lives in Pittsburgh, PA with her husband and cats. Hana teaches writing at conferences and for Osher at CMU. E-mail her at speechless@comcast.net.

Krista Caponigro Harner received her B.S. in Secondary English Education from Millersville University and her MA and MFA in Creative Writing from Wilkes University. She loves reading, writing, dogs, and ice cream. Krista lives in rural Pennsylvania with her husband, three children, and naughty Fox Red Lab.

Joey Held is a writer based in Austin, TX. He's the author of *Kind, But Kind of Weird: Short Stories on Life's Relationships* and the founder of Fun Fact Friyay. When not writing, he's likely planning his next trip, playing basketball, frolicking with his two pups, or rocking onstage with his band, Burning Years.

Nancy Hoag, former English teacher, has seen 1,200 of her stories and devotions published, as well as four inspirational/nonfiction books, including *The Fingerprints of God: Seeing His Hand in the Unexpected* (Fleming H. Revell/Baker books). She's been married to her favorite "cowboy" for forty-nine years and lives in Bozeman, MT.

Joyce Jacobo received her MA in Literature and Writing Studies from Cal State San Marcos. She is a freelance writer and editor who lives out in the Southern California desert, as well as the author of *Literary Observations*, a short story and poetry collection.

Susan Jensen, MD is a retired Physical Medicine and Rehabilitation specialist who graduated from Queens College, C.U.N.Y and Upstate Medical Center, S.U.N.Y. The proud mom of one grown daughter, she is enjoying a second career as a journalist and has a monthly profiles column in an international magazine.

Dr. Ken Jeremiah has been teaching, translating, writing, and working on television shows for the past twenty-three years. He has written fourteen books along with dozens of articles that focus on history, culture, and worldwide religions.

Breon Johnson is currently studying to become a Medical Assistant, preparing for his NHA exam while pursuing personal goals like passing his DMV driver's test and saving for a car. A veteran of the Army National Guard with six years of service, Breon's background as a generator mechanic has shaped his discipline and resilience.

Ric Keller is a former U.S. Congressman. He is also an attorney, award-winning author, speaker, and stand-up comedian who has performed on stages from Florida to New York. His TEDx Talk on humor was the sixth most-watched TEDx Talk in the world in May 2022, and his book, *Chase the Bears*, was a #1 Amazon Bestseller.

Ellen Edwards Kennedy is mentor for NC Scribes, a Zoom authors' group. She edited the award-winning book, *911-That Beautiful, Broken Day* and her Bible-based picture book, *Walk With a Stranger*, won first prize (Middle Reader) in the 2024 Eric Hoffer Book Awards. She has also authored four cozy mysteries as EE Kennedy.

Alice Klies has been a member of Northern Arizona Word Weavers since 2011. She has been published multiple times in the *Chicken Soup for the Soul* series, *Guideposts*, and *Moments* books by Yvonne Lehman. Her book *Pebbles in My Way* was released in 2017. She hopes her stories bring smiles, tears, and hope. She lives in Arizona with her hubby and dog, Lola.

Diane Krieg is a former senior finance executive who ranked consistently on American Banker's "25 Most Powerful Women in Finance" list. She has published numerous articles including: "The Girl with the Draggin' W-2"; "Girls Just Want to Have Funds"; and "CEOs, Don't Dump the Boomers!" She is an avid reader and loves playing piano.

Kristine Laco is a satirist, memoirist, and essayist living in Toronto, Canada. She is currently over-editing a contemporary women's fiction manuscript that will never be perfect. You can follow her on all socials @kristinelaco or subscribe and read some of her favorite pieces at linktr.ee/KristineLaco.

Shannon Leach lives in Tennessee and is the owner of A Repurposed Heart. Her inspirational short stories and books about leadership, life, and loving people focus on encouraging others and reminding them they are not alone. She holds a bachelor's degree in social work and is the cofounder of the nonprofit The Fostered Gift.

Arlene Lassiter Ledbetter earned a Bachelor of Arts in English from Dalton College in Georgia. She has written adult Sunday school curriculum and been published in numerous magazines. Arlene's byline has appeared in nine titles in the *Chicken Soup for the Soul* series. Her favorite moments are those shared with her grandchildren.

Joan Leof has written a memoir titled *Fatal If Swallowed: Reclaiming Creativity and Hope Along the Uncharted Path*. A collection of twenty of her personal essays appears in her book, *Matryoshka: Uncovering Your Many Selves Through Writing*. She facilitates journal workshops for groups and individuals.

L.M. Lush is a writer, professor, and Christian minister. Her heartwarming stories about miracles, angels, and the transformative power of love and positive thinking are featured in multiple titles in the *Chicken Soup for the Soul* series. She plays the piano and enjoys life with her beloved dogs, Sadie and Oliver.

Debbie Maselli is an Air Force veteran who received her master's degree in Christian counseling from Jacksonville Theological Seminary in 2023. She and her husband have three sons and two grandsons. Debbie enjoys knitting, kayaking, and walking the beach. She plans to write Bible studies based on mental health issues.

Jane McBride graduated *summa cum laude* from Brigham Young University. She has five children, ten grandchildren, and one great-grandchild. She loves to play with her grandchildren, write, and go to garage sales.

J. Bryan McGeever is the author of *Small Rooms and Others*, a collection of essays published by Unsolicited Press. His work has appeared in *The New York Times*, *The Southampton Review*, and *New York Daily News*. He teaches Writing and Literature in New York City and lives with his family on Long Island.

Laura McKenzie is a retired kindergarten teacher living in Abilene, TX with her husband Doug. She enjoys traveling and spending time with her children and grandchildren. Laura loves to read, write and volunteer at the local food pantry. She is thrilled to be a part of the Chicken Soup for the Soul family.

Patricia Merewether lives in rural Michigan with her husband, two grown grandchildren and two rescued Havanese pups. She has studied writing and art for many years. Her passion is writing and art, painting in watercolor and acrylic.

Brian Michael's hobbies include writing, graphic design, gardening, and meteorology. He's an avid fan of both the Philadelphia Phillies and the West Virginia Mountaineer's football team. Most evenings you can find Brian walking his sweet Chocolate Lab, Dawson, or perhaps watching a sporting event with his cat, Athena, close by his side.

Whittier Mikkelsen holds an MA in Psychology and had a career in emergency mental health until pain secondary to cerebral palsy caused her to slow down and pursue writing. She is a wife and mother of two. Whittier finds joy in nature, photography, writing, and being a storyteller and is focused on writing her memoir, due to release 2025.

Marya Morin is a freelance writer. Her stories and poems have appeared in publications such as *Woman's World* and Hallmark. Marya also penned a weekly humorous column for an online newsletter and writes custom poetry on request. She lives in the country with her husband. E-mail her at Akushla514@hotmail.com.

S.K. Naus has been writing since grade school where she enjoyed being a member of the school newspaper team. Words are important and arranging them in the right order can create wonderful stories and that's her favourite part of writing.

A recovering academic, **Christine Overall** has published extensively in philosophy. Her fiction and creative nonfiction have appeared in magazines and journals. She is now working on a memoir about having children, caregiving, and disability.

Celeste Palmer is the founder of Bridging the Gap, a nonprofit providing resources for traumatic brain injury survivors and their families. Online support groups, individual support and many other resources can be found through the website at www.tbibridge.org. She hopes awareness about the subject will help us all to understand. She enjoys art and canasta.

Sr. Josephine Palmeri has been teaching for six decades and still enjoys teaching Spanish to teenagers who love the language. Her jewels are her students who help the poor in Latin America. She has written two joke books in honor of her dad, who was a barber and professional comedian.

Dorian Leigh Quillen, M.Ed., LPC, is a licensed professional counselor. She is a *magna cum laude* graduate of the University of Oklahoma, where she earned a Bachelor of Arts in Journalism, and a Master of Education degree. She enjoys cycling, reading, and encouraging people. E-mail her at dorianquillen@att.net.

An avid road-tripper, **Rachel Remick** gets many of the ideas for her stories while traveling cross-country. Both her fiction and nonfiction have appeared in several literary magazines, and she is a proud multiple contributor to the *Chicken Soup for the Soul* series. Follow her on Instagram @tampawritergirl.

Timothy T.R. Robinson is a writer living in Cleveland, OH with his wife Maggie. He earned his B.A. from Baldwin Wallace College and his M.A. from Drew University. He went on to have a successful career in business before retiring to write blogs on current event topics at www.tim-the-author.com.

Judy Salcewicz is a writer, poet, and teacher who lives and gardens in New Jersey. She is a cancer survivor who has found her strength and is proud to be part of eight titles in the *Chicken Soup for the Soul* series.

Michael Jordan Segal, who defied all odds after being shot in the head, is a husband, father, social worker, freelance author, and inspirational speaker, sharing his recipe for happiness, recovery and success before conferences and businesses. To contact Mike, or to order his CD, please visit www.InspirationByMike.com.

Patricia Senkiw-Rudowsky is part writer, part educator, part artist. She holds a B.A. in English and lives at the Jersey shore. Patricia's goal is to inspire positive behavior, especially for her grandkids whom she adores: Parker and Summer.

Dr. Daniel H. Shapiro received his Doctorate in Education and has served as a teacher, counselor, and mentor for over twenty-five years. He is the author of the book, *The 5 Practices of the Caring Mentor*. He lives with his wife and two children in South Florida and continues to pursue his passion for mentoring and keynote speaking.

Judith Shapiro lives half the year on the opposite coast, marveling at the sun setting over the ocean instead of rising. When the novel she's writing looks the other way, she secretly writes anything else. Judith is a Pushcart Prize nominee. Her work has appeared in *The Citron Review*, *The New York Times*, *The Sun* and more. Learn more at PeaceInEveryLeaf.com.

Billie Holladay Skelley received her bachelor's and master's degrees from the University of Wisconsin. A retired clinical nurse specialist, she is the mother of four and grandmother of three. Billie enjoys writing, and her work crosses several genres. She spends her non-writing time reading, gardening, and traveling.

An artist, author, poet, and an inventor with a passion for the arts, **Ed Solomon** surrounds himself with risk takers, storytellers, creators, truth seekers, artists, adventurers and dream-makers. Since 1980 he has devoted all his time and energy as an advocate for Peace. E-mail him at e.t.solomon@gmail.com.

Elizabeth Sowder inherited her love of storytelling from her mother and started writing children's books to teach her children Biblical lessons. She enjoys spending the early mornings reading and journaling and is so thankful for her relationship with Jesus Christ which has brought her through many trials. E-mail her at EAS4Him@yahoo.com.

Elizabeth Anne Brock Springs has a Master's in Elementary Education from West Virginia University. She resides in Virginia Beach, VA with husband Larry, son Robert and their two dogs Sassy and Midgie Scamp. Elizabeth enjoys photography, writing poetry and short stories, as well as teaching children in the Head Start program.

Glenda Standeven is an inspirational speaker, a past contributing author to the *Chicken Soup for the Soul* series and is the author of *I Am Choosing to Smile* as well as *What Men Won't Talk About... And Women*

Need to Know: A Woman's Perspective on Prostate Cancer. E-mail her at glendastandeven@gmail.com.

Diane Stark is a wife, mother of five, grandmother of one, and freelance writer. She is a frequent contributor to the *Chicken Soup for the Soul* series. She loves to write about the important things in life: her family and her faith.

Robert Stermscheg is a former police officer and pilot. He retired in 2006 to devote more time to writing historical fiction. He is married with two adult children. Robert enjoys reading, hiking, and helping others in their writing journey.

Noelle Sterne (PhD) publishes stories, poems, essays, academic, and writing craft articles in many venues. Her *Challenges in Writing Your Dissertation* helps doctoral students fulfill their goals. In *Trust Your Life*, Noelle supports readers in reaching lifelong yearnings. Thankfully pursuing her own, Noelle writes daily.

Deborah Tainsh is a published author of poetry, short stories, a compilation of military family stories, and a personal memoir about the death of a son in the Iraq War and the subsequent journey. Deborah is the widow of a retired U.S. Marine and mom to Phillip. She resides in Long Beach, MS. E-mail her at deborahtainsh@msn.com.

David G. Thoele is a pediatric cardiologist and Co-Director of Narrative Medicine at Advocate Health. He learned the healing power of writing when his daughter got sick and he experienced the medical system from a parent's perspective. He co-founded the program in narrative medicine at ACH in 2013. E-mail him at david.thoele@aah.org.

John Torre did engineering work for the building trades and managed several home-based businesses including freelance copywriting. He has mentored at-risk adolescents, enjoys playing guitar, traveling to Disney World, and spending time with his three daughters and granddaughters. E-mail him at jt0229@mac.com.

Samantha Ducloux Waltz lives in Portland, OR where her family and friends, pets, writing, yoga and gardening keep her busy and happy. Her writings include anthologized and award-winning essays, her SealPress anthology *Blended: Writers on the Stepfamily Experience*, and her novel *The Choice of Men.*

Roz Warren writes for everyone from the *Funny Times* to the *New York Times*, has been featured on both *The Today Show* and *Morning Edition* and is absolutely thrilled that this is the eighteenth *Chicken Soup for the Soul* anthology her stories have been included in. Roz loves to hear from readers. E-mail her at roSwarren@gmail.com.

Benny Wasserman was an aerospace engineer for thirty years. After retirement he spent twenty-five years as an Einstein impersonator. He is the author of the book, *Presidents Were Teenagers Too*. He has been published in the *Los Angeles Times*, *Reminisce*, *Good Old Days*, and other titles in the *Chicken Soup for the Soul* series. He is a voracious reader and ping-pong player.

Dorann Weber is a freelance photographer and writer who lives in New Jersey. She's a contributor for Getty Images, and her verses have been featured on several Hallmark cards. Writing her first story for the *Chicken Soup for the Soul* series ignited her passion for writing. She enjoys hiking with her family and dogs.

David Weiskircher holds a B.A. in English and has contributed to the following publications, among others, *Bark, CURE Today, Sasee, Guideposts, Mobius: The Journal of Social Change, Avalon Literary Review* and the *Chicken Soup for the Soul* series.

Mark Wood spent twenty years working in mental health, supporting people of all ages to achieve their true potential. He found a passion for writing in his forties whilst travelling and published his first book in 2022. He enjoys reading, hiking, wild camping and photography. Mark is now semi-retired and lives in Scotland.

Mandy York is a nurse and writer who lives in Greensboro, NC. Her faith and positive outlook have carried her through many obstacles in life. She is now happier than ever after finding and marrying her true love, Brian, and becoming a stepmom to three beautiful girls.

Meet Amy Newmark

Amy Newmark is the bestselling author, editor-in-chief, and publisher of the *Chicken Soup for the Soul* book series. Since 2008, she has published more than 200 new books, most of them national bestsellers in the U.S. and Canada, more than doubling the number of Chicken Soup for the Soul titles in print today.

Amy is credited with revitalizing the Chicken Soup for the Soul brand, which has been a publishing industry phenomenon since the first book came out in 1993. By compiling inspirational and aspirational true stories curated from ordinary people who have had extraordinary experiences, Amy has kept the thirty-one-year-old Chicken Soup for the Soul brand fresh and relevant.

Amy graduated *magna cum laude* from Harvard University where she majored in Portuguese and minored in French. She then embarked on a three-decade career as a Wall Street analyst, a hedge fund manager, and a corporate executive in the technology field.

Her return to literary pursuits was inevitable, as her honors thesis in college involved traveling throughout Brazil's impoverished northeast region, collecting stories from regular people. She is delighted to have come full circle in her writing career — from collecting stories "from the people" in Brazil as a twenty-year-old to, three decades later, collecting stories "from the people" for Chicken Soup for the Soul.

When Amy and her husband are not working, they are visiting their four grown children and their spouses, and their five grandchildren.

Listen to Amy's free podcast — Chicken Soup for the Soul with Amy Newmark — on Apple, Google, or by using your favorite podcast app on your phone.

Thank You

We owe huge thanks to all our contributors and fans. We received thousands of submissions for this popular topic, and we spent months reading all of them. Laura Dean, Kristiana Pastir, and D'ette Corona read all of them and narrowed down the selection for Publisher and Editor-in-Chief, Amy Newmark. Susan Heim did the first round of editing, and then D'ette chose the perfect quotations to put at the beginning of each story, and Amy edited the stories and shaped the final manuscript.

As we finished our work, D'ette continued to be Amy's right-hand woman in working with all our wonderful writers. Barbara LoMonaco, Kristiana Pastir, and Elaine Kimbler jumped in to proof, proof, proof. And, yes, there will always be typos anyway, so please feel free to let us know about them at webmaster@chickensoupforthesoul.com, and we will correct them in future printings.

The whole publishing team deserves a hand, including our Vice President of Production & COO, Victor Cataldo, and our graphic designer, Daniel Zaccari, who turned our manuscript into this beautiful, inspirational book.

Share with Us

We have all had Chicken Soup for the Soul moments in our lives. If you would like to share your story, go to chickensoup.com and click on Books and then Submit Your Story. You will find our writing guidelines there, along with a list of topics we're working on.

You may be able to help another reader and become a published author at the same time! Some of our past contributors have even launched writing and speaking careers from the publication of their stories in our books.

We only accept story submissions via our website. They are no longer accepted via postal mail or fax. And they are not accepted via e-mail.

To contact us regarding other matters, please send an e-mail to webmaster@chickensoupforthesoul.com, or write us at:

Chicken Soup for the Soul
P.O. Box 700
Cos Cob, CT 06807-0700

One more note from your friends at Chicken Soup for the Soul: Occasionally, we receive an unsolicited book manuscript from one of our readers, and we would like to respectfully inform you that we do not accept unsolicited manuscripts, and we must discard the ones that are sent to us.

Changing your life one story at a time®
www.chickensoup.com